Glimpses of Phoenix

ALSO BY DAVID WILLIAM FOSTER

*Urban Photography in Argentina: Nine Artists of the
Post–Dictatorship Era* (McFarland, 2007)

*Bibliography in Literature, Folklore, Language and Linguistics:
Essays on the Status of the Field*
(coeditor, James R. Kelly, McFarland, 2003)

Glimpses of Phoenix

The Desert Metropolis in Written and Visual Media

DAVID WILLIAM FOSTER

Foreword by Jon Talton

McFarland & Company, Inc., Publishers

Jefferson, North Carolina, and London

All photographs are by the author unless indicated otherwise. "Erma Bombeck: The Phoenix Suburban Underbelly" was originally published in a slightly different version in *Journal of Popular Culture* 45.1 (2012): 27–40. "Truthful Misrepresentations: Steve Benson Draws Phoenix" originally appeared in *Studies in American Humor* new series 3.21 (2010): 29–45. "Phoenix, Say What? Urban Landscapes in the Chronicles of Laurie Notaro" originally appeared in *Cuadernos de litertaura inglesa y norteamericana* 11.1–2 (2008): 69–83. "Desert Noir: The Detective Fiction of Jon Tarlton" originally appeared in shorter form in the *Rocky Mountain Review* 61.1 (Spring 2007): 73–83. Reprinted by permission of the copyright owner, The Rocky Mountain Modern Language Association. The portion of "Out of the Barrio: Stella Pope Duarte's *Let Their Spirits Dance*" about La Sonorita was originally published as "La Sonorita: Survival of a Chicano Barrio" in *Confluencia* 27.1 (2011): 212–18. The rest of the essay originally appeared in a shorter version in the *Bilingual Review* 27.2 (2003): 171–79. "Phoenix in Guillermo Reyes's *Places to Touch Him*" originally appeared in *Latin American Theatre Review* 43.1 (2009): 71–86. "Phoenix as Dystopia in Cherríe Moraga's *Hungry Woman*" originally appeared in a much shorter version in the *Hispanic Journal* 23.2 (2002 [i.e., 2004]): 91–101. The portions of the essay on Van Buren Street originally appeared in "Can You Get There on Van Buren? Urban Flashes: Phoenix, Arizona," *Border-lines* 2 (2008): 4–22.

LIBRARY OF CONGRESS CATALOGUING-IN-PUBLICATION DATA

Foster, David William.
    Glimpses of Phoenix : the desert metropolis in written and visual media / David William Foster ; foreword by Jon Talton.
        p.   cm.
    Includes bibliographical references and index.

    ISBN 978-0-7864-7364-9
    softcover : acid free paper ∞

    1. Phoenix (Ariz.) — In popular culture.
    2. Phoenix (Ariz.) — In literature.   3. Phoenix (Ariz.) —
    In mass media.   I. Title.
    F819.P57F67 2013
    979.1'73 — dc23   2013009401

BRITISH LIBRARY CATALOGUING DATA ARE AVAILABLE

On the cover: *clockwise from top left* Scottish-rite Masonic Temple, original Channel 5 studios, original IBM building, St. Mary's Basilica, first Phoenix City Hall, Winnie Ruth Judd murder house (photographs by the author); Tovrea Castle (iStockphoto/Thinkstock); Luhrs Tower (photograph by the author)

Manufactured in the United States of America

McFarland & Company, Inc., Publishers
    Box 611, Jefferson, North Carolina 28640
    www.mcfarlandpub.com

Table of Contents

Table of Contents

Foreword: Writing Phoenix
by Jon Talton

In 2011, video of a dust storm descending upon Phoenix captivated television audiences and Internet viewers across America. This majestic, unnerving ten-thousand-foot-tall brown mass eating up the subdivisions seemed like something out of science fiction. It even assumed an exotic name: a haboob. As a fourth-generation Arizonan who was living in Seattle at the time, I fielded questions from many friends and acquaintances about this seemingly strange new phenomenon. Was it dangerous? A result of climate change? I was, they said, fortunate not to have been there and confronted this menacing novelty, the haboob.

To be sure, building a metropolitan area of more than fifteen hundred square miles and four million people in a hostile desert has changed the weather all by itself. The summers are hotter and last longer. The super-heated concrete can make the storms more violent. And the region faces a risky future from climate change. But when I watched the video and its successors — for there was a haboob craze in the aftermath of that first showing — I saw just another Arizona dust storm, a commonplace in the summer monsoon season. And when I was growing up in Phoenix, nobody used the term haboob. That word originates in the Sahara. Our weather events were always called dust storms. Still, it was an instructive moment.

Phoenix has long recorded some of the fastest population growth in America. It also sees a great deal of population "churn," people moving in and out without staying long. Most white newcomers move to new areas of the sprawling metropolis, to subdivisions of look-alike houses in "master planned communities" and, for those with means, gated properties. They drive everywhere. Shopping is done at familiar chain stores in brand-new shopping strips or malls. The fast-food outlets and drug stores are in the same style of building as one would find in Omaha or Des Moines,

1

with perhaps some stucco slapped on. Suburban zoning and the price-points of house builders ensure a high degree of segregation by income, class, and race. It is a prime example of the throwaway built environment called "the geography of nowhere," by social critic James Howard Kunstler. A great deal of self-selection has also taken place. Suburban Phoenix is "the big sort" identified by author Bill Bishop in a book of the same name, where those of like minds and life experiences cluster together. As a result, it is highly conservative, suburban, Midwestern, and almost tribal in its exclusionary character. "Exclusive" is a frequently used adjective, especially in wealthy north Scottsdale. All this is cloaked by the local boosters' promise of a resort lifestyle and no need to shovel sunshine.

One peculiar result of this great Midwestern migration is that "home" for many residents, including the massive retiree cohort and the very wealthy, is where they came from, not Phoenix. The large suburbs surrounding the city, or at least their elected officials, resent even using the name "Phoenix" to describe the metropolitan area, preferring the amorphous "Valley." As the funding difficulties facing local arts and philanthropic organizations attest, most don't adopt Phoenix as their own, however much they enjoy its delightful winters, golf courses, and abundant sunshine. They send their money "back home" to the symphony or museums in Minneapolis, Chicago, or Cincinnati. When they die, they choose to be buried there as well. Politically dominant in the region if not the city itself, they act as a veto elite against most efforts at civic betterment unless they involve building more freeways.

From the new, look-alike built environment and the monoculture of suburban sprawl, to the lack of civic connections, many nominal Phoenicians glide through their lives under the impression that the city has little or no past and no distinctive customs, traditions, and cultures. So it's not surprising that "haboob" would be appended with barely a protest to a timeless and distinctive occurrence in the Sonoran Desert. It reminds me of when I returned to Phoenix in the 2000s and even the news media would term a location "downtown" even though it was miles from the real downtown. I wouldn't do that in their hometowns; for example claiming that Winnetka was in the Chicago Loop. Yet when I would raise these protests to reporters, editors and producers, they were invariably dismissed. "Phoenix has no history," they would say.

They could not be more wrong.

David William Foster's *Glimpses of Phoenix* is a welcome antidote. Phoenix is America's least-examined big city. Yet it is rich in history, national consequence, and a storehouse of many conflicting, competing, and blending cultural traditions that make it a compelling metropolis. These have been good to me as a mystery writer, my muses in creating the six novels in the David Mapstone mystery series. The city is a conscious character in each of these books. I also tried to bring this sensibility to my writing during the seven years that I worked as a columnist for the *Arizona Republic*, the state's largest newspaper, a labor that produced a great deal of controversy. And why not? If Phoenix is not a *tabula rasa*, then it complicates the selling by the prevailing economic and political elites of a Des Moines in the Desert.

Modern Phoenix is centered in the Salt River Valley, one of the world's great alluvial valleys. With soil enriched by the deposits carried from the mountains northeast, it can grow nearly anything. All that's missing is water, for the Salt is a fickle desert river, alternately flooding and drying to a trickle on its way to the Gila and finally the Colorado River and the Sea of Cortez. Capturing the river and making it produce an agricultural bounty is a historic and pre-historic enterprise. It was here that natives created one of the ancient world's most sophisticated hydrological civilizations. We know these canal- and town-builders and farmers as the Hohokam, and their culture reached its zenith between the seventh and fourteenth centuries. Then it went into a relatively sudden decline and the Salt River Valley was largely abandoned around 1375 CE.

For nearly half a millennium, the land lay largely empty, as if waiting. During this time, the United States was established and moved west. Spain laid claim to the land, then Mexico, and finally America. After the Civil War, a motley assortment of American adventurers, idealists, ex–Confederates, and landless farmers arrived and began cleaning out the ancient canals, adding to them, and attempting once again to claim the bounty of the Salt River Valley. Not for nothing was the name Phoenix chosen for a settlement aborning in the ashes of its predecessor. Yet for every promise, the river delivered more curses. In addition to the capricious water flows, summer heat and year-round hardship and isolation were extreme.

In the drought of the 1890s, many settlers considered abandonment, just as the Hohokam had done. But technology had advanced. The Salt River Valley became the first major reclamation project of the Newlands Act of 1902. Theodore Roosevelt Dam was built in the mountains upstream to capture snowmelt water in a reservoir; more dams and canals followed. It's worth noting that whites, blacks, Latinos, and American Indians built the dam. The Apache Trail from Phoenix to the dam was built by Apaches. This extraordinary triumph over nature ensured the rise of the Phoenix. At its height in the 1960s, more than half-a-million acres were under cultivation, sending trainloads of produce and other agricultural commodities to the country. An even more ambitious water scheme, the Central Arizona Project, bringing Colorado River Water hundreds of miles to the city, began in the 1980s. Phoenix is the final triumph, for better and worse, of America's Manifest Destiny.

The other technological breakthrough that ensured Phoenix would not remain a small farm town was air conditioning. After World War II, a population boom began that never even slowed until the Great Recession. No city was changed more by the great Sunbelt migration than Phoenix.

Yet Phoenix was never even an Anglo monoculture. Greeks and Lebanese were among the pioneering business owners. With the rise of cotton farming, African Americans moved there in large numbers. The Salt River Valley included members of native tribes, especially the Pima, who are perhaps descendants of the Hohokam; today's metropolis is bracketed by two American Indian reservations. Chinese migrants came as railroad builders and business owners. The first Asian American elected to a state legislature was Phoenix grocer Wing F. Ong, in 1946. Japanese proved to be skilled farmers, especially in south Phoenix, although many suffered internment during World War II. Owners of sugar-beet fields imported Russian immigrants to work the crop. Latter-day Saints founded nearby Mesa and would become a political force wildly disproportionate to their numbers. And Latinos were always a substantial part of Phoenix.

These cultures coexisted uneasily. Tucson, established by Spain in 1775 and part of Mexico until the 1853 Gadsden Purchase, embraces its Latino heritage and culture. Phoenix, by contrast, was a culturally Southern city into the 1950s. Racism and segregation were widespread, especially toward African Americans and Latinos. The Anglos held economic and social dominance. White settlers in the town's early years snubbed the natural cooling provided by adobe houses, erecting grand Victorians instead. Their goal was to make their new city "American" in its look. Meanwhile, this was a place where "the other side of the tracks" had a literal meaning. The poor black and Latino areas were south of the Southern Pacific Railroad. In the Depression, the slums just south of downtown were identified as some of the worst in America, lacking plumbing or running water. As Phoenix grew, the city located the most polluting industries and toxic dumps near minority neighborhoods. On the other hand, within the black neighborhoods and Latino barrios, even severe poverty, lack of city services, and marginalization did not prevent the emergence of a distinct culture and sense of community. The old Phoenix barrios would, for example, provide author Stella Pope Duarte with a rich vein for her novels. Phoenix was Barry Goldwater's hometown. But it was also the scene of protests led by native Arizonan César Chávez, who is today honored with a public space near City Hall.

This world was swept away by a series of disruptions, including the mechanization of cotton picking, the decline of the old agricultural economy and *de jure* segregation, bulldozing some of the most historic barrios to clear open space near the city's airport, and the mass migrations to the United States of Mexicans and Central Americans from the 1980s through the 2000s. This last event substantially changed the character of the city of Phoenix. The onetime "Anglo city" is now more than 40 percent Latino. Maryvale, the city's first large, post-war suburb, which was once the epitome of the white middle class, is now mostly Hispanic, its modest starter homes being inhabited by people displaced by clearing the old barrios and, more profoundly, by the influx of hundreds of thousands of new immigrants, legal and illegal. The illegal aliens, willing to work cheaply and easy for employers to exploit, were essential to the success of industrial-scale house building, as well as the kitchens and housekeeping staffs of resorts and hotels and the ubiquitous landscaping and lawn-care businesses. Anglos who later joined the Tea Party and the state's campaign against illegal immigration enjoyed inexpensive housing, house cleaners, and gardeners for precisely the same reason.

Whether the "illegals" made more of an economic contribution than they used in schools and health care has been a hot point of debate. What is less discussed is how they disrupted Phoenix's generations-old Mexican American neighborhoods and sense of community. Many Mexican American citizens were ambivalent or even hostile to this mass migration, although they rarely discussed it publicly so as not to give ammunition to racists. Of course, the decisive making of the city into a more diverse place brought considerable cultural flux and benefits, too. Drive along Sixteenth Street today and you'll find blocks of businesses with their signs in Spanish, something that would have been unheard-of in the Phoenix of the 1970s. Visual arts by Latinos are more abundant. Those willing to come into the central core, south Phoenix or Maryvale will find a remarkable variety of great eating. Meanwhile, other sections of the older city abandoned by middle-class whites have seen the creation of what former Mayor Phil Gordon called a "little America" of ethnic neighborhoods, restaurants, and shops run by immigrants from around the world.

To write honestly about Phoenix requires setting aside the city's elaborate mythology. Midwesterners come to embrace what they see as the "rugged individualism" of the Old West. In fact, Phoenix wouldn't exist without massive federal money for everything from the reclamation projects of the early twentieth century to flood control and defense industries. Indeed, the reclamation of the Salt River Valley was the closest thing to large-scale socialism ever attempted in America, as farmers were allotted a fixed number of acres and their farms mortgaged to pay for the dam. Washington's goal was to social engineer a Jeffersonian yeoman farmer community to draw people away from the dirty industrial cities of the era. Another cherished local myth is clean government and lack of organized crime. In fact, City Hall was notoriously corrupt until at least the late 1940s, with one city commissioner running the prostitution racket in south Phoenix. The city was also a mafia stronghold for decades, a back office for the mob in Las Vegas, with attendant hits and bombings, the most infamous being carried out on *Arizona Republic* reporter Don Bolles in July 1976.

It's a commonplace saying that "Phoenix never had a downtown." It did, a quite vibrant one, and allowed it to be destroyed in the 1960s. The city has been trying to recover that essential feature ever since, with varying success. The core has made a remarkable comeback, even if it lags similar sized cities. It also hosts a substantial and growing artist community. Unfortunately, Phoenix came of age in the era of the automobile and cheap gasoline. Its old stewards died off and were replaced by what I call the Real Estate Industrial Complex, pushing sprawl ever farther out, not reinvesting in most older areas, and, thanks to continued population growth, giving the impression of progress and prosperity. "Growth," as measured by local elites, meant adding people and houses, not increasing measures of quality. In reality, Phoenix lost most of its economic diversity and became addicted to the growth Ponzi scheme. When the bubble popped it 2008, it fell into depression.

Another challenge to the writer is how much the city has lost that made it special, even magical. When I was a child in the 1960s, Phoenix retained some coherence: A city core that was an oasis of trees and grass, surrounded by citrus and farm fields and a few smaller towns, followed by the vast emptiness of the desert save for a few dusty hamlets. If we wanted fresh oranges beyond what our two trees produced, we could drive a few miles and buy a box at a roadside stand, surrounded by groves. Sprawl has destroyed all of this, including the enchanting Japanese Flower Gardens at the foot of the South Mountains. Phoenix was once a major railroad center. As late as the 1960s, seven passenger trains a day called at Union Station. Now Phoenix is the largest American city with no Amtrak service. Without the agricultural sector, stockyards and slaughterhouses, it has few rail-based exports, although house building, the last great factory in town before the bust, imported many trainloads of lumber and other building materials. The sky was once so clear and clean it was recommended for people suffering from lung diseases. Now it is infamous for its "brown cloud" and smog inversions, with car emissions and other pollutants trapped by the mountains.

The writer writing about Phoenix faces a city that lacks a self-examining or ironic sensibility and whose Anglo residents are extremely thin-skinned. This isn't surprising considering so much of its economy is based on tourism and real estate, selling the image of unspoiled desert with championship golf. The media are largely tame and investigative reporting, especially focusing on the local elites, is rare. Professor Andrew Ross of New York University, who wrote *Bird on Fire: Lessons from the World's Least Sustainable City*, received a storm of criticism and denial, bolstered by position papers from local "experts" that depend on the real-estate industry for their living. During my years as a columnist there, the newspaper's publisher received repeated demands from powerful people that I be fired. My sins included raising inconvenient facts about an uncompetitive economy and social problems, pushing back against political extremism, and warning of the coming real-estate bust. That I wrote with the standing of one steeped in the city's history only added to the danger that my voice appeared to pose. Despite all this, my column remained highly popular, especially among natives. In 2007, I was finally told that my column would be eliminated, hence my departure. The sensitivity extends even to the noir novels I write. It's not uncommon to receive an email from a reader or a review on Amazon.com castigating me. As one wrote, "There is a negative comment about Phoenix every three or four pages. Obviously Jon Talton, a long time resident (I did have familiarity with his name from his work in the *Arizona Republic*) really hates Phoenix." Does star mystery writer Michael Connelly get this from Angelinos for his gritty depictions of L.A.? I doubt it. Phoenix is a big city with the insecurities of a small town.

I continue to write about Phoenix even though my newspaper

columns made me persona non grata in my hometown. It is irresistible in its beauty, culture, history—and its dysfunction. It is now the nation's sixth most populous city, and for a while in the 2000s passed Philadelphia to occupy the No. 5 slot. Yet it lacks the economic diversity or quality to compete with its peers, to box in its weight class, so to speak. A huge underclass coexists with the palatial opulence of north Scottsdale and Paradise Valley. The politics are extreme and reactionary, so much so that before he died Barry Goldwater said, "I will be remembered as a liberal." And yet most of this emanates from the suburbs. Phoenix itself is reliably Democratic and blue, progressive enough to lead the building of a regional light-rail system. If the large Latino population ever became politically organized, it would turn Arizona from red to blue electorally.

For a mystery writer, Phoenix is a gift with its quirks, cultural mix and wealth of history, as well as its magnetic pull on everyone from criminals to saints to come there and reinvent themselves. It's an important public-policy story that I address on my blog, Rogue Columnist. Mostly, I write about Phoenix because it's in my heart. I still keep a condo on Central Avenue, near the historic neighborhood where I grew up and lived again in the 2000s, with its lovely old houses and shade, near Encanto Park with its comforting City Beautiful Movement layout. I commune with the ghosts of my family and the ghosts of the Hohokam. The latter say be careful, the desert always wins.

Indeed, Phoenix has embarked on a hazardous experiment, with so many people crowded into an ever-hotter frying pan, living—with climate change, dysfunctional politics and an economy too focused on real-estate hustles—on borrowed time. It faces greater sustainability challenges than any other city in America, and failing to address them would bring consequences of national scope. That's the other reason I still write about this city. It matters. Foster makes an important contribution to our understanding of the other city. It will be up to us to realize the stakes in failing to understand Phoenix beyond a place of golf, retirees, subdivisions, and sunshine.

Phoenix native Jon Talton is economics columnist for the Seattle Times *and editor and publisher of the blog "Rogue Columnist." He is the author of nine novels, including the David Mapstone mysteries* Concrete Desert, Cactus Heart, Camelback Falls, Dry Heat, Arizona Dreams *and* South Phoenix Rules.

Introduction

It is probable that the first appearance of Phoenix in American cultural production, aside from some passing references in Western novels, was in the opening twenty minutes of Alfred Hitchcock's *Psycho* (1960). Phoenix before World War II had been mostly known as a place where "lungers" (tuberculosis patients and others afflicted with respiratory ailments) went to be cured in the dry desert air. During the war years, Phoenix had been important for its two military bases (Williams and Luke) and for war-related industries like the Goodyear Tire operation, AiResearch, and Motorola. But Hitchcock's decision to use Phoenix as the starting point for Marion Crane's flight into the desert to meet her fate at the Bates Motel gives moviegoers their first extended image of the city.

Hitchcock opens with a broad pan of the cityscape, and no one seems ever to have determined exactly from where that shot was filmed: perhaps from the Westward Ho hotel, the city's first major downtown tourist hotel and at the time the city's tallest building.[1] The building that the camera zooms in on after the pan, to enter the hotel room where Crane (played by Janet Leigh) and her lover Sam Loomis (John Gavin) are having an afternoon tryst, still stands (it is now called Barrister Square), as does the ground-level connecting office space, between the Luhrs Building and the Luhrs Tower (the first skyscraper in Phoenix and the southwest, built in 1929), where Lila Crane works for a real estate agent. Getting to know Phoenix means becoming familiar with the details of the opening sequence of *Pyscho*. However, where the matter acquires some sort of depth of passing interest is the instability of knowledge as to which building contained the hotel room where the lovers are trysting. It is often claimed that it was the Luhrs Building, when an examination of architectural details demonstrates that it was the building across the street to the west from the Luhrs complex.

The gap in detailed knowledge about the shooting of the opening pan and the prevalent erroneous belief as to where the lovers dallied is typical of so much of the memory and perception of Phoenix. The first Anglo settlers arrived in the 1870s, although the adjectival specification is hardly necessary since their arrival was not in contrast to the presence of any other group: Spaniards and their descendent Mexicans had never settled in what is now called the Valley of the Sun and the Hohokam tribe that once occupied the area had disappeared — it is now believed because of drought — over three centuries previous. Phoenix was incorporated in 1881, and grew slowly as an agricultural community, with the first promise of stable growth ensured by effective water management with the opening of Theodore Roosevelt Dam in 1911. If Phoenix always seemed to be a city about to arrive (as one can realistically say that it did in the high boom years of the 1960s, domestic air conditioning finally having been perfected), it always also seemed to be a city without much in the way of substantial history. What was of interest and what attracted the magic combination of light industry, land developers, and tourists was always what it was at any particular time and what it promised to be in the near future. Phoenix never seems to have invested much in the proposition that "the past is prologue": if newcomers left their past behind them in the (presumably) hostile places from whence they came, Phoenix would always be leaving its less than agreeable past (less agreeable if only because that was before air conditioning and latest tourist installations) behind it in favor of the better life of its blithely assertive nowness.

Certainly cultural attractions have, nevertheless, prospered, in large part because they tie in nicely with the tourist industry or the amenities sought by the sophisticated sector of the middle-class: museums, art galleries, sports venues, music halls, and theaters. Arizona is home to the largest concentration of native American peoples in the U.S., with twenty-one tribes being recognized by the Inter Tribal Council of Arizona, which has its headquarters across the street from the Heard Museum, one of the great anthropological museums of America; nearby is the Steele Indian School Park, built on the site of one of the government Indian Schools, which functioned from 1891 to 1990. Arizona native American culture has been effectively made attractive to tourists, although the same thing cannot be said of either Hispanic or African American culture in the area, even though in the case of the former, Hispanics now make up a third of the state and the greater Phoenix area. But, then, even those who don't like Mexicans (there is a long history of anti–Mexican sentiment in Phoenix, exacerbated in recent years by issues clustering around so-called illegal immigrants) like Mexican food, and Mexican restaurants abound in the Phoenix area.

But culture in general, beyond what is marketable to tourists, has been either a thin proposition in Phoenix or what cultural production does exist has been pretty much ignored. One dimension of the process of ignorance has been to doubt whether what cultural production that occurs even deserves to be called Culture. Thus, while Erma Bombeck's columns may be highly entertaining and even quite informative about modern social life in a city like Phoenix, do they come anywhere near to being "literary" in nature? The same question can be raised about Steve Benson's editorial cartoons or Jon Talton's detective novels. However one might want to relegate to the margins or elevate to the level of the university curriculum such examples, it is an undisputed fact that Arizona is the only state in the nation that has not produced a great novelist. The closest big-name writer associated with Arizona is Zane Grey but he was hardly an Arizonan, despite the prominence of the state in his pacesetting Western writing. A number of writers have passed through the state and written about it, most recently Barbara Kingsolver, who is neither from Arizona nor a resident anymore. But there is no Arizona Faulkner, no Arizona Hemingway, no Arizona Joan Didion, no Arizona Toni Morrison. If this is true of Arizona as a whole, the country's sixth largest state, it is all the more so in the case of Phoenix, the country's sixth most populous metropolitan area. It is significant that Erma Bombeck, who was from Ohio, did all of her mature work in Phoenix, yet rarely spoke directly about the city. And the website ErmaMuseum.org, maintained by the University of Dayton where she was an undergraduate, gives only a glancing reference, without even specifying a date, to her move to Phoenix in the early 1970s.[2]

Thus, this book represents the first attempt to suggest a cultural history for Phoenix. Because there is not a tradition of writing about Phoenix, nor of even discussing in critical detail about what cultural production is associated with Phoenix, my decision was to identify an array of texts that could in some way be called noteworthy and significant and to write about them in detail, guided always by the need to demonstrate with some depth why their relationship to Phoenix[3] is of interest, how it can be identified and commented on, and how the "use" of Phoenix enhances our knowledge about the city and surrounding metropolitan area. In looking back over these texts, I can now perceive a common thread to all of them, and that is the question of urban survival: urban survival in general, survival in an urban area with the geographic and built environment that characterize

Phoenix, and survival in an urban world that, in contrast to the St. Paul of Garrison Keillor's Guy Noir, "a city that knows how to keep its secrets," is compelled to argue insistently (if only by implication) that it has no secrets, no history to remember, and no stories to tell.

I first saw the phrase "Learn Urban Survival" as one of those cautionary messages public service vehicles sport. In this case, it was a standard-issue large red fire engine belonging to the Phoenix Fire Department, and I immediately surmised that it referred to learning to survive fires and other similar emergencies, along the lines of an early ad campaign of the PFD to the effect "Learn Not to Burn," a phrase whose direct and dire eloquence was abetted, as such slogans should be, by the facile rhyming the English language allows for.

Yet, as I thought about this phrase, I began to want to understand it to mean something much broader, with a message relating not just to the important imperative to survive physically the threats and dangers of daily life, but on a subtler level to the kaleidoscope of information, skills, tricks, and simply street-smart savvy that are part of surviving the urbanscape in sociopsychological ways. I don't have so much in mind the idea of an inventory of tips on how to get things done from one end of the day to the other, but, more globally, what are, so to speak, the horizons of knowledge of urban dwellers that make their life possible and even pleasurable. It should be apparent here that by urban I mean the contemporary (post)modern megalopolitan city: I don't know if Phoenix counts as a good example of the latter, but it certainly does win merits for its decentered postmodern sprawl that threatens to give new meaning to the famous dictum that "there is no there there" precisely because one is not always sure where the there is — that is, to what extent Phoenix is adequately or meaningfully "thered."

Perhaps, then, the first unit of urban knowledge one must learn to survive in a city like Phoenix involves grasping its non-theredness. Phoenix does possess a historic downtown area, an original financial and commercial core, and there are serious efforts to revive it, including the major undertaking of opening a downtown campus for Arizona State University and a joint medical training operation involving a partnership between the University of Arizona and Arizona State. Yet, there is no turning back on the proliferation of alternative financial and commercial cores, not just the ones that anchor historical suburbs like Scottsdale, Glendale, and Tempe, but additional concentrations within the city of Phoenix itself. Although I do not want to privilege financial and commercial centers, they inevitably bring with them peripheral residential and arts and cultural activities. Moreover, mega-shopping centers or malls (often called "ghetto malls" for the lower economic stratum to which they appeal) have been integral to the development of Phoenix, and important ones have come and gone, with new even putatively grander ones opening regularly. Arizona Mills, reputed to be one of the largest in the nation, has been a significant, if congested-traffic generating, node for the demographic blurring of southwest Tempe and southeast Phoenix. As Greater Phoenix evolves toward the Greater Los Angeles model of a patchwork of communities, some of which are incorporated and some are not, but all are tightly bonded to others in all directions, the ability to have a sense of this dispersion, and proliferation, of points of identity, to hold in one's mind a sense of the geometry of the urban area, is necessary simply in order to get around.

It is often said that Phoenix is as perfect a checkerboard of street layouts as is possible, given the frequently dramatic geological contours of the valley in which it sits. This is debatable. Yet, nevertheless, there has been the historical attempt, using downtown Phoenix as an anchor, to chart some sort of reasonable distribution of the streets along well-measured axes. The basic pattern is to plot numbered streets to the east of Central Avenue and numbered avenues to the west, with a convergence of a north/south spread at Washington Street. There are main thoroughfares every mile in both directions, secondary ones every half-mile, and tertiary ones every quarter-mile. In part this distribution extends beyond Phoenix proper to include a number of the suburbs, although some of the suburbs have opted for their own numbering and naming system, while often respecting the layout of the thoroughfares. What has most disrupted the geometric grid has been the decision of subdivisions to alter the geometry by introducing streets that do not run in a straight line: some are curved, some create a diamond effect, and in the famous Sun City development, the streets are laid out in concentric circles. There is also the occasional diagonal, such as the much lamented Grand Avenue, which was originally conceived of as a prosperous boulevard that juts out from downtown Phoenix in the fashion of a straight shot to Los Angeles: it was long ago superseded by the interstate, and its character alternates between the funky and the schlocky. "Funky" is an especially accurate adjective to describe the alternative arts and entertainment venues that have for the past five years been attempting to breathe a new life into the strip. Understanding the geometric grid overlay and its derivations, subtleties, and exceptions is part of the degree to which one has a sense of layout of the city and how to get around in it.

Introduction

A third question for urban survival moves beyond abstract geometry into the more directly material of lived human experience, where a crucial strategy for personal security means understanding the distribution of forms of danger within the city. Often this danger is relative or relational. People of color are frequently in danger in upscale so-called white areas of the city because they are likely to become the objects of hostility and even police harassment. But the same is true, although not necessarily for perfect inverse reasons, in the case of individuals who are not perceived as being of color in their forays into areas that are predominantly of color. Since the infrastructure of the latter may be inferior than that of so-called white areas — the absence of sidewalks, inadequate street lighting, poor paving and drainage, defective signage — there is unquestionably an overall disadvantage for both residents and outsiders, but the latter may perceive a greater security risk in accordance with whatever drives their sense of difference and unequally distributed social and symbolic power. Equally such issues affect children, the elderly, women, queers, and anyone else who may suddenly experience vulnerability in moving from what is felt to be a safe zone into what is felt to be a dangerous and threatening one. Since such zones are relational and relative, depending on individual subjectivities and the actual and imagined resources available to them for "getting through" real or imagined areas of danger, there is no way of predicting in a transsubjective way what they will be for any one person or how to navigate them. For some individuals, all ethnic areas are danger zones, while for others all upscale areas, noted for increased security, bring the threat of surveillance and harassment. Others may find industrial parks problematical (e.g., when having to go to a theater or gallery located in a warehouse district), while some are put off by downtown areas, which they may associate with beggars, street-people, and the homeless. Leaving aside the way in which such sentiments are driven by irrational fear and even classism, racism, and ethnocentricity, an important dimension of urban survival must necessarily be both understanding one's comfort zone in the cityscape and knowing how to avoid those realms that produce discomfort. Raymond Chandler's dictum about how one must walk the mean streets of the city (Chandler 991–92) may not properly apply to a city like Phoenix, where few walk, but the streets are no less mean even behind the locked doors of an automobile.

Urban survival must also surely mean having a sense of how efficiently and effectively to conduct the business of life within the maze that it is the city. Most Americans continue to hold onto the notion of Main Street

America, and, indeed, there are residential housing developments that attempt, often with transparent phoniness, to trade on the power of this notion. Yes, it would be nice if one could do a list of the top ten locales of one's daily life — commercial establishments, the grocery store, doctors' offices, the bank, the dry cleaner, and so on — and then have them all lined up in two rows on both sides of a block-long stretch of Main Street or to have everything concentrated in Main Street's immediate successor, the shopping mall. The problem is that no two individuals have the same needs, and those who ever had the experience of meeting the needs of life with a small-town Main Street are likely to remember the limited selection and the simple lack of services (the Sears Catalog and other mail order businesses of a bygone era existed for some reason: which is not the reason their contemporary versions exist). It may now be possible to order all the books one needs from Amazon rather than run across town to a bookstore and to refill most prescriptions with Walgreens' online service, but the complex business of everyday life in the early twenty-first century cannot be accomplished without a large measure of running around, whether within a city or, if one continues to live in a town or hamlet, by running over to the nearest city, which for some towns or hamlets may involve several nearby cities: when I lived in Columbia, Missouri, in the mid–1960s, we were always dividing our time between Kansas City to the west and St. Louis to the east, both roughly equidistant away from what at that time was a definitely resources-deprived Columbia. One can spend an enormous amount of time on such intra- and intercity running around, and a serious amount of strategizing is in order. My wife says that, in Phoenix, she doesn't go where the freeway doesn't go, believing implicitly that all of the important facilities and resources she requires for her complex urban life are within earshot of the roar of the eight-lane. This may not necessarily be true, but at least she has a car to find out. There is a particular brand of urban misery associated with a city like Phoenix if you don't have a car — even temporarily — and where public transportation is still mostly a phantom proposition, especially on weekends and in the summer.

Meeting the rigorous demands for the survival of modern life in the maze of the city segues into meeting the demands for pleasure, which may arguably be almost as imperious a demand as knowing where the grocery stores are and how to do the calculus of successful access to them when taking into consideration other errands, rush hour traffic jams, never-ending street repairs, and the street closures for marathon races, festive parades, fund-raising and similar marches, and the motorcades of endless dignitaries. By pleasure I mean anything that nourishes and satisfies the mind and soul, ranging from myriad cultural events to religious needs and including libraries, galleries, and museums; parks and other recreational sites; and the scenic aspects of the city. To be sure, cities usually provide good information about cultural events, and institutions, both commercial and nonprofit, can be counted on to advertise widely their presence: after all, in a city like Phoenix that thrives on tourism, the nonprofit Heard Museum and Scottsdale Center for the Performing Arts are simply good for that business. As for churches, they are sometimes among the most prominent presences in the American cityscape. Making it on time to Sunday-morning church service may not require that complex a transportation strategy, but making a movie showing or play across town during the week demands honed instincts that begin with knowledge about traffic flows and the drama of finding parking with enough time to spare. As much as I enjoy the event once I am settled into my seat, undertaking the trek can be as unsettling as getting ready to face oral surgery.

Phoenix is fortunate to have a downtown international airport, which means for many a very short trip from the airport to residences, commercial and financial establishments, tourist sites, and the state university. But departing from the airport may not be as joyful as arriving at it. True, the actual distance may be minimal by comparison to, say, nearby Denver, whose international airport is, not to put too fine a point on it, to hell and gone. But heightened security measures and the advised lead-time they have prompted bring once again into play the advanced calculus required to negotiate traffic and, once again, the never-ending street repairs and the lane restrictions, street closures, and detours they impose, in addition to the unknown variable of potential accidents. This again is urban knowledge that Phoenix requires that is a close parallel to Los Angeles. LAX may not be quite as in-town as Sky Harbor is, but citizens of both cities who frequent the airport have internalized complex charts that include all known variables. Or they just simply go way early and sit around until boarding time, content that they have allowed themselves plenty of time.

Every urban survivor has a tale to tell about strategies for survival, including how a particularly dramatic crisis was met by skill, ingenuity, and plain street-smart intelligence. Every city has its own challenges. I may think the urbanscape in terms of Phoenix because I have lived it for forty years — and attempted to refine my skills as it has become increasingly complex, diversified, and (pardon the bit of overdramatization) harrowing. But all cities, in addition to all the nice things that get into the guidebooks and tourist brochures, have their unique horrors. Each city in America seems to take morbid pride in having the worst drivers by whatever rational index is deployed, but the circumstances for the inferno of driving in any city vary widely from locale to locale, and perhaps that is the first principle of survival that one learns in moving from one city to another. But it is only one among a fairly impressive inventory of urban survival skills, and urban survivors hardly have to be told that they need to learn those skills: the ones who didn't are usually no longer around to tell about their learning deficiencies.

The opening chapter concerns the urban chronicles of Erma Bombeck. Bombeck made few specific references to Phoenix. Yet the immense national popularity of her chronicles and their spin-offs (television shows, interviews, public lectures, and an overall very agreeable public persona) made her, nevertheless, very much of an icon for the wide interest in the Phoenix phenomenon during the boom years of Valley growth during the decades following World War II. Bombeck, however, did not always have a benign view of the so-called middle-class Good Life, and her chronicles employ a biting humor, without ever indulging in parody or sarcasm, to underscore the stains on the fabric of this sort of social life.

The Wallace and Ladmo Show is, without question, one of the most famous cultural products ever associated with Phoenix. It was the longest running locally produced children's show in U.S. television history, running from 1954 to 1989. Watching the show and enjoying the whole *W&L* phenomenon became a rite of passage for Phoenix (and Arizona) children, as well as something they continued to savor even as adults. Indeed, the humor of the show often aimed above the heads of the children to an older audience, giving the various characters portrayed and the various genres of skits a denser texture than found on most television programming for children, both before and after *Sesame Street.* Pat McMahon, who joined the show in 1961 and who continues to be a Valley personality long after the death of Ladmo and the retirement from public life of Wallace, was responsible for much of the increasing topicalness and sophistication of the show during the last three decades of its run (see the extensive interview with him by Bergelin).

Discussed next is Steve Benson, award-winning political cartoonist of the *Arizona Republic*, the one remaining major daily in the Valley. Claiming that the purpose of his cartooning is to "kill the wounded," his imaginative artistry and jaundiced wit go far beyond the generally conservative nature of the editorial staff of the *Republic*, heirs to the decidedly reactionary views of the paper when it was the property of Phoenix shaker and mover Eugene Pulliam. Benson's work ranges over a spectrum of national events, but he returns frequently to his base in Phoenix local news. One of the thematic clusters of his editorial cartoons is featured here, his interpretation of the so-called snow birds: the out-of-state winter visitors alternatively praised for their contributions to state taxes and derided as unrepentant and ridiculous outsiders.

The humorous vein of local commentary is plumbed to its extremes in the chronicles of Laurie Notaro. Unlike Bombeck, Notaro was raised in Phoenix, and unlike Bombeck, Notaro has no qualms about addressing specific features of Phoenix life in a lustily parodic and sarcastic voice. Bombeck's concern for "women's issues" is supplanted in Notaro's writing by a frankly in-your-face feminism that stands in stark contrast to the paeans to the Sun Belt's Good Life propagated by a still male-dominated Chamber of Commerce and assorted booster clubs. Nowhere is urban survival more grimly funny than in Notaro's idiot girl commentary.

Jon Talton's great-grandparents, born and raised in Phoenix, in the historic districts just north of downtown, homesteaded near Alma School and Southern in what is now Mesa. Talton resides in Seattle after finally — and much to the relief of the land development industry and its allies — being removed by the *Republic* from his highly eloquent tenure as the business editorial writer. Talton's adventures and misadventures with the *Republic* are a separate story, however. Of interest are his detective novels driven by the need to uncover the dirty secrets of Phoenix and to tell the stories that presumably do not exist. Built around the conceit of a washed-up historian assigned to pursue criminal cases that have gone cold (and there are those determined they remain cold), Talton's highly crafted narratives provide the opportunity to see beyond the supposedly flawless All American-city façade of Phoenix.

Jana Bommersbach is easily one of the most acclaimed investigative journalists in Phoenix, as well as a columnist who comments on current events and the social history of the city. Her extensive investigation into the cover up of the real facts of the 1931 murders attributed to Winnie Ruth Judd, who was railroaded first into the death house and then the state mental asylum, is one of the most intriguing narratives about Phoenix. It is also the seamiest story the city has yet produced. Of particular note is the way in which Bommersbach effects a feminist interpretation of one of the most egregious examples of the exercise of masculinist power in the city's history.

The Winnie Ruth Judd murder case in the early 1930s was Phoenix's first really notorious crime event, and the fact that the accused was a woman was a boon to the yellow journalism of the day. Although Judd was found guilty of the murder of two women friends (one of whose bodies was dismembered), she escaped the gallows by being subsequently declared insane in exchange for her silence as to who the powerful man was who constituted the backstory of the crime. Judd died sixty years later, taking her real story to the grave. Yet Bommersbach, a journalistic phenomenon of Phoenix, pieced together most of the story in a process that she marvelously characterizes as a "look up the dirty skirts of Phoenix."

Stella Pope Duarte is the first Chicana novelist produced by Phoenix, a city that has a slim record of novelists to begin with, a slimmer record of novelists of color, and an even slimmer record of women novelists of color. Coming out of the one of the few downtown historical Chicano barrios to have survived the vertiginous development of Phoenix during and after World War II — Sky Harbor International Airport is a symbol of that development — Duarte includes the survival of urban life by Chicanos in many of her writings. My chapter deals with a young man from the barrio who becomes a Vietnam casualty, and his story is one version of an exit from the barrio, as is the story of his family that attempts to reconstruct the trajectory from his departure from the Sonorita barrio just south of the Phoenix downtown to the inclusion of his name on the Wall of the Vietnam Memorial in Washington, D.C.

The theater of Guillermo Reyes focuses on Hispanic life in the U.S. Southwest. Although many of his highly creative comic texts focus on life in Los Angeles, where he first developed his dramatic skills, his tenure as a professor of dramatic scriptwriting at Arizona State University has brought him to focus also on Phoenix life. By intersecting issues involving both Hispanics and gay men, the sort of dramatic work examined here provides a particularly complex node of urban survival where the personal and the political are deeply intertwined with the backdrop of the prevalent hegemony of white and straight.

Cherríe Moraga's apocalyptic vision of Phoenix, the refuge in a post-utopian American Southwest for a lesbian couple from the Mechicano Nation of Aztlán, now ruled by a solidly entrenched *raza* patriarchy, is examined next. Moraga has written extensively about the machismo of Mexican American culture and the need for it to accommodate a lesbian motherhood. Arguing in her play from the rhetorical question "What ever rose up from the ashes of destruction," Moraga undercuts the underlying

Introduction

mythic credo of Phoenix urban history while using that city as a dystopian backdrop to her hard-edged interpretation of the lesbian struggle within Chicano society. Although Moraga is not a Phoenix-based author (she is based in Los Angeles), it is important to include commentary on her important play as an example of the growing importance of Phoenix as a national imaginary. What is particularly significant about her novel is that it is set around the decaying commercial area of East Van Buren, what is left of the segment of the old Dixie-Overland Highway (U.S. 80) that passed through Phoenix, a fitting setting for Moraga's views regarding an apocalyptic America.

The final chapter deals with Cecilia Esquer's personal memoir about her role as a Chicana activist in the Phoenix area. Set against the backdrop of the problematic history of racial (and, in this case also gender) discrimination in Phoenix, Esquer's narrative characterizes major events in Chicano history as they played out in Phoenix. Her account of her activism is grounded on the strategies of personal resistance and rhetorical contestation that allowed her, first, to bring out the mostly silenced discourse of oppression and, second, to articulate a principled response to it.

Appendix I is about Glendon Swarthout's minor Phoenix classic, *Cadillac Cowboys* (1964). Swarthout, who was for a time somewhat of a celebrity writer in Phoenix, devoted his very broadly satiric voice to characterizing one of the first of several generations of unchecked land speculation in Phoenix. In this case it was the speculation that created the North Phoenix/Scottsdale/Paradise Valley areas that are the setting for so many of Erma Bombeck's chronicles. Between them, they characterize, albeit in a critical way, the imaginary middle-class life in the sun-drenched Phoenix paradise that emerged with the post-World War II boom years.

Appendix II discusses a John Meyers Meyers novel on Jack Swilling, the carpetbagger to whom is attributed the founding of Phoenix and whose Mexican American son is the first citizen of the new settlement.

This volume would not have been possible if it were not for a large number of personal relationships and friendships in Phoenix. Aside from the enormous encouragement and interest of my wife, Virginia, our son, David Raúl, and his wife, Anni, there has been the direct involvement of the students who have taken various incarnations of my course on Phoenix and Cultural Production at Arizona State University. Arizona State's research programs, as always, have provided invaluable material support to this project. Many of the individuals whose work is studied here have contributed to it directly, especially Stella Pope Duarte, Jon Talton, and

Guillermo Reyes. Their gratitude that I might be interested in writing on them has been a very important stimulus to get things right. Various individuals have provided logistical support: Patricia Hopkins, a great first reader; Kyle Black, Charles St-Georges, Edith Marsiglia, Paul Bergelin, and Daniel Holcombe have all been my research assistants on various components; and colleagues Philip VanderMeer, Dan Arreola, Eduardo Pagán, all exceptionally fine scholars on Phoenix, have given generous input. William S. Brashears has been an exciting "native" informant on many aspects of Phoenix, and Max Underwood made possible my teaching on Phoenix in the College of Architecture. Finally, my greatest debt of scholarly gratitude goes to the fine students who have participated in the various versions at Arizona State of my seminar on Phoenix and Cultural Production.

Erma Bombeck: The Phoenix Suburban Underbelly

> A few weeks later [after hearing a lecture by Betty Friedan in 1964], I walked into a suburban weekly newspaper and asked for a job as housewife-columnist who "reveled in a comic world of children's pranks, eccentric washing machines, and parents' night at the PTA."
>
> Later, when my husband came home, I said, "Guess what? I got a part-time job today."
>
> "Doing what?" he asked.
>
> "I'm going to write funny things that happen to our family."
>
> "You can't be serious," he said. "You're going to expose our personal lives to the public, exploit our children, and hold up our intimate moments together for the world to see?"
>
> "I get three bucks a column," I said.
>
> He smiled. "Why didn't you say so?" (*A Marriage Made in Heaven ... or Too Tired for an Affair* 103)[1]

Although there is a museum in her native Dayton, Ohio, devoted to the wit and wisdom of Erma Bombeck, one of the most beloved journalistic chroniclers of American middle-class life in the late twentieth century, it is in Phoenix, Arizona, where her career flourished the most. Arriving in the city in 1971, at a time when its urban growth was reaching a sustained explosive level, Bombeck was first and foremost an icon of the shift of the middle-class suburban consciousness from its centers in the Northeast and the Mid-West to the Southwest. In this sense, she is part of an Arizona tradition that harks back to Martha Summerhayes's eloquent 1908 memoir on the transition from the frontier West, garrisoned by the U.S. Army in which her husband was an officer. This memoir bears the title Vanished Arizona because of how much Southwest lives changed between the end of the Civil War and World War I. But there was no one to write a memoir about the changes in Phoenix from the onset of World

War II and the halcyon sixties, an equivalent Vanished Phoenix. Bombeck belongs unquestionably to the post-vanished Phoenix in which agriculture is replaced by urban sprawl and in which the old core of central Phoenix power and prestige is replaced by north Phoenix enclaves, by trendy Scottsdale, and by ritzy Paradise Valley, three contiguous areas of the city that, while newer areas are now steadily emerging all around the Valley of the Sun, constitute the paradigm of the sun-belt suburbia.

The respect and, indeed, considerable personal affection, generated by Bombeck with her writings about suburbia in general, but certainly specifically about the Southwest suburbia, derived from the enormous cleverness of her adopted narrative voice, which moved easily from self-deprecation — she typically wrote in the first-person, describing her own engagement with the social realms she was characterizing — to a sense of the multilayered absurdity of suburban life, where trivial features of that life are magnified into earth-shattering crises. It is not that suburban life is necessarily trivial, since all human existence is essentially driven by trivia, but that the suburban ethos is predicated on the assumption that trivia must be treated as magnificent obsessions, worthy of enormous human endeavor and unquestionably fascinating to behold. This is clearly evident in Bombeck's writing when, for example, the messiness of children — a recurrent theme in the novel — threatens to bring down the domestic establishment in almost Götterdammerung fashion. Or when customary matrimonial strife assumes the proportions of Greek tragedy.

In one sense, Bombeck's writing is cruelly classist and racist, sexist and heterosexist. Hers is a world in which only straight families exist, presided over by a working and only discreetly present Dad and a fully engaged managing Mom — the *Reader's Digest* and *Ladies Home Journal* fantasy; moreover such families are unreflectively white and, of course, inhabit the promised transcendently ordered world of suburbia. If suburbia is the post–World War II dream of still mostly white America, Bombeck is one of its loyal chroniclers. Such chroniclers of the dream — like other forms of cultural production tied to reduplicating its ideology: *Father Knows Best* and *The Ozzie and Harriet Show* are routinely cited in this regard — present a bemused detachment from the tensions and foibles generated by the Great American Lifestyle. But the latter is generally treated as an unquestionable given in which surface description is in order but not deep-structure analysis.

Yet, already in the 1950s, there were famous examples of such analyses, such as the excellent study by Robert Beuka on the interpretation of sub-

24

urbia in American film and fiction. Sloan Wilson's 1955 novel *The Man in the Gray Flannel Suit* stands out as one of the most unsettling because of its image of mind-numbing, and ultimately psychologically annihilating, conformity, as symbolized by the standard business suit of the day. In retrospect, one can clearly understand how so much of the best cultural production of the period, whether in fiction, film, theater, and even some television, engaged in a relentless critique of the so-called suburban mentality. Although set at a time in which suburbia still had not prevailed definitively, part of the deconstruction, in terms of inherent hypocrisy and self-delusion, of the American Dream in Arthur Miller's 1948 *Death of a Salesman* involves the nuclear family that would be essential to attempts at survival in both the middle-class city and then its suburbs. A culminating vision like Ira Levin's *The Stepford Wives* (1972) had so many tragic dimensions because it was working off of what were the unquestioned values of suburbia (which is why the remake was an unsuccessful farce: there was no longer any dramatic tension, since the underlying values of Stepford were no longer held by the majority to be universal: Bombeck specifically indexes *Stepford Wives* in the essay "The Sexual Revolution" (*Marriage* 158).

While Erma Bombeck's columns certainly never aspired to a rigorous deconstruction of the tragic dimensions of America suburbia, there is, nevertheless, very much of a dark streak in her writing, one in which the aura of a benevolent grandmother that was used so effectively to market her voice, can give way to a sense of terror over the very foundations of suburbia. If one of her most characteristic collections is *Life is Always Greener over the Septic Tank* (1976), a moment's serious reflection on what the septic tank really functions to retain and what it might mean to ground life in/over the septic tank (surely a functional detail that made a good part of suburbia possible) allows the perception of a metaphoric construction inappropriate to the benevolent grandmother. Septic tanks do exist in Phoenix, but they were never much of a detail of Phoenix mass-produced suburbia (the landscape perhaps lent itself better to the installation of sewer lines than in other parts of the country), but perhaps the abstract nature of the metaphor, rather than the literal overflowing possibilities of its everyday reality, renders it more useful: the perception of its full meaning is more trenchant if it is slower in coming.

A selection of Erma Bombeck's chronicles may be examined in terms of the slippage — overflowing septic tanks do lead to the possibility of foul slipping and sliding — between urbane humor and everyday terror. Pursuing successfully such a slippage will not erase the social flaws of Bombeck's writing and the nearly hermetic universe it characterizes, but it can contribute to undermining the presumed idyll such a universe purports to construct. One of the first mainstream popular magazine articles on Bombeck, in *Life* in October 1971, ties her to the domestic sphere: the article is entitled "The Socrates of the Ironing Board." It is difficult to know what is less flattering: the metonym of the ironing board or the inevitable comparison to a male role model. The article is written by a woman, since that would have been the standard writing assignment of the day. Bombeck received much coverage from the popular press, and major observations are summarized in the *Contemporary Authors Online* entry, "Erma (Louise) Bombeck." But it is when Bombeck's description yields to the beginnings of analysis, such writing becomes less journalistic column filling and begins to have some sort of serious and significant engagement with the social reality it is reporting on.

Among Bombeck's many books — approximately a dozen, most of which remain in print in hardback, paperback, and both gathered and sampler anthologies[2] — it is reasonable to begin with *A Marriage Made in Heaven, or Too Tired for an Affair* (1993). Not only is this among the last books published before her death in 1996 (several titles were brought out posthumously), but it is, to judge from biographical information (see, for example, the Wikipedia entry, which reliably conforms to other sources), quite straightforwardly autobiographical as regards the details of her marriage and family life (her husband and children, for example, are identified by name); the beginnings of her journalistic career after hearing Betty Friedan in Dayton, Ohio, in 1964 and being inspired by her call for a feminist revolution; and the Bombecks' move to Phoenix, Arizona, in 1971.

But there is another reason to give privilege to this collection of thirty-three columns, divided into eleven chronological groupings that run from her marriage to Bill Bombeck in 1949 to the marriage of her son (which one is not specified) in 1992, especially when one considers the degree to which, by this point in her career, Bombeck is so thoroughly identified with the Arizona sociocultural landscape. What I am referring to is the topic of marriage in a state that refused to pass the Equal Rights Amendment (Bombeck campaigned for it) and that has gone on legal record as prohibiting any version of marriage that is not between one man and one woman. Phoenix specifically, and Arizona in general, is dominated by three socially conservative religious groups that monumentalize marriage as at or near the core of their theological teaching: the conservative Hispanic Catholics who predate the Anglo presence in the state and who include a high percentage of recent Hispanic arrivals, who may not necessarily be churchgoers, but who subscribe to a traditional interpretation, centered in the Virgen de Guadalupe, of women's roles in marriage[3]; Southern Baptist versions of Christianity and affiliated fundamentalist groups, as the consequence of the enormous importance immigrants from the South and Midwest have had in the development of the local population base; and the Church of Jesus Christ of Latter-day Saints (the Mormon Church), which counts the Mesa suburb of Phoenix as the second most important temple site of their institutional presence. From Sts. Simon and Jude Catholic Cathedral (Bombeck was a convert to Catholicism), to the Valley Cathedral, to the Mesa temple, there is a powerful network of conservative, fundamentalist, and pronounced traditional Christianity in the Greater Phoenix area for which matrimony and its attendant practices (compulsory heterosexuality, procreation, the discouragement of divorce and, above all else, the subscription of the hegemonic privilege such Christian beliefs are absolutely beyond either reproach or question). Not that there are not ample alternatives to such privilege (Phoenix has an ever-increasing Jewish community) and there is an official establishment public endorsement of the Interfaith Council principle, but it takes only issues like the ERA, abortion, and gay marriage to bring back into focus the hegemony I am characterizing.

It is impossible to discern any from-the-pulpit denunciations by Bombeck. She seems to have stayed steadfastly away from the abortion debate; and there is no question that, in a book like *Marriage*, she essentially subscribes to a romantic and often even sentimental version of matrimony (despite the hilariously described conflicts of the state), which is most surely the consequence of the evident success of her almost fifty-year relationship with her husband and the way in which her chronicles recognize the unstinting, unselfish, and thoroughly nonsexist way in which he supported her career. Yet, Bombeck is honest in the characterization of the strains of matrimony, spousal conflict and discord, and many forms of in- and miscommunication, such as the loss of communication as spouses drift apart, the ways in which it would appear that children speak an alien tongue (or speak in tongues), the invisibility of women in public spaces, the futility of verbal irony when so much of the world is humorless. More importantly — especially when viewed from the perspective of traditional religion — there is a frank depiction of the female body in the sense of the other side of the tapestry of the feminine mystique that remained overtly unchallenged in the first decades on which Bombeck reports. Moreover, while so much of her humor is predicated on the sly exaggeration, clever wordplay, and perfect punch line timing, Bombeck does not shy away from being bawdy, although she is certainly never vulgar, and she has no reservations about making judicious use of bathroom humor and accompanying references to bodily functions. Furthermore, there is unquestionably an assimilation throughout her career of the basic principles of the ERA and the right to a strongly feminine and unconventional — perhaps even on occasion feminist — voice that was strategically attenuated, or legitimated, by her carefully maintained grandmotherly appearance and generous smile, which is why Nancy A. Walker makes numerous references to her as a form of critique of women's domestic roles in American society. Bombeck, it would seem, occupied essentially the moderate end of the spectrum of second-wave feminism.

Susan Gubar, a noted third-wave feminist, uses Bombeck's name in her survival guide for women professors, based on what she has observed since Gubar began her career in 1973; otherwise, Bombeck is not discussed beyond beginning an observation to the effect that "If the maddened housewife Erma Bombeck were morphed into a harried associate or full professor, she would throw up her hands in despair" (433) and a handful of follow up references.[4] If first-wave feminism is the movement for women's suffrage and laws of equality, second-wave feminism addresses the multiply repressive and oppressive social, historical, and cultural constructs of woman and proposes significant reinterpretations of them. Since second-wave feminism is often considered essentializing, third-wave feminism engages in theoretical debates on gender identity, gender construction, and queer issues. In practice, the three waves intersect to a considerable degree and run on parallel, rather than sequential, tracks.

Cynical manipulation of the public persona was not at issue here. Indeed, an overwhelming measure of Bombeck's success as the narrating voice of suburban wifehood and motherhood was the unmovable conviction on the part of her audience that she was always and absolutely genuine and sincere in her chronicles. There is no reason to hold the belief that the details of Bombeck's chronicles are necessarily autobiographical in the strictest sense, although many do seem to relate, in a straightforward or exaggerated way, to her daily family and public life. Rather, there is something that can be called a sincerity effect in her writing that validates everything she says as though it were routinely and completely verifiable.

Bombeck's public demeanor, which one would do well to accept as completely authentic, is what allowed her to take risks in certain moments of hard-edged analysis and to indulge a marked propensity for dark — never bleak, but surely far from jejune — humor in the face of the details of "her" alleged life that cannot be dismissed with a bemused smile.

Bombeck never really achieved great success until after she and her family moved to Phoenix in 1971: her first huge success was *The Grass Is Always Greener over the Septic Tank* (with McGraw Hill in 1976). Yet, the publicity convention has been to retain her tied to her Midwestern roots, and the official Erma Bombeck site (ermabombeck.org) makes only the scantest reference to her residence in Phoenix. Even when the biographical section of the site deals with the strains of her weekly commute to Burbank to write and produce for the short-lived television sitcom *Maggie* (1981–82), based on her chronicles, the details of the commute and her Friday return to her family for the weekend glaringly omit any reference to where her family resided, as though they had not moved ten years previously from Dayton to Phoenix.[5] Now, it is true that Bombeck did not directly write much about Phoenix or the actual Paradise Valley where she lived: she remained true throughout her career to the rather manic image of a typically Midwestern — that is, typical suburban — American family. Thus, one of the visual icons on the cover of *Four of a Kind*, which brings together four of Bombeck's favorite collections of chronicles, is a white picket fence, grass, and posies, an all–American conjunction of landscape items rarely seen in Phoenix, and certainly much less in the suburbs, where open lawns or desert landscaping is the norm. Perhaps recounting many of the details of actually living in Arizona, often part of the renunciation by transplants of the iconic Midwest, could have had a disruptive influence on her already firmly established (although not yet widely successful) access to the American reader. It is important to note that Bombeck did not go the route of *Arizona Republic* editorial cartoonist Reg Manning in his introductions to Arizona for tourists and newcomers: *Reg Mannings's Cartoon Guide of Arizona* (1938) or *What Is Arizona Really Like?* (1968), the latter published a few years before the Bombecks moved to Arizona. The *Arizona Republic*'s current columnist Clay Thompson, whose "Valley 101" runs daily and has been gathered into two published books, has a running gag about educating newcomers to Phoenix life; he has recently also initiated a weekly column called "Arizona 101," which deals with Arizona history, again with a particular slant toward the tenderfoots. Nevertheless, Arizona is indexed explicitly in *Marriage*, first in the reference to the 1971 move after a disastrous three-year-long experience with a monstrosity of a fix-up house in the suburbs ("The Fixer-Upper" 183).

"A House Morally Divided Cannot Stand One Another" belongs to one of the eleven chronological periods covered by *Marriage* (1974), which places it in the context of the already well established residency of the Bombecks in Phoenix. The fact that the title is syntactically incoherent may serve to announce the narrator's amazement at the fact of the incomprehensible modifications in the rituals of marriage she confronts in the unconventional hippie wedding of a girlfriend of her daughter. The chronicle is built around the conceit that the narrator is pleased to see a return to the institution of marriage, when Dawn announces her marriage plans. This pleasure is noticeable because previously a hippie entourage had crashed for a few days at the Bombecks,' where they were obliged to abide by the house rules: "No drugs. No booze. And no one sleeps with a person of the opposite sex to whom he or she is not currently married" (197).[6]

Bombeck's narrative voice in this chronicle and elsewhere in her writings never seems to consider the possibility of lesbian or gay marriage. This is not an insignificant detail, since chronicle signals a confrontation with the "generation split" (197), one aspect of which is the revision in the rules of marriage. Such a revision inevitably includes new gender conjugations, which in turn inevitably include newer forms of marriage. Indeed, gay marriage is predicated on the very conservative concept of the marriage imperative Bombeck explicitly defends in "A House Morally Divided" when she provides a zany version of the commitment to see one's children through the rituals of marriage, as though these were the compelling reasons to await anxiously their entry into the sacred institution: "How did [our children] expect us to get on with our lives until we had done our job ... getting them saddled down with a thirty-year mortgage, a bad back, and a couple of kids to support?" (196–97).

Although certainly the hippie movement must have had its adherents back in Dayton, Ohio, the move to the big city of Phoenix (which, by the early 1970s, was well into its megalopolitan population surge; the Phoenix *New Times* carries a section on "Megalopolitan Life") is an eye-opener in terms of the laid-back mores of Southwestern living. The Chamber of Commerce-type discourses tout only those laid-back morals that do not contradict the overarching religious conservatism that maintains itself so vigorously in Arizona. However, the broader meanings of being laid-back are amply evident in the alternative press and the trappings of local youth bars and the music scene (Alice Cooper is from Phoenix, and a major watering hole bears his name) and it is important to grasp all of the varieties of entertainment captured by an unofficial Phoenix slogan, "Fun in the Sun." The clash between conventionally solid suburb values and hippie culture is captured metonymically by the image of the narrator's car — presumably paradigmatically standard-issue respectable — and the "pink van with purple scorpions painted all over its body" (197). Equally jarring is her transcription of the van's bumper sticker "If you haven't seen God lately, guess who moved?" (197). Bombeck may not have subscribed to the "God is my co-pilot" worldview and she certainly was unlikely to have bumper stickers on her car, but her self-characterization establishes the irreconcilable contrast in belief systems: "I had a strong feeling this vehicle did not belong to the pest control company" (197), even though Truly Nolan Pest Control vehicles, prominent on the Valley cityscape, do come decorated with large insects, either their image or mock versions of them.

The structure of the chronicle is the movement from the initial shock of the "discovery" of such denizens of local hippie culture; to pleasure that, nevertheless, the institution of marriage has not been forsaken by Dawn and company ("[marriage] is getting in the game and playing by all the rules" [199]); to the traumatic experience of the sort of ritual of marriage Dawn has in mind: "If I thought tradition was making a comeback, I was wrong. Dawn was married in a meadow just off the highway. Both read a passage from *Catcher in the Rye*, and a minister from the Church of What's Happening officiated" (203).

A perfect companion volume to *Marriage* is the 1987 collection, *Family: The Ties that Bind ... and Gag!*, since the family is the monumentalization that accompanies marriage. The two opening pieces contain internal information that allows the reader to date them and, therefore, to compare their pared nature in terms of a then-and-now set of experiences: the then of a typical Midwestern family in 1939, when Bombeck would have been a pre-teenage girl of twelve, and the 1987 suburban family, now living in the Southwest. The contrasting link between "The Family: 1939" and "The Family: 1987" is the living room. In typical old-school fashion, the 1939 living room was never used, except for the major social event of the funeral of the narrator's always silent and never quite there stepfather. It is not clear how much more the 1987 suburban family uses the living room (comfortably-off Phoenix families all have an Arizona room, the local equivalent of the family room), but by then the major social event staged there is the Christmas card photograph, usually produced months prior to distribution. Although no reference is made to the absurdity of posing for a Christmas photo when it is still 100° in the shade — Sunbelt Christmases anyway are hardly characterized by jingle bells at Farmer John's — the whole family setting is decidedly laid back: "[My son] was wearing a wrinkled jacket with sleeves pushed up to the elbow, Hawaiian shirt, and balloon pants that revealed white ankles and bare feet" (9).

When everyone is finally assembled and husband Bill is checking out his human tableaux through the lens, he responds to his wife's query as to how the composition looks: "It looks like a group of illegal aliens hauled in for questioning. 'What are you doing in a tennis dress?' he asked our daughter" (10).

Hawaiian shirts, tennis dress, and references to illegal aliens represent a conjunction of elements that do seem typically Southwestern, especially when cast against the formal living room where the man of the house must remove his shoes before entering (7). Perhaps the group would have looked less motley had it been photographed in the Arizona room, meant to provide a relaxed contrast to the formal living room that, although it may be decorated in Southwestern motifs (i.e., indigenous and/or Mexican), is customarily generic *Home Beautiful* in its décor. This is, in fact, the way in which the narrator characterizes it, with: "The white sofas facing one another, the pristine plush carpet, and the plump pillows that peaked like fresh meringue" (7). As the camera clicks, daughter asks mother about the snake in the utility room. We learn in subsequent chronicles that one of the sons has brought it with him to the annual family ritual, announcing that he plans on leaving it behind for safekeeping before, as he says in good Phoenix-speak, "I'm going over to the coast for a couple of days to catch some rays" (9; elsewhere in the country, one goes "out to the coast"). But when the matter of the snake is first brought up, the reader, at the moment of reading "The Family: 1987," may well think of one of the major inconveniences of desert suburbia: the fauna of the desert checking into houses. This is why the reference in the text to a pest control service in the text discussed above — Truly Nolan and his commercial brethren do a very brisk business in Phoenix — has a particular resonance for the Phoenix reader.

Part of Bombeck's often rather maniacal humor is that some of her interpretations of things do not really tally with the verisimilar. So as the shutter clicks, the image it produces is of the narrator reacting to the news of the snake: "My lips were forming what looked like the SH word ... when in fact it was the SN word. They photograph the same" (12). This is not quite true, since the shape of the mouth anticipates, in customary phonetic fashion, the upcoming vowels, [I] versus [æ], quite differently positioned in the buccal cavity, whose different configurations affect the exterior appearance of the mouth and face. But the point is made without saying as much: they all look like shit in the photograph — or, alternately, they look so bad that "shit" rather than "cheese" should be the photographer's injunction. Modern-day Christmas — and Christmas in the Sunbelt (like Christmas in Miami) undermines the traditional images of the holiday in multiple ways — never looked so bad.

The reader could assiduously troll the dozen published books by Erma Bombeck, but little would be found that specifically indexes Phoenix, much less discuss the parameters of the Phoenix lifestyle. But the reader should not let this marvelous humorist get off free in regard to how the Arizona megalopolis appears in her writing. After all, she did spend twenty-five years in Phoenix, and it was the home base for the mature peak of her career, which began with the publication of *The Grass Is Always Greener* five years after her arrival in the Valley of the Sun. Moreover, Phoenix readers always understood that her image of suburbia during the following two decades was all about their lifestyles and its tribulations and quirks, even if she did not refer to them specifically. But, then, one assumes that her readers everywhere must have felt the same. The reaction was, undoubtedly, one of the major bases of her popularity. Norman King, in his chatty book about Bombeck, quotes her: "The most flattering thing to me is that people think I live in the town where they read me" (19). She goes on to observe that once when she spoke of looking out the window at a swollen abandoned garden hose, her Ohio readers knew it was because the water in it had swollen the hose as a result of the cold, while her readers in Arizona were convinced that it was a consequence of the desert heat (King 19).

Yet Bombeck is irrevocably associated with Phoenix, to the degree that she was one of the forces — sociocultural in her explanation of women's issues and her defense of their equal rights; literary in the sense of the quality of her writing — that brought Phoenix to national attention as having outgrown the images of orange groves, tuberculosis sanatoriums, and trailer parks for the snow birds. Few of the latter remain, although perhaps the most prominent reminders are the TB-related guest houses along the downtown end of West Roosevelt, which have been transformed, in the main, into offices. With the displacement of trailer parks and orange groves by housing developments, which have taken over most other agricultural installations and a good share of the open desert around Phoenix, the metropolitan area looks more and more like the all–American suburbia Bombeck scrutinized in such detail. Phoenix in a sense has caught up with the general spirit of Bombeck's writings, and this is why there is no compelling need for her to have named what her hometown readers instantly recognized as their own.[7]

Wallace and Ladmo: Dark Shadows of Irreverent Humor in the Valley of the Sun

"There's a lot of cartoons and a couple of goons." (From the opening jingle of the *Wallace and Ladmo Show*)

In an interview on life in Arizona in the 1970s,[1] the ineffable Alice Cooper (although born in Detroit in 1948, Cooper counts Phoenix as his hometown since 1958) asserts that the "dark, subversive sense of humor" in his music is the result of a childhood watching *The Wallace and Ladmo Show*.[2] *The Wallace and Ladmo Show*, created by Bill Thompson as Wallace,[3] and Vladimir Kwiatkowski as Ladmo ran from April 1, 1954, to December 29, 1989 — the longest-running locally produced children's television show in American TV history.[4] In 1960, Pat McMahon joined the show, and the trio developed a programming that entranced children in the Phoenix area (popularly called the Valley of the Sun); their audience also included many adult viewers also who had first seen the show as children.

Predominantly zany and wacky, *The Wallace and Ladmo Show* manifested qualities that undoubtedly appealed to children who soon tired of far blander network shows apparently aimed toward the youngest viewers in the lowest common sense-of-the-world denominator. There is little doubt that *Wallace and Ladmo* (as the show is mostly known), which predated the sophisticated programming of *Sesame Street* by fifteen years, was an index of the growing worldliness of TV audiences of all ages in the United States. The nearly four decades of the *Show*, in essence, grew up with American television and paralleled its emergence as the dominant entertainment medium in the world.[5] Because it ran so long, it would take

35

many pages to catalog the rank of programming the show involved, the recurring characters, the various narrative and musical formats, the types of advertising and public-service tie-ins, plus the various venues of the show from studio productions to visiting locales. Since Richard Ruelas and Michael K. Sweeney have done this in what one might call a keepsake coffee-table volume, the reader is referred to that invaluable source. Suffice it to say that the show was held together by the Wallace (Bill Thompson) and Ladmo duo, and they have become permanent icons of Phoenix cultural history.

What I would like to pursue are the implications of Alice Cooper's tribute to *Wallace and Ladmo*'s influence on his music, because it represents a profound paradox of the show: how could a show produced in Phoenix, Arizona in the 1950s and 1960s remain on the air, given so much of its over-the-top parody — and, indeed, mockery — of the all–American values that were the cornerstone of Barry Goldwater's Arizona. Even in the 1970s and 1980s, as the Valley of the Sun lost its self-styled innocence and began to contemplate tragic dimensions of its national identity and local history (e.g., race relations and the broad implications of the Vietnam war), the conservative/reactionary matrix of Arizona kept many of those discussions out of the sphere of public discourse: certainly they could hardly have been welcome on commercial television programming for children and young adolescents. One only need recall the serious reservations about the politics of *Sesame Street* when it began airing in 1970 to understand the stakes at issue. In the case of Arizona, and more specifically Phoenix, the early decades of the show coincided with the emergence of the Republican Party as dominant in Arizona.

While it had not yet been taken over by Christian fundamentalist ideologues, the party was dominated by Goldwater's "conscience of a conservative" and the touting of the proposition that extremism in the defense of liberty was a virtue. It was the nostalgic Arizona of the ultra-right-wing Minutemen, whose crosshair's icon could be found stenciled all over on the landscape, from rock formations in Sedona to concrete irrigation standpipes in metropolitan areas. The John Birch Society counted one of its founding members from Phoenix (Frank Cullen Brophy, Sr.), and his estate on North Central was a regular meeting place for the group, whose troops went door-to-door peddling their tracts like a religious sect. The Society's American Opinion Libraries were some of the busiest bookstores in town, and Reg Manning's editorial cartoons in the *Arizona Republic*, owned by Eugene Pulliam, one of the three most powerful men in Phoenix[6] and grandfather of George H.W. Bush's second vice president, Dan Quayle, touted in broad pen strokes the purported virtues of a small-town America that Phoenix had already for a couple decades ceased to resemble. It was the period in which the likes of John F. Long and Del Webb began a land development boon in Phoenix that brooked no criticism, and it was the time in which Phoenix refused federal funds for so-called urban development because it would have allowed people of color to "invade" central Phoenix from across the railroad tracks and the Salt River from the South Phoenix of pronounced "dis-amenities" to which they were in the main confined.

Nevertheless, *Wallace and Ladmo* became a cultural repository of snarky commentary on many of the sacred values of All-American Phoenix. The dynamics of this process is one of the truly amazing dimensions of the show's history. Although it would be a mistake to attribute to the show what, at least at that time, would have been called a "subversive" agenda, one is impressed, when viewing the recorded and print material available, by the insouciant manner in which ongoing threads of the program built around specific characters and situations, as well as extemporaneous asides peppered throughout a particular show, casually questioning prevailing essentialist categories of human nature and undermined clichés of civic and patriotic responsibility. Much of the humor of the show was in direct contrast to the seriousness with which Phoenix took itself as an all–American city in which there was a categorical distinction between the good and the bad, "Us" and "Them," and friend and enemy. Overlaying these disjunctions was the mythification of so-called Western values (in the American West, not in the Occidental sense) that was essential to the creation of the Arizona mystique and subcategories of it, such as the wholecloth fabrication of Scottsdale as "The West's most Western town" and various Chamber of Commerce and Tourist Commission promotions of the much touted Arizona way and Phoenix lifestyle. Although the show never presented anything like a sustained and hard-hitting critique of these parameters, as, say a social novel or noir film might, the fun of the show was that it did constitute a site for poking fun at what so much of what Phoenix locally and Arizona statewide took as unimpeachable, self-satisfied community gospel.

Since the program depended so much on the appeal to children, and the coding within the show of children's real and potential interests, it is important to consider in detail what the show seemed to be saying about mid–1950s childhood and its subsequent interpretations. As I have written elsewhere regarding the religious culture of Phoenix, there is a predominance of conservative and traditional religious belief, which was undoubtedly even more pronounced at the time the show was inaugurated. Phoenix has always been a city dominated by spectacular churches, from St. Francis on Central and Camelback, to the Church of Latter-day Saints Temple in Mesa, to the massive Central Baptist installation on North Central Avenue. At a time when political and commercial life was ruled by sober-minded white men and social values that were undergoing transition from the influence of Southern Democrats to Eisenhower (and, then, Goldwater) Republicans, it was only in the late '80s that the cultural life of the city ceased to be controlled by the self-styled morally righteous. A famous historical anecdote is that when an African dance troupe performed at the Frank Lloyd Wright-designed Grady Gammage Auditorium at Arizona State University in the mid–1960s, the women in the troupe, who had danced bare-breasted in venues across America, were required to don brassieres ("Gammage Controversy").

It is in this context that one needs to understand how pretty much of an essentialist conception of moral and social values prevailed in the Phoenix of the mid–1950s. Perhaps this climate was no different from that of the majority of America, but it was not in Peoria, Illinois, where there was emerging a local TV program of the nature of *The Wallace and Ladmo Show*, whose formulas of zany and often simply wacko humor were being developed against the backdrop of what was considered appropriate for children at the time. As Ellen Seiter has pointed out, parents are the primary audience targeted for children's television.[7] That is, if parents are looking over the shoulder of their children at what they are watching, TV producers are, so to speak, looking over the shoulder of their products to gauge what the reaction of parents will be. Dissatisfied or upset parents will, at least, attempt to prevent their children from viewing shows they find inappropriate and, at worst, pressure stations directly or through the media or through the political process to comply with the standards they and the community they feel they represent wish to enforce. KPHO, the local station (Channel 5) that produced *Wallace and Ladmo* knew very well what prevailing conceptions of childhood were and what the costs of treading the terrain of racial, sexual, and other social issues were. One had simply to change the channel to the other shows on the market available for children to ascertain quickly what prevailing assumptions were.

It is when Pat McMahon joined the show in 1960 that the format began to get more experimental and to assume the shape that most remember.

Although Kwiatkowski died in 1994 and Thompson is in retirement out of the public eye,[8] McMahon continues to be very much of a visible personality on the Phoenix entertainment scene, and he will occasionally evoke some of the famous personae he created for the show. The routines tagged between Wallace and Ladmo had much of the vaudeville about them, with Wallace playing the straight man to Ladmo's fall guy. The considerable amount of plain silliness and clownish shtick characterizing their exchanges was of the sort that young audiences are likely to easily identify with. McMahon, by contrast, began to develop a cast of characters that, while hardly featuring any subtlety of personality, possessed definable traits that gave them continuity from one enactment to another. These characters included:

Marshall Good, an incompetent town sheriff, which permitted all manner of parodies of the clichés of cowboy movies, some vintage examples of which were routinely included in the programming. Undermining the superior prowess of frontier law-and-order, which included much of the racism beginning to be seriously questioned in the 1960s, especially with reference to "Indians" and "Mexicans," Marshall Good invited the children to revel in his buffoonishness.

Captain Super was easily one of the most salient of McMahon's impersonations. On the one hand, it parodied Superman and other similar larger-than-life action heroes that were the staple of pulp comic books of the era. And, tying in with the underlying ideological assumption of the Superman motif that he was, in reality, American manhood at its quintessential best, McMahon's Captain Super mouthed exaggerated patriotic slogans. Without ever moving into the realm of desecration, Captain Super nevertheless managed consistently to mock some of the more exaggerated bywords of the day regarding the dangers of more imaginary than demonstrably real enemies of the nation. In this regard, McMahon was intentionally winking over the shoulders of the immediate juvenile audience at older viewers who had only to be following the jingoistic editorial cartoons of Reg Manning in the *Arizona Republic* to know what Captain Super was referring to.

Aunt Maud[9] is perhaps one of the most resonant of McMahon's characters, both in terms of the assumptions of childhood and a significant detail of Phoenix society. Based on an amalgam of Elmira Gulch (from the *Wizard of Oz*) and figures from a long sexist tradition of elderly women (in the main, spinsters), Aunt Maud is the antithesis of every child's favorite doting aunt or grandmother. Because of the venue, Aunt Maud could hardly have been foul-mouthed, she always looked like she wanted to be. Although in appearance a saintly older woman, Aunt Maud was the neighborhood curmudgeon, with never a nice word to say about anyone but always a mean commentary and a vociferous complaint about everything. Since her routines highlighted the transgressions of spirited children, the audience appeared to delight in her scolding without any real-world consequences.

Feminist issues were a controversial matter in Arizona in the 1970s and 1980s, and, despite the presence of local celebrity writer Erma Bombeck on a Carter administration commission to promote women's rights, Arizona was one of the states that refused to ratify the Equal Rights Amendment. Part of the recurring routines of Aunt Maud is as an irreverent woman who refuses to recognize male authority and rebels against the image of domestic housewives and womanly matters like cosmetic surgery. And, in addition to outrageous comments, there is no overlooking the role that drag played in the case of this character, despite the intense homophobia still prevalent socially and officially in Phoenix throughout Aunt Maud's presence on the show.[10]

But Aunt Maud also referenced the senior-citizen population of Phoenix and the Valley of the Sun, both a permanent segment of the local demographics and the so-called snowbirds who descend on the area during the winter months each year. There are running jokes about the snowbirds and retirees (e.g., they drive like they are still on a tractor out on the farm; they can't tolerate having anyone younger than fifty around them; they want everything free or as cheap as possible).[11] Generational conflict is the basis of Aunt Maud's ludicrous complaints, and McMahon's character plays off the particular presence — if not in actual statistics, at least in terms of the Phoenix imaginary — of elderly discontents.

Finally, there is **Gerald**. Gerald is the riskiest of McMahon's representations, both in terms of class conflict and latent homophobia. Gerald is a spoiled brat, dressed outrageously in a red velveteen Little Lord Fauntleroy outfit with ruffled collar and sleeves. He wears oversized horn-rimmed glasses, and has buckteeth and silky blond hair cut pageboy style. His family seems to own everything, and his standard retort to the taunts of the other children — i.e., the children in the audience assuming the role of his classmates — is to appeal to his family for retaliation against his tormentors. Projecting a persona that is categorically in opposition to Beaver-like all–American boyhood (let's leave aside for the moment the sexism of this all-boy dynamic), Gerald is the queer everyone is invited to smear.

Although, to be sure, no overt reference is made to gender nonconformity, McMahon's performance of Gerald leaves little doubt, in terms of clothes, mannerisms, attitude, and speech that Gerald is the odd man out whose social dissonance cannot go unnoted and unpunished. While the show does allow for the sort of direct physical torment meted out to the Geralds of the world, the audience is invited to jeer Gerald as something like a metonym for real-world bullying. Moreover, the routines play off of an unquestioned unhealthy symbiosis between Gerald's behavior and peer reaction: one feeds the other, such that it is impossible to understand either Gerald's inappropriate behavior or his peers' mean response to it. This is, to be sure, all meant to be in good fun. However, recent attention to the question of bullying in schools makes this perhaps the most dated of McMahon's personae and, upon retrospection, the most socially questionable. Yet one notable characteristic of Gerald is the way in which he is something of a metacommentary device, deriding much of the very material of *Wallace and Ladmo*: cartoons, PBS programming, the general middle-class demographic of the real children who make up the audience of the show.[12]

Whereas Wallace and Ladmo often played off of each other in routines before McMahon's joining the show, although he never received star billing, at least as part of the name of the show, his inventiveness and expansive personality seemed to take over the show, with Wallace and Ladmo now playing straight men to his various characters.[13] These various characters, who also interacted with guests on the show that provided civic messages for the children, such as Sergeant Harry Florian from the Phoenix Police Department, were some of the most memorable moments of the show. Indeed, McMahon, in the full drag of Aunt Maud, flirted outrageously with Florian in one sketch included in the thirty-fifth anniversary DVD.[14] It is not surprising to discover that the often self-reflexive nature of McMahon's characters and routines began to attract an older more sophisticated audience that was able to grasp his social and political references, most of which indexed issues current in public discourse, such as the patriotic shibboleths Captain Super parodied. The audience made up of children would have identified with the physical enactment, the sillier the better, of cartoon superheroes, while more mature viewers savored the broad humor of his one-liners. This circumstance explains how McMahon has gone on to have a career as a local TV personality beyond the final demise of the show, the death of Ladmo, and the reclusion of Wallace (Bill Thompson).

Certainly, Phoenix is physically prominent throughout the show, and not just in terms of internal references made explicitly or to the tie-in of certain routines or dimensions of certain routines with the prevailing values and concerns of public discourse in the city and its greater metropolitan area. The fact that the show traveled beyond its downtown (and then suburban) studio (the original KPHO building at North First Avenue and West Roosevelt has recently been restored) and was recorded in outdoor settings brought recognizable landmarks into the programs and, indeed, on occasion, into the sketches. Broadcasting the show in places like Encanto Park (Kiddyland and the old band shell), Park Central Mall (one of the city's first shopping malls), and other similar venues inscribed in the programs — and the archival copies that are still available — signaled a recognition of the place in which it was anchored. Most children's programs did not do this: exactly where is Mister Rogers's neighborhood located? Recognizable locales of cities like New York or Los Angeles made sense. But even today, as Phoenix has grown to become the fifth largest metropolitan area of the country, there is not much one could claim as landmarks. Many films and TV programs may be made in Phoenix, but Phoenix is rarely the actual named locale of these filmings. The opening sequences of Alfred Hitchcock's *Psycho* (1960) remains one of the few films in which Phoenix is where the action really takes place and where recognizable buildings that the film identifies as being in Phoenix still exist. One would not want to exaggerate the presence of out-of-studio locales in the programs of the *Wallace and Ladmo Show*, but the point is nevertheless valid that there is an awareness of Phoenix on various levels in the show's history.

Since others have provided extensive anecdotal and descriptive information about the show, I would now like to turn to a closer analysis of one of its important characters, Aunt Maud Garntz, who first appeared in 1961, at the very beginning of McMahon's participation in the show. More specifically, I would like to analyze the written material relating to her as gathered in *Aunt Maud's Storybook* (2000). Based in part on textual and situational material from the almost three decades of this character's participation on the show, the *Storybook*, with its brief foreword by Alice Cooper, an important archive of the nature of that show, of McMahon as a creative force, and Aunt Maud as an iconic figure, with her grey hair done up in a bun, her spectacles, a flowered housedress and shawl.

The *Storybook* includes forty texts, all around only 200-words in length, as appropriate to a program built around brief sketches that took into mind the short attention span of a restless pre-teenage audience. One typical story refers to one of the paradigmatic Phoenix traditions, the Arizona State Fair, held every year at the State Fairgrounds in downtown Phoenix (the northeast corner of West McDowell and North 19th Avenue):

> THE FIRST STATE FAIR
> Now, we all know that the opening of the State Fair is a very special day.... But, this is the story about the very first State Fair back in 1878.
> Electricity had just been invented and everyone was waiting for the fair to open so they could see all the new rides. There was a Ferris Wheel and a Merry Go Round. All the children were looking forward to the Fair. It was going to be great fun.
> But, an hour before the Fair opened, there was a power failure. Without electricity the rides couldn't operate. While everybody was waiting for the power to be turned on, it started to rain! Everyone was soaked, but they still waited. They waited and waited. Even in the cold, night air, they waited.
> Finally, when everyone had just about given up hope, the finance company came and repossessed the rides. They took away the Ferris Wheel and the Merry Go Round. All the children went home crying. No State Fair. And, late that night, when everyone was asleep, the power came back on. But, of course, by then it was too late [Thompson and McMahon, *Aunt Maud's Storybook* 69].

The Arizona State Fair, while it may now compete with many other attractions in what is now a significantly more sophisticated city than Phoenix was in 1878 (it had only begun to be settled in the early 1870s and was not incorporated until 1881), continues to be one of the signal features of municipal culture. Since it is held in the capital of the state and the seat of Arizona's dominant Maricopa County, it represents the interests, material and symbolic, of the state as a whole. But it is unquestionably a local event that draws on both the nostalgia for a state fair that may or may not accurately mirror what the city and the region once were and the need to constantly update the format of the fair to reflect changing entertainment tastes.[15] Billed as a family attraction, it may not always actually direct itself toward that social component, and some even question (particularly when attendance falls off in a particular year) whether or not it continues to serve any perceptible function. Moreover, part of the way in which it is driven by the sort of nostalgia a city like Phoenix appears to need,[16] every time the matter arises about moving the fair toward a more modern and less urban setting, nostalgia for keeping it where it has always been — including its appearance in Joshua Logan's 1956 film *Bus Stop*, starring Marilyn Monroe and Don Murray — wins out.

As in all of Aunt Maud's tales, narrative emphasis lies with attacking the assumptions of a childhood of prelapsarian and carefree innocence, one in which the dark forces of life do not intrude. Yet they do intrude in Maud's stories, with the result that, in her narrative universe, children are bitterly disappointed and brought up short as regards their naïve expectation that the adult world will ensure that everything is sunny and rosy for children. Maud views it as necessary that children be reduced frequently to tears in order to understand that life will always disappoint them: this would appear to be her objective correlative to the proposition that children will be spoiled if not made to cry with the proper and frequent application of the rod. While corporal punishment was still prevalent in the Arizona of Maud's storytelling career (with recurring unsuccessful attempts to outlaw it in public schools), this was not likely to be a topic of discussion on a comedy show. But it is not difficult to discern the stern moral principle behind Maud's selection of stories. Of course, the actual audiences of children would have none of this nonsense, and the reaction was always one of hilarious rejection of the so-called moral of Aunt Maud's exemplary tales: Ladmo, as a frequent direct narrate of the tales and as a stand-in for the carefree child, may have always been reduced to tears, but the audience for which he stood in, the real children, would deride both the moral and the tears it produced. The result was, as over and over again in McMahon's sketches, to elicit a critical burst of laughter in the face of presumably sober social, moral, cultural, or political values. That is, it's funny that children are portrayed by the adult world of Maud as in need of the reality check that tears bring, and the humor functions here and in other sketches on the principle that children are not as naive as the adult world the *Wallace and Ladmo Show* is mocking believes them to be.

In the case of "The First State Fair," it is as though the disaster of the inaugural 1878 somehow sets the tone for the entire history of the Fair, which like any event held over the span of a hundred years, has in fact had its ups and downs. But the proposition of the Fair as a disaster-struck event from its inception is an effective way of poking fun at what, in the jingoist parlance of Phoenix civic leaders, is a local "Point of Pride." What makes it all the funnier is that the first state fair was not held until 1884: settlers arriving in the early 1870s could hardly have had enough time to bring forth crops meriting such a celebration in barely a half-dozen years. Since Maud's story is based on an invented history ("we all know"), the repossession of child-attracting rides by the finance company, the false date (hardly of interest to an audience of children) is, nevertheless, a wink toward McMahon's adult fans. What is more, the story makes specific reference to the Ferris Wheel, which was not inaugurated until 1893 at the World's Columbian Exposition in Chicago: one even wonders if there would have been enough customers at a state fair in Phoenix in 1878, with or without electricity, to make it profitable.

Thus, this story is doubly outrageous. It is outrageous in Aunt Maud's apparently unquenchable need to find stories about how unpleasant and disappointing life is that will make her audience of children cry. And it is outrageous because those stories are based on wildly inaccurate, but quite transparent, allegations of historical fact. Indeed, one could add to the matter of the date of the first Arizona State Fair and the matter of the Ferris Wheel the fact that the fair is scheduled precisely when the weather is still mild in Phoenix in October, with little likelihood of either cold (more properly, chilly) nights of December and January or the rain of the so-called monsoon season of late summer.

"The Littlest Cowboy" is a particularly perverse take-off on the themes of children's pluck and the perseverance of dreams, rounded out by the cynicism of American capitalist ingenuity. While the child in the story comes to a typically painful realization of his limitations, there is, in the entrepreneurial spirit of the Jaycee establishment, in this case, a happy ending.

The Phoenix Jaycee Rodeo, like so much of the popular culture of the Phoenix area, is grounded in fiction rather than actual historical fact. In this case, it is any belief that Phoenix was ever a cowboy town and that the skills showcased by the rodeo were ever an actual issue of day-to-day life and survival in the Valley, whose prosperity has, through most of its history, been based on agriculture. Agriculture becomes complemented by tourism sometime in the early twentieth century. One of its major traces is the creation of the glossy magazine *Arizona Highways* (1925–) to promote national and then international tourist interest in the beauty of the state, made more beautifous, thanks to the technical marvels of professional photography. Another trace is the invention of a cowboy past for the urban area, something that the suburb of Scottsdale, "The West's Most Western Town," amplifies shamelessly. The latter's Parada del Sol complements other events like the Phoenix Jaycee Rodeo, which came to be formally billed as the Rodeo of Rodeos.[17] The Rodeo lasted seventy years, from 1927–97, although the Parada del Sol, which dates from 1953, is still going strong and is held every year down Scottsdale Road in February.

Maud's story plays off the intersection between cowboy tradition and the financial dimensions of any such event in contemporary America. While Buster Bob is not really a child, but a diminutive four-foot would-be rider, his height and his resort to a childlike temper tantrum to get his way are undoubtedly meant to have a "suturing" effect for the children of Maud's audience: it provides them with a point of contact, identity, and participation, to the extent that Buster Bob is as though he were a child (and note the down-home nature of his nickname, Buster) vying for legitimate participation in the adventures of the adult world. Children are plucky to the extent that they aspire to more demanding achievements, often against overwhelming odds. And children are persevering to the extent that they will not take no for an answer. And children are foolhardy to the extent that they would undertake what they are not prepared for. But, in the end, children are admirably triumphant if they succeed in overcoming the odds, objections, and barriers to accomplishing their goals.

Buster Bob is bucked by the Brahma bull in a mere 1.6 seconds and stomped and trampled in such a way that he loses a sixth of his already diminutive height, such that, subsequently his only possible gainful employment is that of a bellhop — as though the children in the audience even knew what a bellhop was anymore... In other of Maud's narratives, this might have been the end of Buster Bob's sorry story. Yet the moral here is different, although no less outrageous: Buster Bob is able to sue the Jaycees and use his settlement to open a Brahma Burger franchise. Ladmo would have cried first and then clapped upon hearing this story. Yet while Buster Bob turns suffering to profit, Maud as narrator is still able to savor the misbehavior of his tantrum and the just desserts of his physical suffering and reduced employment opportunities. There is again the presence of Maud's wink toward the divided audience: Buster Bob comes off "happy" in the end for the children, but there is the inevitable dig at the system, in the form of the boosterish Phoenix Jaycees, getting stomped and trampled on in the end.

Aunt Maud's stories do not routinely make explicit reference to Phoenix, and I have expressly chosen two of the few that do (one might also consult "The Lady and the Cat Burglar" which takes place in a Senior City like Phoenix's Sun City; Sgt. Harry is also mentioned). Indeed, some of the stories make reference to snowmen and the beach, very non–Phoenix details. Nevertheless, Aunt Maud, as one of Pat McMahon's two most successful creations (along with Gerald), remains as one of the icons of the show, and she is particularly illustrative of the irreverence, twin-level (children and adults) humor, and overall outrageousness of the show. As the text "Meet Aunt Maud" that closes the *Storybook* notes: "Before *Monty Python*, before *Saturday Night Live*, Arizona had *The Wallace and Ladmo Show* ... and Aunt Maud" (86).[18]

Truthful Misrepresentations: Steve Benson Draws Phoenix

I don't aim to please, I just aim. (Steve Benson)
My goal is to shoot the wounded. (Steve Benson)

Arizona and Editorial Cartooning

In a lecture at Ohio State University (1998), *Arizona Republic* editorial cartoonist Steve Benson[1] enumerates many of the characteristics that distinguish fine editorial cartooning, such being on target and keeping some level of pertinence to the topic at hand. But perhaps one of Benson's most important points is his discussion of "truthful misrepresentation." Although he does not elaborate on exactly what he means by such a possible oxymoron, one can think immediately of phrases such as Aristotle's dictum on his *Poetics* to the effect that poets do not describe things as they are, but how they might be. Another possibility is the rather elastic category of allegory, where one is to understand a higher meaning or a meaning beyond that which is being explicitly told. Or, seeking yet another way to approach the essence of Benson's art is to turn to the concept of hyperbole. In hyperbole, certain metonymical or metaphoric aspects of the subject are strategically exaggerated in order for the viewer/reader to concentrate on an aspect of the subject. This allows for a satisfying leap of interpretation, which is nothing more than "getting the point" of the text.

It is my intention to explore some of the dimensions of Benson's truthful misrepresentations in order to understand how he makes use of particular strategies of distortion to make a sociopolitical point. One of the features of Benson's cartoons is that there is often a lot going on in

48

them visually. They may be line drawings, but they are very complex compositionally, and it is this complexity that reinforces his often egregious rhetoric. My goal is to provide, through a detailed analysis of six panels, an understanding of why Benson is one of the most prominent editorial cartoonists working in the United States today.

Benson is particularly adept at hyperbole,[2] and his view of matters is colored by the desire to draw without concessions, if not to good taste, to the sensitivities of persons and institutions, whether public figures and elected representatives of government or private parties whose affairs represent something that Benson deems attackable. In the aforementioned Ohio State presentation, Benson contrasted with his audience some of the cartoons that his editor considered too offensive for publication with the versions he, in fact, saw published. Whatever the statistics might be as regards to what Benson draws and what his editor accepts, the point is that part of the genius of his art is his willingness to push his point as far as possible.[3] Benson won the Pulitzer Prize for editorial cartooning in 1993,[4] and many other awards have since come his way.

There are a number of consequences resulting from such a stance, in addition to the risk of editorial disapproval. Such disapproval does not really amount to censorship, since visual hyperbole seems to be more the issue than rejection of either topics or verbal text.[5] One is that Benson, by taking such extreme positions in much of his work, often arrives at contradictory editorial positions, such as can be charted over the course of his work on topics like gay rights, feminism, stem cell research, women's reproductive rights, and other similar high-stakes ideological issues. But, then, as Benson also insists in his Ohio State speech, he subscribes to "equal opportunity offensiveness." Thus, he stands in contrast to other editorial cartoonists whose work rests on specific ideological principles, such as a categorical pro-life position. Benson ranges all over the social, political, and cultural map in his search for what, by his standards, constitutes outstanding cartoon fodder.

The availability of editorial cartoon targets is particularly evident in the case of Arizona politics: like most local politics, mainline political positions in Arizona are supplemented by a rich vein of kookiness. The back cover of *Where Do You Draw the Line* (1992) contains testimonies (of a sort) from nine representative functionaries, from the clueless Ev Mecham to the outrageous Rose Mofford, from the hapless Dennis DeConcini to the feckless Fyfe Symington. Part of Benson's exceptional talent has been to focus in particular on Arizona, as state history in recent decades has followed so well national concerns. Tolstoy enjoined the author to write about his own village, because, in so doing, one writes about all of mankind. And as Tip O'Neill always insisted, all politics are local. It is in both these senses that no matter how local the target of an editorial cartoonist may be, there is always likely to be a resonance with larger national issues. It is not only Arizona whose governors are often injudicious and outrageous, and if Phoenix residents must put up with the invasion of winter visitors, Martha's Vineyard has long had to cope with the swell of summer visitors. There is no issue of high-profile varsity sports that is not the replay of something that happened elsewhere or the foreshadowing of something that is going to happen somewhere else.

The result is a wealth of Arizona material in Benson's personal archive, made all the more extensive because of the exceptional case of Governor Ev Mecham, who came to power in 1986 in a three-way contest in which no one candidate achieved a simple majority and who proceeded to govern with what seemed at times such willful malfeasance that he was subsequently impeached in 1987. *Evanly Days!* (1988; which carries the cover explanation, "A cartoon journey into the wacky world of Arizona politics — and beyond!")[6] does not deal only with the Mecham administration, but with national and international issues as well, underscoring the seamless web connecting the local to what lies beyond, thereby charting the continuity between Mecham, Reagan, the Ayatollah Khomeni, and even the Pope.

However, as rich a vein that this Arizona/world conjunction could prove to be for an analysis of the Benson oeuvre, my interest here is with the local at even a more local level — to wit, particular aspects of Phoenix life and times that the cartoonist has dealt with. If there is a continuity between Arizona and what lies beyond its borders, this is also true for the relationship between Phoenix and the state as a whole. This is not only true because Phoenix is the largest city in the state (a little bit more than half of Arizonans lives in the Greater Phoenix area), it is also the state capital, the capital of the state's largest county (Maricopa), and an important federal administrative base. It may be questionable whether as goes Phoenix, so goes Arizona. There has long been considerable historical resistance to Phoenix domination and concerted efforts by non–Phoenicians to make it clear that Arizona and Phoenix are not commutable terms. But because of its sheer size, what Phoenix is all about is necessarily of importance to the rest of the state.

Arizona State University and Frank Kush

For example, the development of Arizona State University, located in the Phoenix suburb of Tempe, as a major educational institution has been vital. The university not only provides expertise to programs of the city, but it also complements the contributions made at a state level by the University of Arizona, located in the state's second most populous city, Tucson. The conversion of Arizona State College to Arizona State University in 1959 was fought in part by exclusivist interests at UA. Yet the explosive growth of Phoenix during the past fifty years has made ASU not only vital to the education needs of the city, but also to specialized knowledge that only a dynamic university can provide. The development of ASU into what is called a Research Intensive institution, with accompanying teaching and service programs such a status implies, was not without difficult moments, and the men's athletic programs, football in particular, were often seen as a throw-back to earlier more good-ole-boy days. It is not coincidental that the legendary Frank Kush, who would coach men's football at ASU for over two decades, from 1958 to 1979, coincided with the definitive transformation of ASC into ASU in 1959. Part of this transformation also involved participation in the PAC 10 athletic league, which is reputed to entail higher professional standards, including academic ones, for the league's athletes. Yet, questions over professional standards plagued ASU's football program throughout the period, and the controversies that led to Kush's summary dismissal in 1979 were viewed by many as only the tip of the iceberg.

Benson's cartoon (from *Fencin' with Benson*, p. 137) is indicative of the bases of criticism that the Kush regime had to endure. Kush had the support of some of the most powerful citizens of Phoenix, but it did not prevent Benson from taking him on. One assumes that Benson, all–American eagle scout that he is, has no aversion to college football (as does a measurable portion of the professorate), but to those practices that detract from whatever intrinsic value, institutional or otherwise, that college football has. Kush's problem was that it was precisely elements of detraction — and, therefore, distraction — that became paramount as part of his enormously successful coaching career. In Benson's cartoons, one dimension of what detractors said about Kush is evident: the way in which players were recruited less for their academic profile than for their athletic ability.

Benson's representation of Kush's recruits relies on three strategies of

51

Arizona State head football coach Frank Kush addresses new team members (by permission of Steve Benson and Creators Syndicate, Inc.).

representation. The first plays off the necessary qualities of football players as brawny and excellent physical specimens. However, the four players Benson includes in his drawing are hardly men on the cutting edge of physical development. They are more examples of a certain buffoonish version of Neanderthal man, grossly pumped up, low of brow, and cranially challenged. We see that two are missing teeth, signaling that brawl rather than brawn has been their interest. The representation of Kush is equally ludicrous. Kush himself was always a man's man, always in tough muscular shape. However, in Benson's merciless interpretation, Kush is as less than athletic as his recruits, with balloon buttocks and prominent paunch, with spindly arms and legs complementing his hayseed face.

The second representational aspect of the cartoon involves the recruit's demonstration of academic accomplishment. While Kush, in good standard English, welcomes them to the team at ASU and asks if they have any questions, we see one of them "reading" a play book upside down, while a second inquires how to spell "A-S-U"; a third echoes part of the Kush-

ASU football mystique, "We're No. 1" while holding up three fingers. Finally, the third representational device is to portray the recruits, in addition to being moronic, as sophomoric: someone from a row behind the recruits sails a paper airplane into the frame. Certainly, none of the elements of this portrayal could account for ASU's league status,[7] which is typical of Benson's recourse to outrageous, over-the-top rhetoric in his portrayal. But the cartoon is effective in bringing out the ugly side of intercollegiate men's sports. Moreover, Benson pointed to many of the things that those who were not Kush fans and who were not convinced by university officials' protestations that everything was fine and above-board in its imperial athletic domain.

The cartoon regarding the quality of ASU men's football recruits is complemented by a second cartoon (p. 138), which addresses itself to the real issue of Kush's demise: not the quality of his recruits, but the tenor of his training practices, akin to those of the old Parris Island Marine boot camp. Kush's dismissal came in mid–October, and the controversy over it dragged on for some time subsequently. ASU's decision was attacked by

Former Arizona State head football coach Frank Kush takes his training methods to the Canadian Football League (by permission of Steve Benson and Creators Syndicate, Inc.).

Kush's powerful supporters and ASU defended its decision. This self-defense was a bit self-righteous, some would argue, since it had condoned Kush's practices for two decades. In Benson's cartoon Kush's testosterone-poisoned violence is shown being taken out on a snowman: Kush is walking away from, to use appropriate vernacular, knocking the snowman's block off. He is mumbling "Dumb Canuck couldn't punt."

The reference to Canada is reduplicated by the fact that what the recruit Kush has attacked is a snowman, set against a wintry landscape hardly characteristic of the Phoenix desert. The head of the snowman is wearing a typical football helmet, with the image of a tiger rather than ASU's Sun Devil; Kush's assignment with the Canadian Football League was to coach for the Hamilton Tiger-Cats. The latter supports the way in which Benson's cartoon represents how Kush's violent form of training was an integral part of his career legacy. Finally, the contrast between the violent act that has taken place and the paradigmatic snowman smile and carrot nose is a particularly successful juxtaposition. The outrage expressed by six of the eight comments from readers that accompany this panel is indicative of Benson's skillful offensiveness. Because of Kush's disgrace with ASU, this cartoon is surely a particularly eloquent example of "shooting the wounded."

Snowbirds and the Valley of the Sun

Snowbirds are an integral part of the tourist and retirement industries in Phoenix, as elsewhere in the so-called Sun Belt that stretches between Los Angeles and Houston and passes through Yuma, Tucson, and Phoenix. At one point in his career, Benson seems to have had almost a pathological obsession with them. One might think that such an obsession is a harmless crankiness, but his images on the subject provoked the same sort of offended outrage as did his work dealing with apparently more urgent social and political issues. This is somewhat understandable, since tourist and retirement facilities are a major segment of Arizona's economy, with tourism and its infrastructure customarily counted as the state's largest industry.

Since apparently time immemorial "snowbird" has been the designation used for those individuals who regularly migrate from northern climes (in both United States and Canada, although there are certainly many seasonal visitors from other countries) to the southwest, typically between the onset of cold weather in the late northern fall and until hot weather begins to be the norm in the southwestern mid-spring: in the Valley of the Sun, where Phoenix is located, this usually means the six months from mid–October until mid–April. As one can easily appreciate, this represents an appreciable amount of tourist dollars.

There are many diverse facets to this industry. Seasonal visitors complement the permanent residential retirement community, both long-time Arizonans and people who have come to Arizona to retire. While tourists may stay in the broad spectrum of hotels and rentals available, many arrive in mobile homes of varying degrees of luxury. RV camps, often in satellite communities, have long been a part of the Valley landscape, along with trailer parks for permanent residences. Winter tourism unquestionably accounts for a large part of the passenger travel at the downtown Sky Harbor International Airport, one of the ten busiest airports in the country.

One of the prominent points of reference for the snowbirds is Sun City, located approximately 10 miles from downtown Phoenix. Sun City was built in 1960 by developer Del E. Web exclusively for people 55 and older (followed in the late 1970s by Sun City West and, in 1996, by Sun City Grand; there are now other such communities in the Valley).[8] The development is distinctive in the design of its street patterns. Most characteristic are the concentric streets that look like a vast labyrinth, a pattern that breaks with the dominant checkerboard layout of so much of the Greater Phoenix Area. Sun City has also been a highly innovative design experiment for the Valley, constituting one of the prominent symbols of the metropolitan area with a well elaborated mystique of retirement living. Yet it has also been highly controversial both for its restrictive policies, the de facto racial segregation it represents, and the communal sentiment that it inhabits a sphere of life separate from the rest of the area, such that, for example, it should not be held to the same tax code as other residents are. This is a sentiment grounded in both the "I paid taxes back home for years" and "I now live on a fixed income that rising taxes would devastate." While the snowbirds do not all flock to Sun City, Sun City West, and similar communities, seasonal tourists and the sometimes stridently contrarian attitudes of those communities are customarily linked in the Phoenix imaginary. Benson's cartoons relating to snowbirds often play off of this firmly entrenched imaginary.

One of Benson's most well known cartoons about snowbirds appears in *Fencin' with Benson* (p. 133). A monster RV with Minnesota plates is hogging three lanes of traffic; about to be caught in road kill is a "normal" size car, with Arizona license plates, traveling down the presumably safe

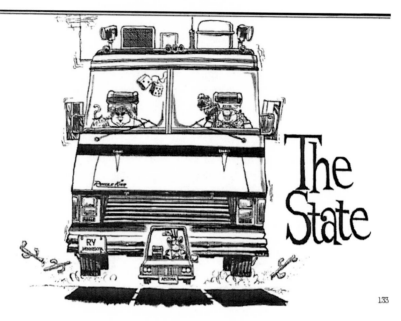

The arrival of Minnesota winter visitors to the Valley of the Sun (by permission of Steve Benson and Creators Syndicate, Inc.).

middle lane. The RV, brand name Rumble King, is appropriately outfitted for the rigors of the road: huge side mirrors, top-mounted powerful auxiliary lights, air horns, and two types of antenna, one for TV and the other apparently for CB. With plush dice swinging from the mirror between them, the passengers are the standard-issue geezers[9] snowbird couples are attributed to be.

Dressed for the southwest road (she wears a halter and he a loud patterned shirt), they are oblivious to the swath they are cutting. While she clutches a cat, he has his booty-topped gold clubs slung over his shoulder even as he drives. As good snowbirds are supposed to be, these are ready-for-action retirees, and he clenches a pipe between his teeth, while her lips are lipsticked bee-stung fashion. Rumbling down the highway — the horse-power they are expending is signaled by the vibrating side mirrors and dust-generating wheels — they sheer off saguaro cactuses as they go. This is a particularly eloquent detail, since the saguaro cactus is one of the icons of the Arizona landscape and a venerable symbol of the state; its blossom is the Arizona State Flower and there is a Saguaro National Park (in two locales, one east and one west of Tucson). Since it often takes a saguaro a hundred years to attain its full growth, the stateliness of this aged natural growth contrasts with the ridiculous demeanor of the two aging tourists. Moreover, part of the stateliness of the saguaro is its well proportioned trunks and limbs, while Benson's snowbirds are always grossly overweight: the trim artist seems to find overweight people particularly repellent and a ready shorthand for the point he is making.

The Arizona driver, significantly portrayed in what we can see of him in Uncle Sam garb, contemplates with troubled eyes what he sees in his rear-view mirror. As the affirmation goes, "objects in the mirror may be closer than they appear," and Joe Citizen has every reason to believe that he is going to end up a squishy spot on the road as the tourists barrel blithely on their way. It is rarely clear in Benson's anti-snowbird cartoons what the threat of the elderly is, although I will consider in a moment a cartoon that has to do with the resistance to paying school taxes. Is it the belief that they somehow "corrupt" the landscape? As though the explosive growth in the last fifty years needed anyone else's help to do that, with, for example, virtually all of the once extensive farming in the Phoenix area relentlessly obliterated by residential and commercial building. Everyone in Phoenix has a favorite story about a street that used to end a few blocks away but now goes on for miles and miles of ticky-tack. Is it because the much vaunted youth culture of the Valley is somehow squelched by the oldsters? Newspaper stories a decade ago about the sexual high-jinks (including back-seat acrobatics in golf carts) among the residents of Sun City gave an added meaning to the tourist cliché of "fun in the sun" (Benson did a few choice drawings on these reports). Or do their sagging bodies and often overstated vacation clothes offend local aesthetics? Such a proposition would be outlandish in a city almost devoid of design sophistication and in which it is only a 25,000-square foot monstrosity in the desert foothills à la Mike Tyson or Magic Johnson that produces a frisson of the beautiful. I realize that I have lapsed into some hyperbole here, but I mean it to echo efficiently the depth of venom with which Benson attacks the snowbirds.

A reprise of the bloated figures of the cartoon I have just discussed including pipe and bee-stung painted lips, is to be found in another panel, also in *Fencin'* (p. 149). No specific mention is made to the determined resistance Sun City residents have expressed over paying school taxes.[10] Yet the force of the panel turns on the literal hounding of the children by Mr. and Mrs. Snowbird, she swinging her crutch, as they ride to the hounds. They are accompanied in the distance by an ambulance, but not for the

Residents of retirement community Sun City, Arizona, take aim on unwanted children in their community (by permission of Steve Benson and Creators Syndicate, Inc.).

children, one assumes, but rather in case one of the two senior-citizen riders requires emergency attention: pointing in the direction of the hunt's pursuit is a sign that read "Oxygen tank / 500 feet." Mrs. Snowbird calls out "Tallyho! Hunting in Sun City is such sport!" The prey of the hunt — they are preceded by eight snarling hounds — are two small children, eyes bugging with the effort to get away from the ten animals. Jane has already stumbled to the ground, and Dick has lost one of his shoes.

The panel seems to address itself to one of the pertinent regulations governing the Sun City-type enclaves, a ban on any resident younger than a certain age that excludes all children. The ban also provides only for a tightly defined maximum stay in one of the residences of a relative — such as a grandchild — below the minimum age. One of the effects of the regulations of homeowners associations is to encourage snoops and snitches, who are only too happy to report to the manager violations of those regulations. Since retirees often have plenty of time on their hands to indulge in such pastimes, the formation of a posse-like hunt to hound down offending children is, while an outrageous extrapolation on Benson's, one that is quickly grasped by the reader. Like the bloodhounds of southern sheriffs of yore, today's retirees and their snowbird counterparts are, in Benson's view, only too happy to keep the demographic order.

It is not uncommon for political cartoons, in order to focus on a particular social problem or political event, to trope an existing cultural referent. In Benson's multifaceted attack on snowbirds, it is understandable that he might have recourse to a recognized reference to the malevolence of birds. This he does by evoking Alfred Hitchcock's 1963 film *The Birds*, where suddenly and inexplicably flocks of birds began attacking humans. While some birds (mockingbirds, starlings, crows) have been known to attack individuals they feel may be threatening their nest, birds tend to avoid human contact. Hitchcock uses the birds in his film as metaphors of the unknown natural forces human beings are wont to ignore because they think they do not impinge on human society or they believe that they have tamed them. Within the context of the film, the arbitrary malevolence of the birds is a correlate of the viciousness human behavior can manifest and a cautionary reminder that birds and humans are both part of an atavistic drive.

In Benson's cartoon (*Evanly Days!*, p. 127), the allusion to Hitchcock's birds is essential to its cleverness. One understands that the snowbirds' arrival in Phoenix is an annual phenomenon, but it is not clear how their arrival signifies malevolence or violence, much less a threat to established social order. I suppose one might conclude that the phenomenon of the snowbirds and the larger tourist/retirement industry in which they are participants speaks to errors of judgment with respect to the economic stability of Phoenix and Arizona, an inherent danger in relying on unpredictable clients as a major source of the state's income in revenues and taxes.[11] Whatever the precise motor of Benson's may be, it is one of his most entertaining as regards the bane of the snowbird. The cartoon, making explicit use of the Hitchcock reference, is headed with the screaming banner "Just when you thought it was safe to go back on the streets ... 'The Birds.'" There is also a banner along the bottom of the cartoon proclaiming "Coming soon to a R.V. park near you!!," a statement that is also a direct film reference, troping as it does the advertisement of a "film coming soon to a theater near you."

A detail of the trope involved in Benson's header banner is significant: one of the greatest complaints against snowbirds and those thought to be snowbirds (i.e., all retirees and anyone elderly in appearance) is the erratic

They're b-a-a-ck.

The ominous fall arrival of northern-clime snow birds as winter visitors in Phoenix (by permission of Steve Benson and Creators Syndicate, Inc.).

nature of their driving. It is as though most of the year they drove a tractor through farm fields and only drove a car on civilized city streets when in Phoenix for the winter. Correlating alleged sins of the road (driving too slowly, failure to yield, inappropriate or non-existent direction signals, gawking, and the like) with out-of-state vehicles and tell-tale license plates is a veritable road-trip game in Phoenix, with extra points awarded for license plates from Minnesota and any of the Canadian provinces. The sensation that in the winter months the streets of greater Phoenix are congested with demon drivers from the northern wastelands may be more subjective than statistically grounded, but it is one of the driving forces of Phoenix popular culture.

Benson's cartoon makes full use of a series of images that reinforce the proposition that the arrival of the snowbirds constitutes the advent of winged conquerors. Over a dozen luggage-laden and most overweight winged creatures descend on a frantic citizenry. This Biblical scourge is

60

met with wailing and overwrought gestures. The violence of the plague is to be seen in the way one man's head has been bashed. Like the window panes attacked by the birds in the Hitchcock film, the lenses of his glasses have been shattered. Statistically, there are more descending snowbirds than assembled citizens, underscoring the sense of invading hordes. Benson typically represents the snowbirds as obese, men with paunches and women with gargantuan breasts. Only one woman is portrayed as other than obese, although her breasts do not escape highlighting. The luggage borne aloft by the arrivals includes, in addition to typical forms of luggage, a portable TV, a bird cage, golf clubs, and, in one pertinent touch, a portable barbecue pit.

Certainly, Benson's anti-snowbird drawings do not overwhelm the weightier issues of local, national, and international news. Yet their insistent presence in his published work is virtually a defining characteristic of his view of life in Phoenix.[12]

The Homeless and Friends

Another Phoenix social phenomenon, not unrelated to the snowbirds, is that of the transients, a percentage of whom come during the winter months from elsewhere, following the changes in climate. They may no longer be the now folkloric demographic of hobos riding the rails, but their very name of "transients" indicates that we are still dealing with a relatively mobile population. When Phoenix was home to extensive agriculture, one component consisted of the migratory farm workers who were preponderantly Mexican/Mexican-American and who followed the crops around the country. Today, unemployed farm workers join a large pool of the homeless that includes individuals with mental problems, people who have fallen into poverty because of economic hard times, and those with drug dependency and other medical problems. The fact that a segment of the transients who come and go with the weather could allow for their correlation with the snow-birds[13] means that they are equally blights on the Valley landscape. The importance of the Phoenix cityscape as attractive to tourists is brought out by the central image of the panel (*Fencin' with Benson*, p. 141), a downtown tour bus filled with tourists picking out the points of interest recited into his microphone by the driver. In addition to the bus sign stating that it is the Downtown tour, we see the bus flanked by typical central-core features like a bus stop, traffic light, lamp post,

WE ARE NOW PASSING THROUGH AN AREA OF BOLD, INNOVATIVE URBAN REDEVELOPMENT. ON YOUR LEFT IS PHOENIX'S NEW HOBO PARK, FLANKED BY DERELICT PARK AND HOOKER PARK. STRAIGHT AHEAD TO THE RIGHT IS OUR SPACIOUS ILLEGAL ALIEN PARK AND, OF COURSE, OUR DRUNK DRIVERS PARK. COMING INTO VIEW ON THE LEFT IS OUR ATTRACTIVE MUGGERS PARK AND COMBINATION GYPSY-SNOWBIRD PARK. NOW, IF YOU'LL LOOK TO THE RIGHT...

Downtown Phoenix as a slumming attraction for tourists (by permission of Steve Benson and Creators Syndicate, Inc.).

power lines, and the like. On the other side of the street, although mostly covered over by the cartoon balloon, the Valley's signature palm trees, along with more lamp posts, are to be seen.

Anyone who has taken such a city tour knows what to expect: museums and symphony halls, major landmarks and monuments, important administrative and executive buildings, the homes of the rich and famous, parks and gardens, historical sites, major commercial locales, amusement and entertainment venues. But in the case of Benson's drawing, Phoenix's bold and innovative urban redevelopment (itself a questionable proposition in the early 1980s when the panel was drawn) features seven parks, one for hobos, derelicts, hookers, illegal aliens, and drunk drivers, along with parks for gypsy-snowbirds and muggers. Downtown parks are precisely what Phoenix has not had in any abundance, and certainly much fewer than seven of them. But the cartoon glosses over the fact that muggers, hookers, drunks, and even illegal aliens may not necessarily be transients. Some of the cream of the city's elite are drunk drivers....

But what Benson's cartoon does effectively, if perhaps disingenuously, is play off of the semantic chaining that urban fears generate. Criminal justice statistics may not support those fears, but they are part of a compelling imaginary that serves to define Phoenix. Such an imaginary has resulted in the abandonment and often fitful redevelopment of the downtown core. The quality of downtown Phoenix life may be much better at the end of the first decade of the twenty-first century, but the transients, no matter how one breaks down their demographics, are still very much on display for the tourists' attention.

Steve Benson is unquestionably one of the most eloquent editorial cartoonists working today in the United States, and, despite the endless stream of outraged letters to the Editor of the *Arizona Republic*, one of the Valley's most treasured cultural assets.[14] His cartoons play an important role in shaping opinion: in conventional journalistic fashion, they run alongside the paper's official editorial positions. Benson's cartoons are the first thing many readers look at in the morning paper. Because Benson makes unstinting use of the editorial cartoonist's license to hyberbolize, distort, and willfully misinterpret, one would be disappointed if his panels were held as reasoned examples of civil discourse. Indeed, the very presence of questionable motives, possible venality, and rampant snarkiness are what make them both entertaining and meaningful.

Phoenix, Say What? Urban Landscapes in the Chronicles of Laurie Notaro

When my best friend Jamie finally broke up with her evil boyfriend who had the personality of a raw potato, I considered it a hallowed day. It was the kind of relationship in which she had to carefully hide all of her best qualities, the qualities which I most admired in her: her pack-a-day devotion to Benson & Hedges, the talent she possessed to effortlessly paint a verbal masterpiece of profanity that could rival the mouth of any dockworker, and the facet of her that we called "Fun and Frolic Jamie," that portion of her personality that could be easily talked into anything after a twelve-pack. Like the night we found her drunk, topless, and unconscious in a neighbor's desert front yard, a photo of which may have contributed to the disintegration of the love between Jamie and Potato Boy. (*Idiot Girl's Action-Adventure* 45)

Hope for the best; expect the worst. (Russian proverb)

Idiot Girls in a Man-Made World

Laurie Notaro (b. 1970? in Brooklyn, New York) has been wont to say that she grew up "on the wrong side of the tracks in Paradise Valley, Arizona." This is an immediately catchy use of a metaphor that has a long lineage in American culture, evoking as it does major economic, social, and racial differences.[1] If one always lives on the "right side of the tracks," one is decent and respectable in an appreciable calculus of the ingredients at play, such as being at least somewhat middle class (including a family and personal history that is respectable enough not to be cast out over the tracks to a no man's land of shady identity); not constrained by grinding poverty; and, most importantly, not be of color, whatever the spectrum

64

of color is at play in a community that invests in such a rigorous, if often imaginary, dividing line. Such a sociogeographic positioning ensures social and legal fairness.

Indeed, like most American cities of any size, Phoenix does have a set of railroad tracks: the railroad is now reduced mostly to freight service. However, other dividing lines, such as the Salt River, the ground-zero Washington St., and even the only-decades old Interstate 10 all in one way or another fulfill that function. But these are all dividing lines that pass through downtown Phoenix, which lies at quite a far remove from the Northeast enclave known as Paradise Valley, Phoenix's equivalent of Beverly Hills, where the only train whistles heard are those of high-end model train collectors. Yet, in a major Southwest American city, where the railroads played at one time a very important role in the opening of the West, in the development of a commodity-based economy, and in the first stages of the tourist industry (which is now the number-one industry of the State of Arizona), a reference to the train tracks evokes a history of Us vs. Them that is probably more racial than anything else: the Chinese got to be on the "right" side of the tracks, as did some Mexicans, while the majority of Mexicans and most blacks came to be systematically consigned to the "wrong side," what has historically been called South Phoenix.

To be sure, Notaro's metaphor is just that, a metaphor, although certainly not drained of the segregationist politics that once dominated Phoenix with an iron fist (Whitaker; Luckingham, *Minorities*). Rather, Notaro's metaphor in reality refers to the vagaries of the development of residential areas in a city like Phoenix, where the imaginary and political entities collide. Paradise Valley is, thus, both a general denomination for open desert to the Northeast of Phoenix as it began to be developed as residential neighborhoods and the operant part of the name of the Town of Paradise Valley, incorporated in 1961, as a separate municipality bound today on the north, south, and west by the city of Phoenix proper (the western boundary is the Piestawa [formerly Squaw Peak] City Park); and bounded on the east by the Town of Scottsdale. Hemmed in by its neighbors (two of the largest cities in the metropolitan Phoenix area; the other is Mesa), the Town of Paradise Valley sought to create its own exclusive character, much tonier than the upscale areas of Phoenix and Scottsdale that bound it — something like a Phoenix equivalent of Beverly Hills, but more residential, in the fashion of Bel Air located to the north.

As Phoenix began its dramatic demographic expansion in the context of the postwar prosperity of the 1950s and 1960s, it was inevitable that it expand more and more into what had previously been open desert. With major agriculture communities to the west and south and with the university town of Tempe to the east, with Mesa and other agricultural communities to the east, expansion to the north and northwest was inevitable. Today, new waves of expansion have gone on to doom the once protected agricultural communities all over the Valley of the Sun, where the Phoenix metropolitan area is located, as agriculture was replaced by other sources of wealth in the area. With the perfection of domestic air-conditioning in the early mid-fifties, the stage was set for more and more development of the open desert, where the canals, old acequias, and lush greenery were no longer needed to attenuate the 100 degree-plus weather Phoenix has five to six months out of the year (May until well into October). The creation of residential areas with fairly large lots, swimming pools, irrigated lawns, and, blessedly, refrigerated air-conditioning meant housing opportunities for the middle class in this Northwest "paradise valley" in place of the smaller homes on cramped lots with, at best, swamp cooling that characterized the former middle-class residential area around the downtown Phoenix financial and commercial core.

An Idiot Girl's Sociogeographic Coordinates

Notaro's family moved to Arizona from Brooklyn when she was seven, in the late 1960s or early 1970s (the record is silent about her year of birth), purchasing one of the ranch-style houses in the northeast bedroom communities I have been describing. As Phoenix has grown and neighborhoods have consolidated, commercial venues have shifted, and by the time Notaro moved into the area, most of the power structure of the city lived in the best enclaves of north Phoenix, in Scottsdale, and in the young Town of Paradise Valley. Commercial establishments moved with them, and downtown Phoenix, as it lost much of the power structure as residents, lost also the shopping areas, to the many, mostly high-class, malls that now cluster in the northeast valley. It is into this so-called paradise valley of perpetual newness that the Notaro family moved from New York. While only the few could afford the gilded addresses of the Town of Paradise Valley, most were content to live "across the tracks." That is, not really in Paradise Valley, but enough away from older Phoenix such that in the pursuit of most aspects of daily life, they would never have to venture into the former central core/corridor. The fact that Notaro will subsequently move into the old downtown and make it the base of much of her most recent chronicles set in Phoenix will be taken up below.

The touch of geographic schizophrenia that characterizes Notaro's autobiographical persona is one of the most distinctive elements of her writing about Phoenix. Although she has now lived in Eugene, Oregon, for several years because of her husband's doctoral studies, she remains inextricably identified with Phoenix and with the experiences of coming of age and surviving in an urban landscape that she depicts as mostly populated by the brain-dead who conspire against her legitimate aspirations toward sound personal happiness and fulfillment. The fact that her family — especially her often outrageously nonsensical Italian American mother — is part of that conspiracy only makes her sense of being an alien in the land of fun in the sun that much more acute. One might be tempted to identify Notaro (and here I will use simply her last name to refer to the autobiographical narrator in her chronicles) with Generation X, but that might not be a very useful connection, since it is important to underscore how Notaro is not talking about the collective feelings and experiences of a generation, but of a persecuted minority in a precisely identified cityscape.

While some of Notaro's experiences, her characteristic discourse, and her worldview might coincide with the vague pop-cult notion of Generation X, there is a specificity of the relationship between Phoenix as lived urban space and her misadventures that affords her chronicles a far more nuanced sense than coincidence with a series of generation markers would imply.[2] Notaro's chronicles are found in the collections *The Idiot Girls' Action-Adventure Club: True Tales from a Magnificent and Clumsy Life* (2002); *Autobiography of a Fat Bride: True Tales of a Pretend Adulthood* (2003); *I Love Everybody (and Other Atrocious Lies): True Tales of a Loudmouth Girl* (2004); *An Idiot Girl's Christmas: True Tales from the Top of the Naughty List* (2005); *We Thought You Would Be Prettier: Tall Tales of the Dorkiest Girl Alive* (2005); *The Idiot Girl and the Flaming Tantrum of Death: Reflections on Revenge, Germophobia, and Laser Hair Removal* (2008). There is also a novel, which is not set in Phoenix: *There's a (Slight) Chance I Might Be Going to Hell; A Novel of Sewer Pipes, Pageant Queens, and Big Trouble* (2007).

Because Notaro is an autobiographical persona of a series of chronicles of place, it is important to specify the way in which she undertakes a self-characterization as a voice in antiphonic relationship to the world around her, that of the extensively inventoried spaces she inhabits, beginning with her mother's own home. Notaro's first collection of essays, *The Idiot Girls Action-Adventure Club: True Tales from a Magnificent and Clumsy Life*, established with considerable success this voice. It is that of the so-called idiot girl. The idiot girl is the nonconformist woman who, consciously or otherwise, is out of synch with prevailing norms of thought, speech, and general behavior. The idiot girl is unable or unwilling to study the social discourse adequately and to assimilate to it accordingly. The idiot girl has interests, desires, impulses, goals that are "ungrammatical" as far as the acceptable norm is concerned. The non-idiot girl cannot lose time analyzing the "grammar" of what might be called appropriate girlness, but must quickly internalize with a requisite degree of proficiency and fluency the structure of whatever rite that, at a given moment, is considered appropriate to her being in the world. If she does not, she is an idiot.[3] The idiot girl (and, of course, there exists her parallel in the form of the idiot boy, who may also be called a nerd; who may also be called a geek or a creep or a dweeb; who may also be called a queer) is unable to negotiate the most basic of life's situations; unable to conduct the day-to-day business of life; unable to engage in the social commerce that keeps one moving smoothly through the dangerous shoals of social interaction. The idiot girl is unprepared for — and, therefore, unfit for — the world she inhabits.

Notaro's narrative voice fairly luxuriates in her recounting of the accumulated score card of her ineptitude, as though she possessed an unerring ability to demonstrate, once again, her idiocy. Rather than her internal social grammar leading her to efficiently realize and reinforce the appropriate norms, it is as though it were a powerful dynamic that propelled her toward ever finer idiocy of nonfulfillment and non-achievement. One of the recurring motifs of this dysfunctional life, iterated from one collection to the other in some form of a blurb, is the way in which Notaro lost an impressive number of jobs in journalism, her university major, whether it was at Arizona State University's daily, the *State Press*; the major Phoenix daily, *The Arizona Republic*; the widely distributed free alternative weekly, *The New Times*; and some local glossy magazines, such as *The Phoenix Magazine*. The strict accuracy of this self-characterization may include some strategic resignations and rhetorical highlighting, but it is meant to serve as a vivid summary of her handicapped life skills.

But all of this is very much tongue-in-cheek.

Idiot Girls Against a Man-Made World

Notaro's idiot girl is, when viewed with a different interpretive optic, the symbol of a higher idiocy: a masculinist world dominated by a social norm that is inimical to any manifestation of independence, creativity, and self-expression on the part of what ought to remain as robot integers in a placid society of absolute conformity. It is inevitable to evoke Ira Levin's by-now paradigmatic Stepford Wife whose every particle of feminist rebellion has been programmed out of her. The idiot girl is the counterimage of the Stepford Wife because the particles of rebellion in the face of imperious conformity remain intact, whatever their source may be, whether determined resistance or unconscious noncompliance. Just as many social subjects have resemanticized as a badge of courage the epithet most stridently employed to characterize their nonconformity — queer being a particularly vivid example; one thinks also of a tee-shirt legend such as "I'm a witch spelled with a capital b"[4] — behind the often self-flagellating voice of the idiot girl is that of the determined assertion: "I'm an idiot girl and damn proud of it." By which one understands that (1) "idiot girl" is the interpellation of certain women by a patriarchal society that hails them, while at the same time inserting them into a particular slot in the social dynamic; (2) the hailing may be executed by anyone (self-) empowered to perform such interpellation, whether male authority figures or other women engaged in duplicating such male authority figures (Mary Daly's "token torturers"); (3) the idiot girl is principally and primarily hailed as such by the mother, secure in the knowledge of the importance of her role in making sure her daughter adheres to the grammar of social interaction she herself believes effectively to embody; (4) the idiot girl, in defiance of such interpellations, fulfills the behavior that legitimates, for those who are or would be in control, the assignment of the quality of being or acting like an idiot; (5) that the enhanced performance of such idiocy by the idiot girl, as much unconscious as it is deliberate, stands in reality as an eloquent denunciation and refutation of any such legitimacy of interpellation; and (6) being an idiot girl emerges, after all, as a program for social defiance in which being an idiot girl is not a hindrance in navigating the dangerous shoals of social existence, but rather an enhanced strategy for wrecking them. Like any such social movement, it calls for an energetic organizing practice, and hence the emergence of the Idiot Girls' Action-Adventure Club: idiot girls arise and give them hell. Resemanticizing the passive condition of being called an idiot into the call for concerted sisterly action is the guiding principle of Laurie Notaro's chronicles, in which each of her now over one-hundred sketches constitutes a front-line report on idiot girl's skirmishes with life.[5]

The fact that those skirmishes take place in Phoenix, Arizona is an integral part of the idiot girl's story, as there is very much the proposition that Phoenix is a place propitious to having to organize a resistance to the higher idiocy of social conformity. There is something about the rigors of "the hot, dry dust bowl of Phoenix, Arizona" ("About the Author," *Idiot Girl's Action-Adventure* 227) that seems to require an increased militancy on the part of the alleged idiot girl for sanity and survival. Wherever Notaro moves through the Valley, whether organized spaces such as her mother's household, shopping malls, cultural establishments, or the random sunbathed expanse of urban sprawl, the narrator is confronted with multiple opportunities to reconfirm her status as an idiot and face the challenges of countering it. Much like those series of detective stories, especially of a formulaic nature — one thinks of the Carolyn Keene's proto- or pre-feminist heroine Nancy Drew — where no matter where the main character is, there just happens to be a pressing mystery to be solved. It is as though mystery stalked the otherwise mundane protagonist (Agatha Christie's Miss Marple, for example), and there is no alterative but to deal with it as a strong and effective woman. In a similar vein, the idiot girl is stalked by events, no matter how much she might wish to avoid them, that require her renewed expressions of feminine fortitude to deal with them. Computer keyboard in hand, Notaro goes forth to avenge, in the name of the Club, the attributions of idiot girl.

Among the thirty-nine chronicles that make up *The Idiot Girls' Action-Adventure Club*, which held a place on the *New York Times* Best Seller List when it was first published (2002), there is ample evidence of the narrative pattern that underlies Notaro's chronicles, including the privileged characterization of Phoenix as a source of particular idiocy. While there is less specificity of place in *Idiot* than in other of Notaro's chronicles analyzed below, there is the general ambience of the Southwest, of the transient here-today-gone-tomorrow nature of people and businesses, and, in general, some sort of intangible shallowness of desert living. One chronicle is worth commenting on in detail because of certain primes of Phoenix living it evokes, "Waiting for the Bug Man." The title is, surely, a trope on Samuel Beckett's *Waiting for Godot*, and for the desert dweller the Bug Man occupies, if not a godly niche in the urban landscape, he at least has a major stake in one's salvation: not freedom from sin and despair, but freedom from being consumed alive by the teaming hoards of insects that inhabit the Valley floor.

The Bug Man Cometh

The bug man is as ubiquitous in the residential areas of the deserts as the vegetation those areas replaced: the vegetation may have been replaced, but most of the bugs stayed on, and they thrive particularly in new residential areas and all areas that border open desert where the houses may function essentially as incubators. Most fastidious housekeepers have the bug man come by every few months to keep the unwanted guests, outside and inside, at bay, and one of the major companies emphasize the omnipresence of the bug man by decking out its vehicles to resemble enormous desert insects and vermin. The cockroach is a favored theme. Thus, waiting for the bug man becomes virtually an existential experience: will a new family of cockroaches make for the crumbs or moisture left on a counter before the bug man arrives? Fittingly, Notaro's text opens with sparse Becketian language: "We are waiting for the bug man. / Again" (154):

> The service demeanor, physical appearance, and general freakishness of the bug man define his passage through the house. He is unreliable, incoherent, behaves in unexpected ways, and — crucially — seems to be ineffective in addressing the momentous problem for which he was contracted. He is a veritable mysterious stranger:
> Fred ... finished spraying around the house, and then left without even saying goodbye. Just jumped in his truck and drove away. But the fleas didn't.
> As soon as he walked out the door, complete familial colonies of fleas that had been in temporary hiding sprang out of the living room carpet and bit our ankles, executing bitter revenge, and it didn't stop there.
> I've never been bitten in such private places by anything that didn't at least pay for dinner first [156].

This sets the stage for a three-way battle against the fleas between Notaro, the bug man, and the resistant fleas, which always seem to reappear within the hour of the bug man's departure. This is a typical idiot girl adventure because of the way in which the narrator is, yet once again, caught between an overwhelming problem and the truly idiot people sent to deal with it. When Fred, who routinely appears to underspray just enough to have to be called back in short order, accidentally leaves behind the canister of his "potent insecticide that would 'actually kill them this time'" (157), Notaro decides to take action on her own and works the spray mechanism with determination:

"I gasped. I was so excited. The stuff was straight from the manufacturer, which meant no dilution, no sparse spraying. It meant no more fleas. No more bites. No more itching. No more scabs, only cancer!" (159). Of course, the idiot girl prevails and, despite the protestations of her boyfriend that "I was going to kill all of us with that stuff" (160), she is happy to announce that she did: but only the fleas.

As a sample chronicle of the misadventures of the idiot girl, "Waiting for the Bug Man" follows the curve of the recognition of a grave matter, in this case one integral to desert living; the series of reversals that accompany the attempt to resolve the problem in a rational, professional, urbane fashion; and the introduction of a reversal that allows, serendipitously, for the idiot girl herself to prevail against both the odds of the problem and those of the superior idiots who would be her saviors. All with only the circumstantial risk of cancer from inhaling her excessively diligent application of the poisonous spray. This last detail is a significant one, because, unlike high-minded and serious (that is, noncomical and nonself-parodying) feminist writing, none of the idiot girl's solutions constitute an unmitigated triumph. If one might want to insist that there is a feminist dimension to Notaro's chronicles, it comes, as in the case of this chronicle, in conjunction with the narrator's highly contingent and markedly limited prevailing against the masculinist world of the repugnant but yet still authoritarian bug man, whose canister she is able, only through accident and temporarily, to expropriate, but which, in the end, she must return. In this fashion, the domain of the bug man remains intact, even if she did get rid of the fleas on her own.

This Old House

One of Notaro's most successful compilations of chronicles is *Autobiography of a Fat Bride: True Tales of a Pretend Adulthood*. These chronicles describe the marriage of Notaro and the couple's installation in a small home in one of the oldest working-class residential areas of downtown Phoenix, in a neighborhood that is called Coronado, one of the city's thirty-five officially recognized historic districts.[6] Although there are properties in the Coronado district that qualify individually for a historic designation, the majority of the homes are modest, in poor repair, with yards and landscaping that do not receive the intense attention any green space requires to thrive in the desert, such as one finds in two residential areas to the west of Coronado, the Willo and Encanto-Palmcroft districts, two of the most prestigious residential areas of Phoenix's urban core. Many of the properties are surrounded by chain-link fences, have debris (including old cars) in the front yard, and display details such as blankets or tinfoil in the windows and decaying furniture spread out on the porch and in the front yard. Many owners (and, perhaps, a large number are renters) are on one sort or another of limited income, whether retirees, migrants, or widows/widowers, and are simply unable to maintain their property in an optimal manner. The major neighborhood park, Coron-

Cover of Laurie Notaro's *Autobiography of a Fat Bride* (used by permission of Villard Books, a division of Random House, Inc.).

ado, is minimally maintained by the city, drug plagued, and often the site of nighttime violence.

I realize that the forgoing is rather a grim portrayal of Notaro's Coronado, and, indeed, residents of the area could well protest angrily that she is off by a mile, that these features are more to be found in the surrounding nonhistorical areas to the east and south, including the much more economically modest Garfield and North Garfield areas. Yet, Notaro's fictional narrator characterizes the area in these terms, with a consistent exclusion of any reference to those properties that may belie such a description. The point, of course, must be that Notaro is not engaging in an ethnographic report on the Coronado district, but rather is evoking it in terms of her own particular idiot girl experiences. It is one in which the neighbors appear to be biological throw-backs, the houses themselves are threatening monsters, particularly her own, which seems to be a machine of discomfort and dysfunction, and in which one of the major details of the environment is the noise pollution produced by the random firing of handguns throughout the night. What is particularly hilarious about this neighborhood of horrors is the way in which it is unqualifiedly the consequence of taking up residence on the so-called wrong side of the tracks. If the wrong side of the tracks in Paradise Valley means simply smaller lots, more modest homes, and humbler cars, residence in Coronado represents residence in a marginal sector of the inner-city in which the suspect zone is not on the other side of materially visible tracks, but over here on the near side of an invisible demarcation line of urban decline. In this case, in some vague sense north-south Central Avenue is the "track," where residential areas west of it (Encanto-Palmcroft, Willo) are on the right side, and residential areas east of it (Coronado, Garfield) are on the wrong side. As a consequence, the opportunities for challenges to the ability of an idiot girl have increased exponentially in number.

For example, in "The Retainer" she delves head-on into the questionable joys of owning an older home, often called a fix-up. In this case, it is her friend who proudly announces such a purchase. In a city like Phoenix, where the housing and realty industries have worked hard to convince up-and-coming middle-class clients that they ought to prefer ticky-tack on the outskirts of the city and abandon the old inner-core residential areas to the destitute and illegal immigrants,[7] it is a badge of courage to take on an "older home in central Phoenix," a trope that Notaro cites with precision:

> "It's a great house," [my friend] added, "but it's a little dated. The kitchen needs some polish, the floor in the dining room needs to be replaced, and I'm going to have the paneling in the living room removed. I'll have to hire someone. But it's just a little work, I don't think it will take more than a couple of weeks" [114].

These fives sentences could be subject to the sort of semantic unpacking normally reserved for surrealist poetry. And if the analysis of poetry frequently involves the identification of a dominant motif or key signifier, it is, in Notaro's chronicle, surely that of "I'll have to hire someone." Who that someone is to be, what his qualifications might be, and what the limitations of his craft are — and, most crucially, how long it will take for those limitations to be made evident — is part of the ever-expanding commitment of time and money to the renovation project. It is often said that people who invest in an older home of the fix-up variety end up retaining a carpenter like others retain a lawyer, and in both cases the experience turns out to be much more expensive than anyone could have originally thought.

Hence, Notaro's title, "The Retainer," anticipates the frustrations ahead for her friend. If many of the problems associated with redoing an old house are universal, there are some that are particularly pertinent to Phoenix, such as the lack of infrastructure (many areas were never wired for 220V appliances), the high mineral content of desert water that rots out original steel piping, and dry rot and insect infestation (cf. "The Bug Man" discussed above); these features present almost insurmountable obstacles. Termites have done very well in the Valley of the Sun, and it is a problem old-home dwellers will experience sometime during their ownership.

Carpenters and contractors are not all that hard to come by in Phoenix, since working people from around the country have flooded into the Valley as much as the well-to-do and professionals have. They are almost exclusively men (hence my restricted pronoun use above), but not of the phenotype Notaro has in mind. So when Notaro and her husband purchase a "lonely brown house not far from my friend's" (114), she experiences first hand this new idiot girl's adventure:

> I imagined [the contractor] driving up in his truck, and out would step a dead ringer for Norm Abrams, the loveable expert carpenter from *This Old House*. In years to come, I envisioned, Paul would stop by the homestead on Christmas Day armed with a fruit basket and roam around the house to make sure that all of his repairs were still working properly. We'd laugh about the good old days of restoring my house, recounting tender vignettes and drinking brandy in front of the blazing fireplace [115].

As in the case of the quote referring to Notaro's friend's purchase, one can search for the operant phrase in this one. It appears in the form of the parenthetical observation "I imagined," since the scene the fragment creates is one of pure fantasy, down to the homey cliche of the "burning fireplace," which is not often to be found on Phoenix Christmas Days, where the daytime temperature may reach 75+ degrees.

Such a fantasy is a recipe for disaster to the second degree, since it squares the disaster that will flow naturally — and, it certainly seems so, unable to be staunched — from the pulling of the first nail in the renovation process. Here the idiot girl is an agent in her own nightmare, as she turns home and checkbook over to an exemplar of the building trades who is the alternative-universe version of Norm Abrams. Notaro spares no effort in her portrayal of the crew as incompetent Neanderthals, beginning merely with their physical appearance: "[The contractor] arrived to start working with his partner in tow, a man named Len, who had occasional teeth" (115). The remainder of Notaro's chronicle is thankfully sparse in details, as one disaster follows another, including the contractor ending up hiding in the house from hit men because of unpaid bills, to shoddy work, to eventually abandoning the house in less repair than when he arrived; subsequently he sends a bill for work not even undertaken. This time around, the idiot girl is unable to prevail against the Sisyphean rock of home repair Phoenix-style.

Although *Autobiography* covers a lot of ground in the bridal and early marriage years of the idiot girl, the chronicles return frequently to the travails of living in Phoenix and in the particular neighborhood they have chosen, as when "Home Sweat Home" describes living in a house in July without air-conditioning: "Who, in their right mind, buys a house in Phoenix without the necessity of air-conditioning" (123). Many of the houses in downtown Phoenix, often stately historic ones, lack central air-conditioning or have a precarious version of it; there may be window units strategically placed, or the inhabitants may get by with a pre-air-conditioning swamp cooler, which is only effective if the humidity is very low.[8] Articulating what is a common dilemma of the old-home buyer, Notaro goes on to wax dithyrambic about the bungalow they purchased, while at the same time detailing, once again, the disasters of its upkeep and the futile attempts to undertake remodeling. This time, however, after chronicling the near-miss of matrimonial murder, the idiot girl is successful in coming up with a way to afford a new cooler. Since there is no way of repairing the old and always inefficient swamp cooler and after discovering her husband is working late not to rack up extra pay to pay for air-conditioning but because it is cool in his office, she devises an effective financial plan: "I ... was very careful about how many dependents I claimed on my tax forms the next year, and with our refund money, we had a new cooler installed two weeks ago" [125].

Mixing freewheeling hyperbole, a delightfully vicious and unerring eye for gross detail, a take-no-prisoners ironic tone of voice, a self-characterized loudmouth, Notaro's idiot girl must rarely confess defeat at the hands of the real idiots of her world. The fact that the real idiots are in the main men or the agents of a male world (her long-suffering and "nice" husband excepted), gives Notaro's misadventures the particular focus of one variant of the feminist agenda. An important dimension, among the wealth of challenges to a woman just trying to get by in the world, relates to the trials of life in her own home town. It usually isn't a Phoenix the Chamber of Commerce would care to relate to. But whether on the wrong side of the tracks in Paradise Valley or on the wrong side of the tracks in the downtown historical preserves, Notaro provides a very witty take on the Phoenix many of its inhabitants can identify with.

Desert Noir: The Detective
Novels of Jon Talton

> Phoenix is a magnet for rough-hewn faces. Misfits, losers,
> con artists, ex-cons, desperate Oakies and Oaxacans, second-
> chance Johnnies — they all end up here, as if the city is the last
> fence line catching the unattached debris of a windy world. I often
> imagine faces from the streets of Phoenix transported into primitive
> black-and-white photography of the Old West. You couldn't tell
> the difference. Only the clothes give away their place in time. (Jon
> Talton, *Dry Heat* 66)

There are two interesting facts about Phoenix, Arizona. One is that
the city — and, by extension, the Greater Phoenix area and central Arizona
Valley of the Sun in which it is located — reputedly has few interesting
modern stories to tell. At least, no stories that relate to the settlers who
arrived in the empty desert in the early 1870s, some four hundred years
after the mysterious disappearance of the Hohokam Indians. The archeological remains of the Hohokam complementing the primitive canal system successive generations of settlers have converted into part of a major
irrigation system, keep cropping up in the excavations of the burgeoning
megalopolis. The other fact is that, of the approximately two dozen novels
that have been written about Phoenix, something like two-thirds are crime
novels. It is my contention that these two facts are inextricably related.

Although there is an interesting inventory of detective/mystery writers
who set their stories in Phoenix, it is clear that Phoenix is often merely a
circumstantial backdrop for those stories, and there is little contribution
to an understanding of Phoenix as a society with its own history and social
configuration. By contrast — and this will be a major point in arguing for
the importance of his novels — Jon Talton is profoundly committed to the
importance of recounting the particular stories that are relevant to the his-

tory of Phoenix as an interesting postmodern, sunbelt metropolis. As a consequence, his novels make use of the conceit of the mystery story in order to counter the proposition, made both locally and abroad, that such a relatively recent and homogenous city like Phoenix has no interesting stories to tell. Precisely for Talton, the opposite is true, and I will argue that the plot configurations of his novels, grounded as they are in the sub-genre of the detective/mystery story, are designed to counter the, for him, false claim that Phoenix is a "narrativeless society."

I suppose that the sense of what we might call a "narrativeless" society can be accounted for in part with reference to older areas of the country with a concomitant longer accumulated record of human experience, although some West Coast cities like Los Angeles, San Francisco, and even Seattle, as far as their Anglo history goes and discounting the now heavily romanticized Hispanic past in the case of the first two, are not that much older than Phoenix. This despite how Seattle and San Francisco generated great wealth far earlier than sluggish Phoenix, a wealth that allowed for an extensive cultural production and its institutions. Perhaps the way in which so many citizens of Phoenix are what Talton calls second-chance Johnnies displaced from somewhere else instills in them little interest in the historical foundations of their new society, although the West Coast cities I have mentioned are also societies grounded in large measure on adult outsiders, and even more so in the case of the high incidence of for-eign-born immigration they had long before Phoenix (a circumstance that also includes Hispanic groups in the Valley, by the way: if Hispanics or Latinos now make up over one third of the population, this has only been so in the last decade or so).

Rather, I would propose that this narrativeless condition is the result of something like an "ana-narrativity": The opposition to producing nar-ratives, which would require recognizing that there are stories to tell and recognizing the nature of such stories. True, there does exist a trove of narratives about Phoenix that, in addition to serious fiction, are continually recycled as part of the tourist industry, such as those relating to the cowboy West (the abiding theme of Scottsdale's self-image), surviving the summer heat before refrigerated air-conditioning, the Goldwater legacy, and the occasional monumentalized scandal such as the ax-murderess Winnie Ruth Judd and the two trunks of body parts put on the train to Los Angeles in the middle of October 1931 (on Judd, see Bommersbach[1]). But not much else gets out from behind the blank stares of old-timers and newcomers alike as regards what an inventory of the interesting stories of Phoenix might look like. If only Phoenix, like San Francisco, had something in its past like the 1906 Earthquake or L.A.'s fabled Hollywood, accompanied by something like the villainous LAPD. Nor does Phoenix supposedly have anything like Seattle's devious Dave Beck and the Teamster's legacy in that city. So rather than invent stories — beyond the disingenuous ones that might appeal to nevertheless rather disinterested tourists — one simply repeats the mantra that Phoenix has no history other than the thin gruel of routine annals.

But there is another way of looking at the matter, and this leads to what is the narrative material of Talton's writing. Talton would have us understand that Phoenix's history, both in its founding instances and current daily reality, is filled with dirty secrets simply waiting to be discovered and told, secrets relating to the treatment of minorities (as evidenced in eternally ongoing spiteful measures to control alleged illegal immigration and perennially unresolved issues such as the teaching of English to those who are not native speakers, even when they may be U.S. citizens), the violent opposition to unionization (most Phoenicians do not know that César Chávez, who co-founded the United Farm Workers in California in the 1960s, was run out of his native Arizona by growers willing to do anything to prevent any form unionization in their state), or the widespread shenanigans of wolfish land developers whose expansive ways go unchecked because they are guarding the hen house in the form of city counsels and the state legislature. Then there's the matter of the Mafia and other crime syndicates... These and many others are stories waiting to be told, but first you have got to acknowledge their existence before anyone might think to tell them and others to read them as anything other than wildly slanderous fictions at the expense of the All American Cities that all the Greater Phoenix communities aspire to be, anchored as they are by their vast churches and equally vast shopping malls that are really two sides to the same coin: Arizona Mills on Saturday and the Valley Cathedral on Sunday.

And what does this have to do with the preponderance of noir fiction that Phoenix seems to stimulate?[2] Precisely the fact that these authors, most of whom are admittedly not viable candidates for the National Book Award, are undertaking to discover these stories, even if they have yet to generate any large audience appeal or to do for Phoenix what Raymond Chandler did for Los Angeles (Reck; Fine 115–52; esp. 120–28[3]) and Dashiell Hammett did for San Francisco. One of the operating principles of noir, either as a fictional mode or a filmic genre, is the bringing out of the shadows of tightly guarded and unsavory secrets. Noir fiction is unaccompanied by music or photographic images (except for signature covers), but the following definition of film noir from the Merriam Webster online Unabridged Dictionary is suitable enough for its novelistic equivalent: "a type of crime film featuring cynical malevolent characters in a sleazy setting and an ominous atmosphere that is conveyed by shadowy photography and foreboding background music." Of course, one will recall that most of the great noir films are based on novels of paradigmatic malevolence and sleaze; some of these novels have been filmed more than once.

Thus, crime noir and Phoenix ana-narrativity attitudes go hand-in-hand, with the former telling the stories the latter jejunely insists do not exist. Since so much of the noir fiction set in Phoenix is literarily very thin — some of it is frankly bad — and none of it has been made into a film, little of it has attracted significant critical attention beyond the brief review note.[4] However, there is one author who is well deserving of such attention for the simple fact that he has interesting stories to tell about Phoenix, tells them well, and transmits a respectable understanding of the social dynamics of the city. That writer is native son Jon Talton.

Talton was born in the late 1950s—1956—and counts himself as a fourth-generation Phoenix native. Although he left the Valley for an extended period as an adult in 1978, he returned in the early September 2000 to assume the post as editorial writer covering business and related issues for *The Arizona Republic*, a Gannett newspaper, covering business and related issues. His tri-weekly columns, which ran until 2007, were often provocative and generated a fair amount of hostile responses, and Talton tells about particularly relishing responding to disgruntled readers who ordered him to go back where he came from to the effect that, in fact, he was where he came from. Throughout the early 2000s, Talton was the only *Republic* editorial writer who was a native of Phoenix. Talton's columns were often backgrounded by the malevolence and sleaze that he has fleshed out in his novels.

Talton has published six crime novels set in Phoenix: *Concrete Desert* (2001), *Camelback Falls* (2003), *Dry Heat* (2004), *Arizona Dreams* (2006), *Cactus Heart* (2007), and *South Phoenix Rules* (2010); all bear the subtitle *A David Mapstone Mystery* (*Dry Heat* won the 2006 Arizona Library Association award for best fiction). One of the traditions of crime novels that cuts across languages and cultures is the practice of tying a group of novels by an author together on the basis of their major figure, whether a lawyer, a district/prosecuting attorney, a private investigator, or some combination of these categories; indeed, some writers will use different *noms-de-plume*, one for each major fictional character in a set of their novels. It is also part of the same tradition that many of their major characters assume a culturally iconic importance beyond the novels so that they become synonymous with some social phenomenon, such as a way of life (the ur–English Agatha Christie's Miss Marple), a way of thought (the hyper-intellectual Sherlock Holmes), or a city (Los Angeles's Philip Marlowe). David Mapstone falls into the latter category. Although a native son of Phoenix, Mapstone leaves the Valley to do graduate work in history, fails to achieve tenure, and returns to Arizona, where he obtains something like a charity post with the Maricopa County Sheriff's Office,[5] where an old friend, Sheriff Mike Peralta,[6] employs Mapstone as a cold case specialist. Not only does Mapstone return to the city of his origins, he reconnects with old friends and even lives in the house he has inherited from his grandparents. It is the house in which he grew up in the historic Willo area of downtown Phoenix (where, incidentally Talton himself lived, around the corner from the house in which he grew up). But — most significantly — his professional employment brings him into contact with many of the unpleasant details of "ancient" Phoenix history. Important figures in Phoenix would just as soon not encourage a return to this past, both because its involves their own unsavory origins and deeds and because its brings to the fore aspects of the city best left unavailable to tourists and investors: mandatory archeological excavations are a bothersome inconvenience to the expansive built environment of Greater Phoenix, but digging around in old police files can be downright dangerous because of the revelations that they might yield regarding the ugly past and deeds of important civic leaders. The strategy of these civic leaders is to pretend that the past does not exist, that, quite simply, there is no past — in short, that there are no stories from the past to be told. As a consequence, Mapstone, whose work on cold cases is meant to be a public relations ploy for the Sheriff's office, is repeatedly exposed to the vengeful violence of those individuals inconvenienced by his diligent investigations into the past, and that violence extends to Lindsey, who is first his girlfriend (in *Camelback Falls*) and then his wife (in *Dry Heat*), and who is also employed by the Sheriff, as an expert in sleuthing in cyberspace.

I do not wish to detail here the plot outlines of Talton's six novels. Let me just say that in one sense it is standard crime-story fare involving revenge killings, corrupt business dealings, and the business activities of the mob (in this case the Russian mafia), along with scheming women and police sculduggery. My interest here is not the originality in Talton's crime themes or in his narrative plotting of them, but the way in which Mapstone serves as a filtering consciousness for the interpretation of Phoenix at the height of its apotheosis-like emergence as the nation's largest state capital, as the sixth demographic concentration in the country, and as an important station along the new Camino Real of the Southwest that stretches from Los Angeles to Houston, the much vaunted Sunbelt that is the consequence of political, economic, and technological forces of the late twentieth century.

Mapstone's role in these novels reminds one of the philosopher Walter Benjamin's view of the fictional detective as a privileged flaneur. The flaneur, as the word is originally conceived in French, is the urban idler, the individual, typically male, who is able to walk the streets of the city, interact comfortably with its diverse spaces, and, most significantly, as the flaneur morphs into the commentator on social customs, render pithy observations about the life he sees around him. The flaneur is closely related to the man about town and to the roundtable raconteur, as his expert idleness allows him entree into all sorts of realms and his glibness allows him to pay his way with his stories. Typically, the flaneur enjoys a disposable wealth that allows him to cultivate idleness as an artistic way of life, but in more democratic American versions, the flaneur, as Damon Runyon's stories teach us, may occupy humbler social conditions. Benjamin recognizes in the detective (of course, his image of the detective is the privileged upper-class intellectual sleuth, such as Sherlock Holmes, Lord Peter Whimsy, and Hercule Poirot, and even the less socially and economically advantaged but nevertheless unmistakably genteel Miss Marple), the individual who moves through society with a privileged analytical eye that allows him to perceive what others either cannot see or, if he does see it, cannot compute its importance. In this sense, then, the detective is a flaneur whose idly inquisitive eye becomes a social virtue. As Rob Sheilds sees it, "Walter Benjamin casts the *flâneur*, or stroller, as a detective of street life" (61), and he continues:

> The *flâneur* is like a detective seeking clues who read people's characters not only from the physiognomy of their faces but via a social physiognomy of the streets. The image and activity of *flânerie* is tied to the emergence of the popular genre of the detective novel and also to the literary practice and social justification of the labour time of journalists who, like the *flâneur*, put their observations both "for sale" on the market and wish to pursue *flânerie* for their own purposes.... Benjamin notes the "Remarkable association of *flânerie* and the detective novel" [Shields 63].[7]

83

Glimpses of Phoenix

The American detective-flaneur, however, merges with Raymond Chandler's rough-and-tumble noble savage of a detective, the man who must walk alone the mean streets of the city — and, like Mapstone, mess around in its mean police archives:

> But down these mean streets a man must go who is not himself mean, who is neither tarnished nor afraid. The detective in this kind of story must be such a man. He is the hero, he is everything. He must be a complete man and a common man, and yet an unusual man.... The story is his adventure in search of a hidden truth, and it would be no adventure if it did not happen to a man fit for adventure. He has a range of awareness that startles you, but it belongs to him by right, because it belongs to the world he lives in [Chandler 991–92].

Certainly, Talton's Mapstone does not get much chance to walk the mean streets of Phoenix: no one walks the mean streets of the city, and "streetwalker" is only a fossilized metonymy for the prostitutes who, like most other sin in the sun, are very much hidden away in air-conditioned shadows (of course, the degree of air conditioning is always relative to the economic standing of the sinners in question). Rather, Mapstone must rove the city in official and personal cars, the only reliable mode of transportation in the urban sprawl that is the Valley. Yet the ethos of the privileged observer is never out of mind for the narrative voice of Talton's novels, and one of the major functions of that voice is to observe the city in terms of both what it is and, relative to its decidedly humble past, what it has become. It is important to note that Mapstone's critical scrutiny of Phoenix is significantly different from Philip Marlowe's relationship to Los Angeles. While Chandler unquestionably is successful in transmitting the gritty texture of post-war Los Angeles and figuring the many dimensions of its official and personal corruption, Marlowe's mean streets are simply those that, perforce, must be experienced as they are, but never as they have become vis-à-vis something else. There is no nostalgia for an idyllic lost Los Angeles, which would connect with (mostly outrageously fanciful) legends of its romantic Spanish heritage and unquestionably none of the historical correlation undertaken between past and present Los Angeles as we have in the case of Roman Polanski's detective Jake, "J.J.," Gittes in Polanski's 1974 film *Chinatown*.

It is not so much that Mapstone entertains any gripping nostalgia for his youth in a prelapsarian Phoenix, although there is unquestionably a certain measure of that: the interrelated Thomas Wolfe motifs of *Look Homeward, Angel* and *You Can't Go Home Again* (novels from 1929 and

84

1940, respectively) animate most of us in our relationship to our home-towns, particularly in a society like the United States where few live in their hometowns and, given the accelerated rate of social change in this country, the way in which many hardly recognize after a while those home-towns, either due to the presumed benefits of progress or as a consequence of economic decay and decline. One of the controlling rhetorical strategies of Talton's novels is to play off the way in which Mapstone repeatedly experiences consternation over the changes in Phoenix since the sleepy desert-town days of his youth in order to describe one of the American cities that has most experienced, as the phrase constantly goes, dramatic change since World War II.[8] Often the commentary that is the narrative realization of that consternation does not contribute significantly to the crime novel plot: it may provide incidental contexts for it, but the main story line would not be significantly impacted by the elimination of that commentary. Rather, in fact, that commentary exemplifies the way in which the crime story is more the pretext for Mapstone's social history observations, rather than how these might be merely grace notes in the playing out of the central plot.

Talton's foregrounding of Mapstone's social history eye is particular evident at the outset of *Dry Heat*, which opens with the discovery of a dead body in a decaying swimming pool in the rough and frayed neigh-borhood of Maryvale on Phoenix's less desirable west side — less desirable, that is, than the old north Central Phoenix corridor and the East Valley communities of Scottsdale, Paradise Valley, and, more lately the southwest quadrant of Mesa, Chandler, and Gilbert suburbs).[9] This less desirable west side is demarcated not by the conventional railroad tracks of so much of the American social imaginary,[10] but rather the north/south axis of U.S. Interstate 17, which in the 1960s created an unbridgeable split between west Phoenix on the one side, and central and east Phoenix on the other. Mapstone arrives on assignment at the site where a body has been discov-ered in Maryvale and remarks as follows (this is the opening page of the novel):

> Maryvale! Fortunate home of the American dream. A single-family detached house in the suburbs: three bedrooms, living room, den, all-electric kitchen and carport, laid out in a neat rectangle of a one-story ranch house. We've got thousands of 'em, ready to sell, on safe winding streets in brand-new Phoenix. New as a hoola hoop. New as a teal '58 Chevy. New as this morning's hope. Leave behind those snow shovels and below-zero winters. Leave behind the old dingy cities of the East

and Midwest, with their crime and racial trouble. Time for a fresh start, thanks to a VA mortgage and the FHA. You've earned it: back-yard lifestyle with a new swimming pool. Here in Phoenix, its eighty degrees in January, and in summer, we've got air-conditioning. Green lawns, blond children, pink sunsets. All in Maryvale.

Until you go out one fine day and find a body facedown in the green water of what was once the swimming pool [*Dry Heat* 1].

There are many things going on in this passage, not the least of which is the mockery of the sales pitch of almost fifty years ago for the new planned community of Maryvale, a name in itself so aggressively all–American, in its steadfast denial of any historically local or indigenous place names. Yet, it is a sales-pitch — certainly stylistic flourishes and design details aside — not unlike those one sees everyday in the pages of the Valley's newspapers for housing developments that offer today the same fantasy fulfillment as Maryvale did a half-century before: my depressing favorite is the mega-development El Verrado. And the implication is unmistakable: in time all

Example of residence in the Maryvale planned community allowed to go to seed, Phoenix west side.

of these planned communities will likely come to experience unremitting decline, pinpointed here with reference to the most salient icon of the mid-twentieth-century ranch-style house, the swimming pool. The aquamarine waters of the backyard pool party, with the bouncing heads of blond children, are replaced — in time, but here, specifically by the demands of narrative logic — with the fetid algae-green scum bearing a facedown floating corpse.

Talton's narrative logic, therefore, makes the corpse a symbol for the "death" of the Maryvale subdivision, at least in terms of its once trumpeting advertisement, and later in this opening chapter, the implied promise of an Anglo safe zone (i.e., no Mexicans allowed) is disrupted by the comment that the house seems to have served as way station or "drop" house for undocumented aliens, who have all fled before the police arrive (*Dry Heat* 4), although neighbors are clustered on the sidewalk, speaking softly in Spanish (*Dry Heat* 2). Both the dated nature of this boosterish example of urban planning (but not, *pace* Jane Jacobs, the grim concept of urban planning) are signaled by the reference to the hoola hoop and the teal '58 Chevy, along with the manifest falsehood of a liberation from crime and racial troubles: the important Maryvale substation of the Phoenix Police Department is not located there by accident (see image included here: a typical tract house in the Maryvale area).

Mapstone continues his assessment of the neighborhood:

> I could have written a fascinating paper on the evolution of the American automobile suburb in Phoenix, how places like Maryvale that once seemed so full of promise had evolved into postmodern slums. How abandonment of place in the West is as old as the Hohokam, the ancient Indians who first settled in the river valley that became Phoenix, and then disappeared. It would seem fascinating to me, at least. But I don't see any need for that skill in what looked like one more dreary west-side killing — the "curse of the Avenues," as my wife Lindsey called it, referring to Phoenix's grid of numbered avenues on the west of Central, numbered streets on the east [*Dry Heat* 5].

Mapstone is speaking here as the professional (albeit, failed academic) historian, and, in one important sense, the novel in which he appears is, in fact, a treatise on the urban destiny of Phoenix, as are the three other Talton novels in which he appears. As the reader will discover, however, the so-called curse of the avenues is, as is always the case with such denominations, mostly symbolic and contains a grain of the disingenuous. That is because said curse does not affect the entire hemisphere of the designated avenues in Phoenix, but only a subset of them: those in places like Maryvale, but not Del Webb's contemporary yet apparently still thriving community a couple miles to the north and a bit to the west (the first Sun City development dates from 1960 and remains a signature event in Phoenix's residential development); there is also a subsequent Sun City West, farther north and west of the original development. Nor does it affect Mapstone's own residential neighborhood, where, as I have said, he has come to live in the grandparents' house he grew up in on West Cypress St. Actually the alleged curse of the avenues seems to move west from North 27th St., immediately west of the railroad-tracks barrier and deep trench of the north–south interstate discussed above. Mapstone, however, lives well to the east of that barrier, as the Willo Historic District (one of the city's thirty-five such neighborhoods) extends only between N. Central Avenue, the point of the east-west divide, and North 7th Ave., and only one mile from West McDowell Road north to West Thomas Road. Mapstone speaks in idyllic terms of this neighborhood, both as it continues to exist today, eighty years or more after the majority of the homes were built, and as it existed when he was a child, one assumes around the time of the Korean War. Then, the area, outside the Phoenix City limits when it was first built up, was still on the fringes of the downtown district, surrounded by citrus groves and little else. While the citrus groves are long gone, the area is still noted for its lush greenery, with, as the real estate pitches proclaim, carefully tended lawns, stately palm tress, and noble citrus and other shade-providing trees.

Mapstone's Phoenix functions, therefore, on two historical planes, which is not surprising, given the narrative conceit of his training as a historian. On the one hand is the Phoenix of his childhood:

> I drove across the Seventh Avenue overpass, made a right on Grant Street, and then turned back north on Ninth. Up through the 1970s, this had been the industrial heart of a much smaller city. The Southern Pacific and Santa Fe railroads sliced through on their way to Union Station. The railroads also served scores of produce warehouses and other agricultural terminals. Old Phoenix was a farm town, where irrigated fields and groves yielded oranges, grapefruits, lemons, lettuce, and cotton for markets back east. Mile-long trains of refrigerator cars were made up here, sending fresh Arizona citrus to the tables of families in Chicago and Dayton and Minneapolis. Now those families seem to have moved to Arizona, and the old produce district had been long abandoned [*Dry Heat* 31].

Having grown up in an area adjacent to the citrus fields that fed the agricultural commerce of the Old Phoenix, it is to be expected that Mapstone

Example of bungalow architecture in the Willo Historic District, downtown Phoenix.

would also wax dithyrambic about the then of what is now the blighted district only a couple of miles southwest of where he lives.

The Then vs. Now deictic axis is very strong in Talton's writing, and no more so in *Dry Heat*, which is why I have focused specifically on this novel, although all of what I have explicated here is equally extensive to the set of four David Mapstone mysteries he has published so far. One of the things that is notable about *Dry Heat* is that the crime story it is based on, the 1948 murder of an FBI agent, whose badge turns up on the derelict found floating in the Maryvale pool, functions as part of the Then vs. Now axis. However, the significant point is that the FBI agent was not murdered by the mob or anyone else of the ilk, but was killed by a child trying to protect her mother. The "historical facts" of the cold case that Mapstone uncovers, an activity that brings very much into play the crime syndicates of contemporary Phoenix, most especially the newly arrived Russian Mafia, was that the mob of the old days lived by a gentleman's agreement that excluded the murder of reporters and cops. Mapstone's boss Peralta, also a long-time Phoenix resident, observes pointedly that "These Russians [who have killed at this point two of his deputies] are on the offensive. They don't follow any of the old rules" (*Dry Heat* 48).

The second axis of the novel is the relative quality of life in surviving Phoenix neighborhoods. While the Willo area is at least three decades older than the Maryvale area, the relative circumstances of their locale — historical core vs. isolated western fringe — account in part for the way in which the first has allowed for an interesting combination of survival and renewal, such that Willo is now considered one of the great bungalow communities of America, while Maryvale has been exposed to a wide array of the features of urban rot and decay see the image above of a typical Willow-area craftsman's bungalow). This process is integral to Phoenix history and cannot be simply attributed to regrettable chance and, indeed, must be correlated with larger patterns relating to the urban configuration of the city.[11]

In the end, while Talton's novels, like Chandler's and other noir writers, turns on a skillfully crafted crime tale, its fundamental interest lies in the interpretation of the circumstance of that tale as part of the dynamics of contemporary urban cities in America, particularly those of the Southwest such as Phoenix. And in the end, the most important literary contribution of Talton's writing is to bring out the historical forces that have shaped contemporary Phoenix and, in the process, to provide it with one set of the stories many, naively or disingenuously, would like to pretend it lacks.[12]

Jana Bommersbach on Winnie Ruth Judd: Woman as Scapegoat for the Dirty Secrets of the City

Investigative reporters each have their own system, but we all start with a basic premise. Something is wrong with this picture. That is what I had always heard about the Winnie Ruth Judd case — that the truth had never been revealed. If those rumors were accurate, then what really happened? (Bommersbach, *The Trunk Murderess* 285)

When Jana Bommersbach (birthdate not available) published the first edition in 1992 with Simon & Schuster of her *The Trunk Murderess: Winnie Ruth Judd: The Truth about an American Crime Legend Revealed at Last*, sixty years had passed since Judd was convicted of the murder of her close friends and former roommates Agnes Anne LeRoi and Hedwig Samuelson (see image, next page, of the murder house). Sentenced to die by hanging in 1932, she was subsequently evaluated as mentally incompetent and sentenced in 1933 to the Arizona State Asylum (about a mile from where the crime occurred, in downtown Phoenix). Judd subsequently escaped six times from the Asylum between 1933 and 1963, thanks to having obtained, apparently from a sympathetic employee, a key to the front door of the institution. Famed criminal attorney Melvin Belli finally obtained her parole and release in 1971 after the longest period, six and a half years, of flight, during which time she worked in California as a maid under an assumed identity. In 1983, Governor Jack Williams of Arizona finally signed a formal discharge from the asylum. Judd died in Phoenix at the age of ninety-three in 1998, sixty-seven years to the day after her surrender

Above: Winnie Ruth Judd murder house, downtown Phoenix. *Bottom*: The trunks, hatbox, and suitcase in which the bodies of Winnie Ruth Judd's murder victims were transported by train to Los Angeles (Arizona State Archives, #94–7383, 13–0058).

to the police in Los Angeles, where she had traveled by train with luggage that included the bodies (one dismembered) of her victims in two trunks, a suitcase and a hat box.

Occurring at a time when American journalism, only recently having moved into truly mass distribution, was particularly keen to pick up on lurid crime stories, especially when there was a manifestly outrageous angle to them. Moreover, the emerging widespread phenomenon of crime photography, pioneered in the period by the likes of Weegee (Arthur Fellig, 1899–1968) in

New York, provided an enormous circulation boost through titillating immediacy to the event. Practitioners like Weegee often arrived on the crime scene before the police, thanks, in his case, to his own police radio hook-up, allowing them unrestricted material access to the crime scene that is unimaginable today. Indeed, part of the story of the investigation surrounding the alleged Judd murders was the loss of evidence, evidence tampering, and the loss of evidentiary integrity that stemmed, first, from the invasion of the crime scene by photographers eager for the lurid scoop and, second, from the commercial sideshow of paid tours of the property the owner quickly organized, capitalizing, precisely, on the excitement produced among readers in large measure thanks to the crime photographs.[1]

There is much about the Judd story that will probably never be cleared

Vulture-like press and public press congregating at the Winnie Ruth Judd murder house, compromising crime-scene evidence (Arizona State Archives, #94–7383, 13–0063).

up, thanks in part to a systematic cover-up by the real perpetrator(s) of the crime and the power structure to which they belonged and thanks to the aforementioned loss of evidence. Judd's own decision to remain silent on many details, despite the close friendship Bommersbach established with her over the years, means that much reliable information has irremediably vanished.[2] But the Judd story was never about what really happened. Rather, it is more about how it impacted the imaginations in Phoenix at the time and how it evolved into an authentic folk tale of a very plucky woman's determination to remake her life, first through her escapes from the insane asylum and then in her persistent anonymity after her final formal discharge. During the thirty years she was confined to the asylum, which went from being on the fringes of the established city to being lost in the urban core of a city that was growing exponentially during the period, her escapes became legendary, and much of the dinner table and cocktail party conversation they provoked was more myth than fact, although it is true that after one of her escapes she did, in fact, walk the entire Southern Pacific train route from downtown Phoenix to Yuma, on the border with California.

Winnie Ruth Judd consulting with her lawyer during her trial (Arizona State Archives, #94–7383, 13–0139).

The fact that Judd was by mid-century an elderly lady and that people really knew that she had been railroaded, first into prison and then into the insane asylum, for crimes she did not commit, made her more attractive as a folk hero. Moreover, newcomers to Phoenix through this period of intense population growth, perhaps tired of recycling stories of cowboys and

Indians that were part of the mystique of the state, were thirsty for some (almost) authentic urban stories in a new found land's apparent total lack of anything interesting to say about it except the last heat wave. Judd's story — Was she really an ax murderer? Was she really demented? How was she engineering all those escapes? Might she not be the frail senior citizen (there often seemed to so many of them) in line in front of you in the supermarket? — was genuinely intriguing, especially when one found out that other stories, such as who really owned the kitschy Tovrea Castle in the middle of a junky industrial area or what the extra little addition was on top of the San Marcos Hotel, were just so much hokum.

Of course, what was most interesting about the Judd story was the fact that it involved a convicted woman killer.[3] The 1932 trial was the biggest crime story that had ever occurred in Phoenix to that date, and the newspapers made the most of it.[4] Feeding stereotypes of murderesses

Crowds outside the courtroom during the trial of Winnie Ruth Judd (Arizona State Archives, #94–7383, 13–0091).

as hysterical jilted lovers, the narratives of the event could only be enriched by the fact that one had been dismembered and that both bodies had been taken by train across the still warm Arizona-California desert of late October in eventually seeping and stinking trunks (with the head of the dismembered victim traveling with Judd on her lap in a hatbox). Judd was supposed to have done away with two rivals, not just one, and that the rivalry involved the attentions of wealthy businessmen toward unattached or, at least, easily available, women (Judd's doctor husband had left her behind in Phoenix to practice elsewhere; LeRoi and Samuelson were unmarried). During the Depression Era and pre–World War II period in Phoenix, such women were wont to entertain such men with cards, illicit liquor, and sexual company during, but not exclusively limited to, the long summer months. Since there was no domestic air-conditioning in those days, well-to-do housewives absented themselves with the children to cool retreats on the beach or in the mountains. The result was a social setting that could readily become the stuff of penny-dreadful pulp fiction.[5] In addition, Judd worked as a medical secretary at the Grunow Medical Clinic (which still exists in all its neo–Alhambra splendor in downtown Phoenix), as did Agnes as an X-ray technician (Samuelson was unemployed, having ended up in Phoenix because of tuberculosis). The possibilities of any sort of affective liaison between two or all three of the women and the subsequent intimations that Judd may have been privy to cases of illegal abortions being practiced at the Clinic helped over the years to spice up the story; the illegal dispensing of narcotics may also have been involved. Yet the background narrative of women on their own in a city notable for its loose morals,[6] women who were no better than they should be, only made the story spicier. And even spicier when it became evident that Judd was a fallen woman who came from good respectable Christian folk (her father was a mid-west Methodist minister of unquestioned probity) and that her husband had, in effect, abandoned her in the pursuit of a medical career ruined by his own dependency on drugs. Probably little of the pulp fiction of the day (which really flourishes after the emergence of the paperback in the post–World War II publishing industry) had such an accumulation of juicy narrative threads, and there is little wonder that there is, albeit modest, a parallel fictional production about Judd.[7]

Winner of a Distinguished Service Award from the Arizona Press Club, Jana Bommersbach is undoubtedly the most ubiquitous freelance journalist in Phoenix, and her many activities (including political activism) have included writing a column regularly for the *Phoenix Magazine*, a forum that, while mostly serving the commercial interests of the city, of the cosmetic surgery and upscale decorating variety, has also striven to include coverage of Phoenix history and the serious arts scene. Bommersbach has achieved considerable local prominence with her book on Judd, and in 2003 the Scottsdale-based Poisoned Pen Press, a prominent publisher and bookseller in the area of crime and mystery fiction, brought out a new edition of the original Simon & Schuster imprint, which went on in 2010 to win the OneBookAz award, a program administered, according to its site, "with funds granted by the Arizona State Library, Archives and Public Records, a Division of the Secretary of State, under the Library Services and Technology Act, which is administered by the Institute of Museum and Library Services." Clearly, Bommersbach's book has struck a chord as equally resonant in local history as the original Judd story did. The new edition contains as an appendix (305–17) "Remember Winnie Ruth Judd," reprinted from the February 1999 issue of the *Phoenix Magazine*, which confirms the strong friendship that developed over the years between Judd and the journalist who attempted to find the truth in a story that had been so sensationalized. Touchingly, Bommersbach relates how Judd presented to her as a Christmas gift the key she had kept throughout the years, the key that had been given to her that allowed her to open the front door of the Arizona State Asylum.

Of course, this key is heavily iconic; indeed, perhaps one might also say fetishistic, in what it came to symbolize as the friendship between the two women. But it is enough that it is iconic of the way in which, as no one else had bothered to attempt to do, Bommersbach had sought to find the key to Judd's story, as to how and why she had been railroaded into jail and into the state asylum for a crime she could not have logically or reasonably committed. As much as she may have been guilty of manslaughter in LeRoi's and Samuelson's death as the consequence of an argument between love-interest rivals, an accomplice to the dismemberment of Samuelson, and the willing agent of the shipment to Los Angeles of the evidence of their dead bodies, Bommersbach is unyielding in her conviction from the outset that the wispy young woman had neither the tools nor the strength to engage in dismemberment or to have alone been able to effect the details of her escape from the city with the bodies. History has tended to point to the person of Jack J. "Happy Jack" Halloran, a prominent businessman and man about town, a heavy drinker and an assiduous participant in all manner of bachelor events, as both the motive for the deadly spat between the three women and the actual person (with or without the collaboration of a doctor from the Grunow Clinic) to dismember Samuelson's body. But the circumstance alone that Judd remained silent over these details for almost seventy years because she believed that she would be protected for her cooperation by the man she loved is enough to allow Bommersbach access to a deep well of feminist pathos in which her narrative is grounded. Judd had apparently agreed never to talk about what had happened, both with Halloran (if it was he who played the central role) and with those who agreed to substitute confinement to the state asylum for the gallows:

> If the woman known today as Marian Lane had her way, this book would never have been written. She would prefer her given name were never spoken again. She would rather live out her last years anonymously, without anyone wondering anymore what happened so long ago.
> There are many times in the last two years I thought she was right. That "stirring things up again," as she puts it, would do nothing but harm an old woman I had no stomach to harm. Even my parents wondered, "Why not just leave her alone?"
> And just when I would decide that I should — that a few peaceful years were the least she was owed — I'd find another piece of this filthy puzzle and I'd get angry all over again [283].

There are three important points of reference raised by this quote that deserve commentary.

One is the matter of "stirring things up." Precisely, the enterprise of investigative journalism is to "stir things up." Based on the principles that everyday reporting is both superficial and dependent to an unseemly extent on information provided by official and other self-interested sources, investigative journalism touts its independence from such controls and its ability to explore behind the scenes and to dredge up the hidden details, often those that have been deliberately hidden. Investigative journalism may also be committed to marginal or subaltern interests that lack due representation in the mainline press and that, by their very nature, may stand in opposition to official channels of information. Investigative journalism touts also its privilege, when necessary and rhetorically effective, to speak in personalist terms that border on the autobiographical (the journalists' involvement with what he or she is reporting on), the testimonial (the exposing and giving witness to excluded or forgotten lives), and the revisionist (to countermand, usurp, and reformulate a story already told).

The Trunk Murderess is driven by the conviction that Judd's fate was that of the victim of a cover-up, one in which she was forced to collaborate in order to, so apparently she was told, escape the gallows. Judd was framed for the crimes of another or others. The event as reported to the standard press of the day, in both Phoenix and nationally, was given a depiction that was disingenuously false and incomplete, and her trial was characterized by evidence that was suppressed and distorted, not to mention the silencing of some evidence, in conjunction with the impossibility of presenting other evidence because it was tampered with, corrupted, or ignored. Bommersbach quotes Hugh Ennis, who was a police officer at the time of the crime. In the course of his long career, Ennis adopted as a "specialty [...] Arizona's spectacular criminal cases" (125). Bommersbach interviewed Ennis extensively on the basis of his extensive review of the 1,700 pages of identifiable testimony, the only record of the trial in existence:

> Hugh Ennis decries the investigation at every single point: how officers collected physical evidence; how they quickly latched onto a theory of the killings and ignored everything that didn't fit; how they blatantly hid all the evidence that undercut their version of what happened that deadly night.
>
> He says the Phoenix Police Department in 1931 botched the case from the moment they stepped into it. And he does not believe it was an accident [whereby Judd, who was herself shot in the hand, supposedly killed the other two women in self-defense during a heated argument over the attentions of Halloran, who may have been providing money to one or all three of the women].
>
> "So much of what happened in this investigation smacks of exactly what it probably was — political interference," Ennis says. "Remember, this was a small town [29,053 in 1920, according to VanderMeer, *Desert Visions* 40] and part of the policeman's job was to know who was doing what to whom — they knew out of self-defense, because that's how you kept your job in those days. They'd know Jack Halloran was prominent. They'd know who his girlfriends were. Some of those cops might even know the victims" [126].
>
> Ennis is blunt about the shameful admissions the officers made on the stand. "They sent officers out there who let reporters traipse all through the place. Right then, they no longer had a crime scene. Any crime scene integrity was gone" [127].

The same sort of ineptitude, coupled with the need to corrupt and destroy evidence, that characterizes Ennis's description of how the police handled the case applies to the trial itself, where Judd's defense was entirely dominated by the judge and prosecution, whom Bommersbach sees as committed not only to protecting Halloran, but, more importantly, the old boy network of which he was a part and that, should he be left unprotected, he would have been compelled to expose. Whether it was a matter of so-called smokers dominated by alcohol, gambling and sex; whether it was a matter of illicit trade in narcotics; whether it was a matter of illegal abortions, it wasn't just Halloran who might be exposed, but the entire core of the Phoenix power system of the day: virtually all of these men involved in the case were a part of this power system. Closing ranks against the convenient scapegoat, a woman by that time of suspect virtue, evidently subject, throughout the trial, to the harsh and unforgiving stares of her parents who had come in from Darlington, Indiana for the trial, the men were determined that no fissure in their story might occur that would cast doubt on the narrative they had agreed to, one that would railroad Judd to the gallows and perpetual silence. Thus, her defense attorney chose at no time to put Judd herself on the stand: who knew what the woman might say that might challenge their story?

As an example of human drama, Bommersbach's account is, consequently, driven by the dramatic principle of the lone individual against society as a whole, with that individual being effectively silenced such that her personal narrative could never challenge the one that had been so effectively elaborated and sold to the mainline press. The fact that it was, in terms of narrative coherence, an unreasonable or counterintuitive one, could be of little consequence. Because what confirmed beyond any shadow of a doubt the seamless nature of that narrative is that it was the one being told by the men in the case, a privileged position of enunciation that could only be enhanced by the undisputed power they wielded in the small town that was Phoenix in 1931–32. As a woman who, in the first place, had a disadvantaged position of social power (a medical secretary from out of town whose morals were suspect and who had, after all, unquestionably fled town by train with two dead bodies in tow), Judd had no options open to her for voice in the social discourse, as of course, virtually no woman did in her day, unless she was the Mrs. of a powerful man, and then only in a limited fashion within well specified thematic possibilities. While her husband Dr. Judd was present for her trial (and to his credit, supported her morally as best he could), he was an outsider and had no local credibility; he had, in fact, abandoned her in Phoenix to pursue his career elsewhere.

Clearly, then, Bommersbach's narrative, as much as it is an untangling of the conspiracy against Judd and the attempt to put forth an alternative narrative, is also a feminist counternarrative. While Bommersbach must in the end concede defeat in the goal of the investigative journalist's attempt to tell the strived-for real story, thanks in great measure to Judd's determination, to the end of her life, to abide by the vow of silence imposed on her (by the same agents of local political power) in exchange for the commutation of her death sentence to that of life in the state mental asylum, she can, nevertheless, effectively rhetoricize her role as a *female* investigative reporter in the face of the *male* narrative of complicitous fabrication.

In this fashion, Bommersbach makes use of two major principles of investigative reporting, personal involvement and subaltern substitution. Personal involvement figures in to the extent that Bommersbach becomes personally involved with Judd. One might say this is a cunning move on her part: get the woman's confidence and she will finally open up. This is why Bommersbach is at pains to convince us of her empathy for Judd and to portray for us the degree to which Judd seems genuinely to develop an affection for the woman who, after all, rather doggedly pursues her, to the extent that her own parents are concerned. But it is not enough, and Judd will never fully allow Bommersbach into her confidence, thus leaving Judd's story, for the time, frustratingly inconclusive. In a word, narrative closure has not been effected.

Secondly, *The Trunk Murderess* is sustained by a principle of subaltern substitution, in this case the substitution for the stonewall narrative of the male participants in the crime and its aftermath,[8] in the sense that the subaltern voice of a woman — Bommersbach, the female investigative journalist — is ranged against the sixty-year primacy of male narrative. While the woman's voice cannot, in the end, prevail categorically, it can mount enough of a contestational response to fill a book and to become a Phoenix literary sensation. Against both Judd's silence and the conspiracy of the male establishment, the voice of the investigative reporter has prevailed. Judd's story may be rewritten in other ways by subsequent historians and journalists, but Bommersbach's account will be the inevitable point of departure because it gave voice to Judd. It may be in a way Judd did not always approve of and it may be self-admittedly a frustrated enterprise in many respects, but there it is as a textual wedge, so to speak, in what was thought to be the fissureless surface of the narrative fabricated in 1931–32 by the male-dominated power structure of Phoenix.

The other point of reference from Bommersbach's eplilogue is the writer's reference to her anger: as she pursued her task, she would get angry all over again, just as she becomes enraged attempting to explain to Judd that she has nothing to fear from the establishment or the mental health

101

board if she finally tells her side of the story: "'Nobody has any right to do this to you,' I raged" (300), so it is no wonder that, at one point Judd breaks off direct contact with the reporter (297). Bommersbach's angry reaction to what she uncovers throughout the course of her investigation exemplifies well the concept of "feminist rage." Feminist rage, while often pinpointed in terms of feminist reactions to the obduracy of male sexism in failing, willfully or otherwise, to understand the stakes of rape for women, is a concept that ranges across a spectrum of principled reactions to the perceived array of male sexism, as a response to how "they just don't get it."[9] Carefully positioned such as not to be merely a female response to male rage (whether conveniently tied to so-called testosterone poisoning or calibrated with reference to myriad sources), feminist rage is a rhetorical ploy to vie for access to a social discourse denied, circumscribed or suppressed for women. As I have attempted to show, Bommersbach's investigative project is grounded on the proposition that Judd's railroading is possible because she has no effective voice and because there was, in 1931–32 in Phoenix, no effective voice to speak for her against that of a power structure threatened by what she might have had to say. Bommersbach's voice of professional investigative journalism may, by the 1990s, be effective enough to counter the narrative of that power structure, all of whom by then were dead, but the reporter decides to invest in the sort of overdetermination, of rhetorical emphasis, provided by her decision to speak out of anger.[10] Interestingly — and eloquently — enough, alongside the wispy twenty-year-old and the frail elderly lady, Bommersbach is physically an imposing presence, with a well deployed booming voice. Although in person Bommersbach speaks in scrupulously professional tones, the persona of *The Trunk Murderess* is that of someone, to put it bluntly, pissed off over the sheer awfulness of what she describes herself discovering. One can only imagine her reaction to her treatment at the hands of Barry Goldwater: "Former U.S. senator Barry Goldwater refused repeated requests for an interview, relaying the message 'You tell that girl to leave that alone'" (9). Professional discretion seems to have kept Bommersbach in check as to commenting on being called 'that girl' by the redoubtable former U.S. senator, unaccustomed to being disobeyed.

Finally, Bommersbach's narrative is framed by two interesting feminine metaphors: "So why did so many people in Phoenix act as though the city was hiding its dirty linen behind her skirts?" (5) and "I felt I'd just looked up the dirty skirts of Phoenix, Arizona" (286).

While the metaphor of "dirty linen" is not necessarily limited to any one sex, the metaphor of concealing skirts is. There is a fundamental ambiguity in the first quote, from the opening pages of *The Trunk Murderess*: whose skirts? Judd's? In which case the morally suspect young woman, whose own linen was for Phoenix society unquestionably stained, both with the blood of murder if not with the detritus of the suspect affairs of the LeRoi-Samuelson household she once shared and then frequented, assimilates, as though that of a medieval sin eater, the dirty linen of Halloran and associates. Or is it Phoenix's dirty linen, with the city being personified as a disreputable woman? This certainly makes sense in terms of the out-of-bounds conduct of Halloran in the licentious Happy Jack moments of his life: decency would have been very heavily invigilated in those days, but Happy Jack and his associates seemed to have found many agreeable ways to circumvent it, which, in turn, would have been consonant with the corruption that prevails in Phoenix until well after World War II.

By contrast, there is hardly any ambiguity to the closing metaphor. The idea of looking up the dirty skirts of the city (here there is no question about the feminine personification involved) is hardly attractive because of what would be understood to be the character of a woman who would put herself in the position to allow for the looking up of her skirts, and much less if her linen were far from impeccable. There's an old Emily Post–type injunction that a one must always go out on the street wearing irreproachable linen, as though one might be run down at any time and have personal linen revealed for all to see. In a sense, Bommersbach's investigation conducts a hit-and-run assault on the historical body of Phoenix, and the consequences are hardly pretty to look at. Of course, hardly anyone wears skirts anymore in Phoenix, but Bommersbach's metaphor is far from reassuring about the cleanliness of the city's social history.

Out of the Barrio:
Stella Pope Duarte's
Let Their Spirits Dance

> We're all children off on an adventure, Americans who have
> never seen America. (Duarte, *Let Their Spirits Dance* 153)

> We've got mainstream American traveling with us now....
> (274)

Phoenix, Arizona (founded early 1870s, incorporated 1881; current
population ca. 1,500,000; national ranking: sixth most populous urban
area[1]), like many cities of the American Southwest, saw historically the
steady increase of a Mexican population, principally as a component of
the development of agriculture and cattle raising. And also like many cities
of the Southwest, modern urbanization, with the shift away from agriculture, meant the destruction of Mexican — by now called Chicano — neighborhoods as the consequence of so-called gentrification and the creation
of middle-class enclaves, including residential housing projects, shopping
centers, parks and other recreational facilities. Although Phoenix never
experienced as dramatic a destruction of a Mexican/Chicano neighborhood
like the demise of Chavez Ravine in Los Angeles for the creation of Dodger
Stadium, there has been a steady erosion and displacement of Chicano
neighborhoods with the emergence of Phoenix as one of the top two growth
areas in the United States and the imposition of the housing industry as
an unchallenged — and unchallengeable — economic engine in the area.
The process has slowed considerably with the economic downturn of the
first decade of the century, but there is no reason to suppose that it will
not resume unabated with the foreseeable return of economic growth.
Only the designation of neighborhoods as historic can provide an immu-

Typical comfortable residence in the Sonorita Barrio of south Phoenix.

nity from the destruction of a barrio, something that has been achieved in the case of the Garfield Historical District, immediately east of downtown Phoenix.

But, in general, Chicano barrios in Phoenix have had little to save them from destruction. The two most notable cases involved the growth of Arizona State University and Sky Harbor International Airport. In the case of the former, what was originally the farming community of Tempe was chosen in the 1890s for the construction of Tempe Normal School, and from its first days, through its evolution into Arizona State College and then Arizona State University, its growth into the largest-enrolling university in the country has been at the expense of what was formerly called San Pablo or, more typically by Anglos, Mexican Town. All that remains as a reminder of the original area, dating back to the early 1870s, is St. Mary's Church, which is part of the Catholic student Newman Center attached to the university. Built in 1903 as Our Lady of Mt. Carmel, it was the first permanent-structure church built in the Phoenix area. Additionally, the names of surrounding parks commemorate the Hispanic presence in Tempe, and there continue to be pockets, east of the university, of Chicano residents.

In the case of Sky Harbor, the enormous growth of the airport, commensurate with the demographic explosion of Phoenix, has been at the cost of a network of Chicano communities in south central Phoenix and north of the Salt River, whose course the landing strips of the airport parallel. These communities with individual names but generally grouped together as the Barrios Unidos, have all but disappeared. The land of the last remaining one, El Campito, is now owned by the airport and is steadily becoming pock-marked with vacant lots as residents move out and structures are torn down. Since the airport has no urgent and immediate use for the land of El Campito, its death agony is a slow but inexorable one. The only major building in the area is Santa Rita Hall. The hall has served as the seat of Chicanos por la Causa, the most active Chicano group in Phoenix. This building is where César Chávez conducted his hunger strike in 1972 as part of his renewed attempt to organize farm workers in the Phoenix area and obtain fair treatment for them.

Perhaps the most notable phenomenon of the barrios destroyed in the name of modern urban progress, as represented by Sky Harbor, has been the fate of the original Sagrado Corazón church just south of downtown Phoenix (a new Sagrado Corazón has been built farther south). Sagrado Corazón was the seat of Catholic worship in the Golden Gate barrio, one of the Barrios Unidos sacrificed to Sky Harbor. However, because of the historic nature of the church, it was never torn down, although all of the other buildings and residences around it were. It has stood in the middle of a vacant lot at South 16th Street and East Buckeye for years, surrounded

Traditional California bungalow residence, with sleeping porch along the front of the house, in the Sonita Barrio of south Phoenix.

Sagrado Corazón Catholic Church in south central Phoenix, "imprisoned" by Phoenix Sky Harbor Airport expansion.

by a chain link fence, its only companions jackrabbits and the interminable stream of jets taking off and landing at the airport a few blocks away. It is anybody's guess what will be the eventual disposition of the original Sagrado Corazón, except to say that its historical status has seemed to save it from the wrecking ball. It stands as a sad but ironic commentary of the fate of so many Chicano barrios in the Phoenix area.

Of all of the still existing and disappeared Chicano barrios of Phoenix, perhaps the most interesting one is La Sonorita, which the city of Phoenix officially recognizes as the Grant Park neighborhood, in reference to the city park of that name that anchors the area. Located immediately south of the main Phoenix financial core, La Sonorita is distinctive in its proximity to the shadow cast by urban horizontal growth. And yet it has managed to survive. Still undesignated as a historical neighborhood, La Sonorita remains unthreatened with destruction for a number of interlocking circumstantial reasons.

In the first place, La Sonorita is located south of the railroad tracks,

View of downtown Phoenix financial/administrative center (old commercial center) from the Sonorita Barrio of south Phoenix.

one of the three physical barriers between north Phoenix, which has been the locus of intense post–World War II development, and south Phoenix, where historically people of color were consigned and where, with the railroad tracks an apparently unbreachable barrier, there has been little interest in the sort of commercial and residential development that destroyed the Barrios Unidos, located north of the railroad tracks. (The other two barriers between north and south Phoenix are the Salt River, south of the tracks, and Washington Street, north of the tracks, the ground zero for the formal designation of north/south streets. More recently, the east-west 202 freeway, over a mile north of Washington Street has been a secondary barrier for the city).

A second reason for the survival of La Sonorita has been its immediate proximity to the Phoenix downtown. Although there has been some central core renewal since the flight to the desert suburbs in the 1950s thanks to the development of effective residential air-conditioning, the downtown, while frequently touted as on the verge of a trendy comeback, has failed to become viable in any meaningful way; the best that can be said is that it has attracted an artist and theater community, with supporting ventures such as funky restaurants and bars. But none of this recent activity represents much of a threat to established installations, since most of what is involved entails the recycling of previously abandoned buildings.

A third significant aspect of La Sonorta is the presence of St. Anthony's Catholic Church. Not only an important architectural landmark but also a vital community center, St. Anthony's is second in community importance only to Inmaculada Concepción de María in terms of the approximately two dozen churches in the Phoenix area where mass is regularly said in Spanish. A distinctive feature of St. Anthony's is the broad set of steps making up the main entrance, which permits the sort of social interaction between individuals that is an important social phenomenon of the Hispanic culture. The lovely grounds of the church, with its green lawns and dense flower beds, moreover, constitute an oasis in the desert landscape that prevails in the barrio, since most homeowners cannot afford the expense entailed in maintaining lawns and gardens in central Phoenix.

Finally, La Sonorita is fortunate to have been home to important Chicano political voices in Phoenix, such as Mary Rose Wilcox, originally a City Council member and now part of the Maricopa Board of Supervisors. She and her husband Earl own El Portal, a major Mexican restaurant in La Sonorita and a vital commercial establishment in the neighborhood. Chicano community organizers have come from the neighborhood, as does Stella Pope Duarte, Phoenix's first native-born Chicana writer. Duarte has set a number of her narratives in La Sonorita, most notably her award winning *Let Their Spirits Dance* (2002), which includes an important seg-

St. Anthony's Catholic Church in the Sonorita Barrio of south Phoenix.

Friendly House, which provides English-language training and civic instruction for Spanish-speaking residents and immigrants in the Sonorita Barrio of south Phoenix.

ment that takes place in St. Anthony's Catholic Church. Duarte also taught at the Lowell Elementary School, one of the other major installations in the barrio. Other major installations like Friendly House, which provides English and civics classes for immigrants, and American Legion Post No. 41 are also prominent. The mural on the latter is a tribute to America's Hispanic Heroes. This combination of installations and politicians and others who support them has afforded important protections to the integrity of La Sonorita. Moreover, the area also includes Maricopa Memorial Hospital, which had the first nurses training program in Arizona, where many women from the barrio studied. Though not a Chicano institution in itself, the Memorial Hospital and accompanying medical center (which caters to many local residents) provide important elements of continuity to the neighborhood.

As one walks or drives through the dozen or so square blocks that make up La Sonorita, the presence of the modern city is very much in evidence. La Sonorita exists as though it were a modest Chicano appendage to the Anglo-dominated downtown urban center, which houses not only important financial and commercial operations, but also, in addition to municipal government, the administration of Maricopa County and regional federal agencies. The downtown Phoenix city skyline is a looming shadow over La Sonorita, and it is virtually impossible to position oneself so that it disappears from sight. But it is especially imposing as one looks due north, where residences can only see the backside fire escape of the Luhrs Tower, the Art Deco fourteen-story office building that was the first skyscraper constructed in Phoenix and, reputedly, in the Southwest. Now dwarfed by other buildings, the Luhrs Tower is a Phoenix symbol, but the fact that, when viewed from La Sonorita, one can only see the backside and not the beautifully designed front façade, is somehow symbolic of La Sonorita's location vis-à-vis the city. Much more imposing are more recent buildings, such as the Collier Center, one of the most recent skyscrapers built in Phoenix, along with the downtown offices of Chase and Wells Fargo banks.

La Sonorita has landscaping amenities like the grounds of St. Anthony's, the eponymous Grant Park (and, a few blocks south, Harmon Park). But its location on the fringes of the megalopolis is very evident in details of both infrastructure and ambient features. Not only are both streets and sidewalks poorly maintained, but the sort of grassy strips between sidewalk and curb maintained by the city in more affluent residential areas are completely lacking, as much as overgrown vacant lots, by contrast, are much in evidence. Moreover, power lines abound, and there is a major substation immediately adjacent to the American Legion post and the park where children play. While scientists may disagree with the proposition that high-tension power lines represent a health hazard, this has been a much debated public policy issue in Phoenix, and all areas where power substations are located are, for many, potential sources of serious illnesses. In addition to the imposing presence of the substation, the high-tension lines fan out across the barrio like a spiderweb.

Since La Sonorita is located close to downtown Phoenix — and close to the downtown Sky Harbor International Airport — air traffic over the area can be heavy. Police helicopters, in addition to patrolling the La Sonorita during operations, overfly coming and going from the nearby central police station. Commercial flights are usually confined to following the bed of the Salt River in takeoffs and landings, but they do wander north (south is less an option because of the proximity to South Mountain). While La Sonorita is not as close to the Salt River as other extant and disappeared Chicano barrios, it is close enough for the planes to be heard. This may not constitute exactly noise pollution, but it is a reminder that La Sonorita is a Chicano residential enclave very much hemmed in by modern Anglo society.

La Sonorita has a firm place in the history of Chicano life in Phoenix, and there is much neighborhood allegiance among its residents. Stella Pope Duarte often tells the anecdote of how, when she was young, her mother called in alarm for her to come see how unfortunate the lives were of some people being shown in a TV news story on depressed areas in Phoenix. Pope Duarte recalls that she told her mother, "Pero, amá, those are our neighbors they're showing." She goes on to say that people in La Sonorita did not feel that they were part of a slum or something often called "urban blight." Rather, they were proud of what they had and the strong human bonds that hold their community together. For the time being, La Sonorita continues to survive, not yet threatened with the bulldozer that has led to an imprisoned church and the devastation of the Barrios Unidos and San Pablo/Mexican Town. The historic and cultural mosaic of central Phoenix would be much impoverished if it were to fall victim to yet one more project of urban sprawl.

In visualizing the setting of *Let Their Spirits Dance* (2002), Stella Pope Duarte immerses readers in the history of Phoenix in relation to the movement of ethnic groups across complex racial and ethnic lines. In large measure, this movement makes an important iconographic use of the physical layout of Phoenix.

Washington Street is a main thoroughfare that cuts across the city of Phoenix from East to West; on the east it ends at the entrance to the suburb of Tempe, and on the west, once you get past the state capitol complex, it peters out into just another residential street. However, in the central corridor, where the original financial district is still located and where the state capitol is located, along with buildings for the City of Phoenix, Maricopa Country, and the federal administrative district, Washington Street is important enough to be a broad one-way street (moving traffic from east to west). At Central Avenue it creates the ground zero for the numbering system that locks Phoenix into the almost perfect geometric grid that has been respected even with the enormous demographic growth in the past fifty years: for example, all numbered avenues still lie to the west, and numbered streets to the east of Central; numbering north of Washington is designated North, while numbering south is designation as South.

The designation of Washington Street goes back to a jejunely patriotic America in which it was frequent for a central plat to be distinguished by the names of the U.S. presidents: in the case of Phoenix, this section of town must have been done in the first decade of the last century, since Theodore Roosevelt is the last president so remembered. Moreover, the person responsible for the designation of streets had the novel, is not very mnemonic idea, of alternating streets north-south between at least a first round of presidents, as Adams is one block north of Washington, Jefferson one block south; yet Monroe lies two blocks north, and Madison two blocks south, despite the fact that pattern logic would have it the other way around.

Whatever the curiously logic of the arrangement of these streets may have been, this presidential constellation, which accounts for a band almost a mile in north-south depth on the city map, constitutes a symbolic swath, an institutional Anglo-American border in which is located the historic core of modern Phoenix, north of which stretch the successive residential districts of the historic ruling bourgeoisie, and south of which lies the no man's land of ethnic margination.[2] Although today, up against and around South Mountain, which marks the southern edge of the so-called Valley of the Sun where Phoenix lies, there is now a bundle of middle-class residential areas that have leap-frogged over the ethnic neighborhoods, there remains the ideological perception that the Phoenix south of the downtown frontier is somehow on the fringes of where the city has gone, which is, literally and in urban terms, north of that frontier. And, while it is true that many things are now happening that have moved the ethnic neighborhoods north just as the white bourgeoisie is taking over the south, with the possibility that those neighborhoods in time will be absorbed, the mental image of many Phoenicians continues to preserve the north-south divide represented by the Washington Street corridor.

In the case of Phoenix's Chicano community (in actuality, now more of a Latino community, as a consequence of the extensive infusions of individuals of Hispanic descent from all over the Americas), although there are large historical communities still tied to the old agricultural areas to the west of the city (which are increasingly disappearing under the onslaught of urban sprawl), south of downtown Phoenix, south of the railroad tracks that cut through the "presidential band," and immediately north and south of the now dry bed of the Rio Salado that cuts east and west through the Valley of the Sun is the locus of what is perceived to be Hispanic Phoenix. Parts of this area, particularly south of the Rio Salado, are also African-American, this ethnic group having come in as part of the services and armed forces contingent during World War II and remaining, completely with their own segregated high school immediately south of downtown; there is also an Asian-American presence.

Duarte's *Let Their Spirits Dance* takes place in what the Chicano community calls La Sonorita and what urban planners have more customarily referred to as the Grant Park District, because of a park in the area of that name (Pancrazio; Reynolds).[3] La Sonorita, which is the oldest Chicano barrio in Phoenix, goes back to the early twentieth century, and many of the houses built in that area, houses whose minimalist architecture is well suited to the Sonoran Desert climate, are still standing and in use today. With the growth of the Phoenix core, what used to be a skyline of a few large buildings (the twelve-story Luhrs Tower, built in 1929, was for decades the tallest building in the Southwest; a building to the east in the next block that is now called Barrister Square was used for the opening sequence of Alfred Hitchcock's *Psycho* [1960]), with a band of warehouses and factories contributing to the physical divide between north and south, is now an increasing dense outline of the sort of skyscrapers associated with the development of a major commercial center like Phoenix. However, with dreadful irony, given the demographics of the American prison population, what most dominates immediately the line of vision as one looks north to the city from La Sonorita, is the Madison Street Jail, a veritable monument to the incarceration mentality that remains part of a residual frontier mind-set still firmly entrenched in Arizona.

Duarte's novel is the first major Chicano novel — the first novel to be published by a mainline American press — to take place in downtown Phoenix and to evoke the lives of this now deeply historical district of the city. *Let Their Spirits Dance* is also a novel about the effects of the Vietnam War on a Chicano family. Sgt. Jesse A. Ramírez was killed in Vietnam, less than a year after having been sent to the front. Although the novel is more concerned with the effects of his death on his family, there are chapters that focus on his experiences in Vietnam, and his letters to his sister are reproduced in the novel. At the end of the novel, we learn that Jesse had married a Vietnamese woman, who eventually made it to California with her son, and she, hers and Jesse's son, and his son are reunited with the Ramírez family at the end of the novel.

It is evident that the novel wishes to evoke a Christological dimension for Jesse, beginning with his name.[4] The time of the Vietnam war was, as is well known, the time of civil unrest in the United States, particularly with regard to racial discrimination against people of color. There was the wide-spread belief that one dimension of the Administration's pursuit of the Vietnam War was because it provided the opportunity to ship off to the Southeast Asian jungle young men "from the ghetto," thereby removing some of the agents of the extensive unrest of the period (see Trujillo for

114

studies on Chicanos and Vietnam). Concomitantly, there was the feeling that men of color paid a higher price than white recruits: not only were the officers in the field mostly white, but their troops of color were far more likely than white soldiers to be in the murderous front lines, being killed and doing the killing[5]:

> By 1968, we were all drowning. La raza was submerged by mainstream America, a submarine drifting under a sea of politics, prejudice, and racism. Barrios like El Cielito, ignored by the U.S. government, suddenly appeared on Uncle Sam's maps. Chicanos, who had never been thought about before were on the list of draftees.... This was a game that said, We're going to pay you for being over there, and if you don't want to go, we'll draft you anyway. So why don't you join up and avoid all the trouble? [56].

One of the significant geographical fault lines of the novel, therefore, involves the correlation between the barrio and Vietnam. The narrator— who is Jesse's sister Teresa—describes the family trip to Sky Harbor Airport to see Jesse off; she has the presentment that he will never return alive, which only serves to enhance his image as a sacrificial victim to yet another exercise in *gabacho* imperialism. The movement from El Cielito to Vietnam is, conceptually, a lateral one. It is not so much that the barrio is a "war zone": the novel engages in a delicate balance between portraying the social and economic margination of life on the Chicano side of the tracks, while at the same time underscoring time and again the complex humanity, with both the good and the bad, of barrio life. Yet, the barrio is marginal to mainstream American life: as the quote above states, it wasn't even on U.S. government maps—just as the Vietnam villages soldiers like Jesse were sent to weren't on any government maps either—not, at least, until they were ready to be bombed.

Such a lateral move from one realm of subalternity to another is an important thematic axis of the novel, and both poles are united in the marriage of Jesse to a Vietnamese woman. Moreover, when Teresa and her family go to see Jesse off, they still remain below the frontier dividing the barrio from the Anglo city, as Sky Harbor International was built along the river bottom, a reasonable location, but one that displaced traditional neighborhoods of people of color. Indeed, as I write this, the Barrios Unidos neighborhood, which lies to the east of the area in which Duarte's novel is set, is targeted for elimination, as Sky Harbor plans for the extension from the east of its runways. In this way, Sky Harbor, which is a major symbol of the modern development of the Phoenix metropolitan area, located in the heart of neighborhoods of color, is the point of reference from the transference of Jesse from one subaltern realm to another: the transference is initially a destructive one — he is sent to kill the Vietnamese opposition — but it becomes a beneficent one, as he forges a relationship with a Vietnamese woman that lasts beyond the grave and constitutes an important second-degree symbolic return of his spirit to the El Cielito barrio.

When Jesse was killed, the Ramírez family was supposed to receive his remains and a $10,000 indemnification. Not only was his body first sent to the wrong address (an effective correlative of how the government is incapable of keeping track of its minority citizens[6]), until finally it is laid to rest properly in the barrio. Since Jesse's remains do return to the barrio, the recovery of his Vietnamese family and what one assumes will be their eventual visit to El Cielito constitute a return in a second-degree of Jesse's spirit to his place of origin.

Additionally, his mother was only paid half of the indemnification she was owed; since she did not know how much she was supposed to have received, it never occurred to her to reclaim the missing half. Yet, the machinery of the bureaucracy is implacable, less toward righting a wrong than in correcting the imbalances on its books. As a consequence, one day Alicia Ramírez receives a phone call from an official to inform her that they have finally caught the error (over thirty years after the fact), and that they will be sending her a check for the amount plus compound interest — almost $100,000 in all.

The receipt of this money becomes the major catalyst for the second half of the novel, which is driven by Jesse's mother's unshakable conviction that the money should be used to enable the entire family, including Jesse's friends, to travel to Washington, D.C. to visit the Vietnam Veterans Memorial: Mrs. Ramírez wishes to take a tracing of her sons name, which then becomes a three-degree symbolic return of his spirit to the barrio. Much space in the novel is taken up by discussing the plans for this journey, the interpersonal conflicts surrounding the details, the choice of the individuals to accompany the caravan, the logistics of setting everything up, and, finally, the actual realization of the cross-country trip from Phoenix to Washington, D.C., the visit to the memorial, Ms. Ramírez's death in a hospital in the D.C. area and, compensatorily, the recovery of Jesse's wife, son, and grandson.

Duarte's description of this highly charged journey across America, with all of the resonance of the discovery of the American heartland, unfolds with full rhetorical panache. Duarte sees this journey as symbolic on several levels. First and obviously, there is the reaffirmation of Jesse's spirit through access to his immortalization — along with that of thousands of other Chicanos and Latinos — in the Vietnam War Memorial, the Wall. Second, there is the consolidation of the extended Ramírez family through the emotional intensity of the experience: Mrs. Ramírez may die, having fulfilled her final burning wish to see her son's name on the Wall, but many conflicts within the family have been resolved, relations have been reestablished between the family and old friends of Jesse's, and even Teresa reconnects with a Chicano she had met in the anti–War protests by Hispanics in San Francisco: there is the promise that this will be a definitive relationship for her.

Then there is the symbolic value not only of a Chicano family enacting a migratory experience across the map of the country, but in a way that is ennobling to them, in contrast to the way in which migration for most Chicanos — whether up from Mexico or within the United States — is an experience of economic exploitation. This migration of the Ramírez family is a triumphal march across the land. Not only is there the notoriety, ever renewed by television coverage and the internet page maintained by one of the Teresa's precocious young nephews; they also attract attention because of the way in which the government has corrected its debt with them. This is the stuff of urban legend. Moreover, there is the way in which they accrue fellow travelers who each have their own reason to join the caravan.

Finally, all of this culminates in a Hispanic self-affirmation on/over the land: the Ramírezes are a Chicano family that has become famous, and in pursuing their collective dream, they attract to themselves a wide array of citizens for whom their story becomes a major point of reference for their own personal experiences. That is, in a word, this one paradigmatic Chicano story emerges, in the universe of the novel, as a narrative — perhaps even mythic — prototype for many others to adhere to. The narrator waxes quite epiphanic in her sense of the culminating meaning of such an adventure, hearing her mother sing, upon their arrival in the nation's capital, for the first time since Jesse's death:

> My mother's voice is rushing in my ears, and I never want her to stop, not now, not ever. Her voice is my lullaby again, caressing my soul. We round the corner onto Constitution Avenue and see the Capitol loom ahead of us, imposing, regal. On either side are buildings that belong to the Smithsonian, some with American flags waving from entrances and

front lawns. The cavalcade of cars curves behind us with my mother's voice announcing to the nation's capital that we are here, the Mexicas of Aztlán, to pay honor to their fallen warriors [292].

In the process of working this narrative out, Duarte figures a new geographical relationship between Phoenix, the barrio, and the nation. The axis of this relationship is the conceptual field of "Washington." The physical journey from El Cielito to the nation's capital is not only a family odyssey that is a multiple recovery of the lost son/brother Jesse, but it becomes also a symbolic enterprise that details the bases for another degree of integration of the Chicano community, on an immediate level, but as well the Latino community and even the broader community of people of color, into the so-called American mainstream. In the process of coming out of the barrio to undertake their journey, the Ramírez's and their friends are inserting themselves in the vast landscape of the United States, literally by traversing it and symbolically by mastering it.

This voyage involves effectively making their way across America, negotiating the details of their itinerary, confronting a potentially ugly encounter with a redneck policeman, manipulating the internet to obtain information, to confirm alliances (one of which turns out to be Jesse's Vietnamese family), and to manipulate television coverage to their advantage. Jesse himself had left the barrio, but under military authority and in a way that impeded his having any control over his own life, so much so that he very promptly looses it, ostensibly defending his country. The Ramírez family's journey is their own freely chosen experience of discovery (albeit driven by Jesse's mother's sense of fulfilling a *manda*, an order received in a vision from God that cannot be ignored or postponed). In the process they assert over and over again their control of their own experiences and destiny:

> La manda, my mother's promise, is changing our landscape forever. It's suffering in motion. We're carrying our burdens on our backs as our Indian ancestors did, adjusting the weight every once in a while to make ourselves feel better. Suffering is our map, it's why we're on the road. Men and women in pain stand close to Christ, the man of sorrow; every procession at St. Anthony's taught us that. We wouldn't be on the road if it weren't for war and suffering. We're part of some unearthly plan to balance the scales of suffering, to release a spring in our souls that will free us from the fear of suffering [165].

While the narrator is clearly using "landscape" in this quote in a metaphorical sense, there is also a literal dimension in the traversing of the landscape, a dimension that assumes its own symbolic meaning in the dynamic of the novel.

One aspect of this literal dimension is the first immediate stage of leaving the barrio. Duarte, evoking Arizona writer Miguel Méndez-M.'s groundbreaking Chicano novel, *Peregrinos de Aztlán* (1979), gives its name to the chapter describing their departure from Phoenix, "Pilgrims of Aztlán," which is the title of the published English translation of Méndez-M.'s novel. This departure not only involves leaving the barrio, but it also involves crossing over the frontier between the barrio and downtown Phoenix. This is necessary in order to pick up Interstate 17 (here identified by its local name, the Black Canyon Highway), which runs through Phoenix to the west of the downtown area on its way north, which is the route to be followed in order to pick up the connecting interstate highways that will take them on into Washington, D.C. While the novel is appropriately vague as to what inner-city route will lead them to the freeway entrance (after all, the narrator is not interested in giving a geography lesson about Phoenix), I-17 cuts through the barrio east-west as it comes up from Tucson, before turning north. By following this route out of the barrio, the caravan necessarily traverses — actually, by freeway, leaps over — what I have called the barrier of the presidential band of streets that broadly separates historical Anglo Phoenix from Chicano Phoenix, the Phoenix of color.

Since the anchor street of this presidential band is Washington Street, by crossing over it within minutes of setting out from their home, the Ramírez family engages unknowingly (since no one in the novel remarks on the coincidence) in a symbolic gesture of leaving the barrio in order to accede to the unknown America (cf. my epigraphic quote taken from this same chapter) beyond the barrio. The odyssey-like nature of this journey is captured in the closing words of the chapter of departure, with a re-evocation of the highly charged title of that chapter:

> We're pilgrims of Aztlán, heading east, following the rising sun, on our own quest, una manda, searching out an invisible trek in a maze of voices calling, prayers, magical words, singsong chants of the ancient world, good wishes, broken promises, pain, traveling through the whiteness of Aztlán. My mother, the beginning of it all, is blind to all she's done. We're pilgrims on a journey to America's wailing wall. Only faith will get us there [157].

Duarte's novel is neither a novel about Phoenix, except only in passing at the outset; nor is it only circumstantially set in Phoenix. The story she tells has many autobiographical dimensions, and she has made it clear that the novel is written in part as a tribute to her own family and her own experiences of growing up in the Sonorita barrio south of downtown Phoenix. As befits a novelistic undertaking, Duarte engages in verifiable identities for her setting, while at the same time engaging in poetic license. The long-time resident of Phoenix will recognize the reference to the Black Canyon Highway and to St. Anthony's Catholic Church in the Sonorita barrio, as well as to presence to the west of the railroad tracks and the city's pioneering days cemetery (Pioneer and Military Memorial Park, where Jesse's remains finally come to rest). But the name of the barrio is fictional, and the name of the neighborhood school were Teresa teaches (Duarte is also herself a public school teacher) is changed. There is little direct evocation of Phoenix outside the barrio: it is simply there as the overwhelming Other of barrio life, the Anglo world that intrudes on and disrupts in so many ways the pursuit of local existence. That disruption is sustainedly there in terms of the long arm of the law that impacts so much on Chicano lives and sends so many Chicano men and women to prison (as captured in films like Edward James Olmos's *American Me* [1992] and Allison Anders's *Mi vida loca* [1993]). This is why I have emphasized the visually imposing presence of the Madison Street Jail and the long — symbolic, if not actual — shadow it casts over the barrio. In one sense, Duarte's novel could be set anywhere in the many places in the United States where there is a historically significant concentration of Chicano life. By placing *Let Their Spirits Dance* in her native Phoenix, Duarte has provided her native city and her native barrio with the first major urban Chicano[7] novel in Phoenix's still lamentably thin literary history. Most significantly, in setting up the dynamics of meaning in the novel to enhance the depiction of the momentous movement of Chicano life into one dimension of the American mainstream, here embodied by Jesse's Vietnam War experience, the Wall, and the epiphanic journey across America to enter into a new level of memory regarding Jesse through seeing his name on the Wall and tracing it on a piece of paper, Duarte makes a judicious use of the material aspects of the city of Phoenix. It is a utilization that contributes directly and effectively to the eloquence of her novel.

Phoenix in Guillermo Reyes's
Places to Touch Him

> I am concerned with what it means to be an outsider, and how this is negotiated with the majority. (Guillermo Reyes, qtd. in Fitch Lockhart, "Living" 120)

> Hacerse visible conlleva un riesgo en tanto que la economía de los especular dicta que una imagen puesta en circulación inmediatamente sale del control de su emisor. Este "exceso suplementario" que proyecta la imagen la hace susceptible de lecturas múltiples que, según en manos de quien caiga, pueden conducir a la opresión o a la resistencia. (Antonio Prieto Stambaugh [parafraseando a Peggy Phelan] 294)

Guillermo Reyes was born in Chile in 1962 and came to the United States in 1971, where he grew up first in Washington, D.C. and then, as a teenager, in Islos — East Los Angeles (Huerta 148). After completing his BA at UCLA and his MFA at UCSD, Reyes accepted a position at Arizona State University in 1996, where he remains a member of the School of Theatre and Film, teaching Playwriting and Screenwriting (see the encyclopedia entry by Pérez, "Reyes, Guillermo"; and the interview with Fitch; Huerta, regrettably, devotes little space to Reyes). In 2000, along with Trino Sandoval and Daniel Enrique Pérez, Reyes launched the first season of Teatro Bravo, an ambitious bilingual theater project that has been an important contribution to a solid presence of theatrical activity in the Valley of the Sun where Phoenix and surrounding suburbs are located (See Pérez, "Dramatizing the Borderlands" on the Teatro Bravo plays anthologized in *Borders on Stage*; see also R. Trujillo).

There are two abiding myths about culture in Phoenix. One is that there really isn't any, and that what there is is transient in nature and little related to what Phoenix is "really all about," which I suppose means enforcing a tacky Chamber of Congress view of carefree Anglo consumers of fun in the sun and its derivatives. The other myth is that, while the Hispanic community continues to grow, thankfully, it has little to say for itself, little to contribute to a cultural dialogue that, anyway, hardly matters.

The work of Teatro Bravo is, remarkably, a stunning contradiction of these two premises. The works generated by those associated directly with Bravo, under the inspiration and sustaining influence of the very talented Guillermo Reyes, and by those from other parts of the U.S. Chicano/Latino community who have seen their works performed by Bravo are outstanding interventions in both a national and local dialogue regarding Hispanic life. And more specifically, the very existence of Teatro Bravo has made a significant contribution to theater in the Phoenix area. Its production schedule is the strong articulation of an impressive local theater talent.

Although prior to Teatro Bravo, there had been various attempts to perform theater in Spanish in the Phoenix area, Teatro Bravo has been the longest lived, and it has amply fulfilled its project to perform theater — both established international texts, but more frequently texts by Reyes and other Latino authors — in versions in both Spanish and English. Although some of the plays performed were written originally in Spanish, most of the plays, as is characteristic of Latino theater in general today, were written originally in English and are performed in Spanish in translations by the authors or others.

Typically, Reyes writes exclusively in English, although, as is the case with Latino cultural production in general, the texts contain an abundant use of Spanish words and phrases, particularly those with a regional or local resonance (that is, various forms of Southwest Chicano Spanish). Reyes has a solid and functional command of Spanish. But English is the dominant language of his dramatic texts, which are oriented essentially toward capturing the contradictions and difficulties of U.S. Latinos in interacting in a social dynamic that plays out essentially in English; indeed, many of his characters, which are represented iconically by the two texts *Men on the Verge of a His-Panic Breakdown* (1994) and *Men on the Verge 2: The Self-Esteem Files* (2004); see also *The Hispanick Zone* [1998]), draw the dramatic tension of their roles from their interaction with the non–Spanish speaking world of Anglo America.

Because of his long association with Southern California and the complex Latino society of that area, it is not surprising that the bulk of Reyes's dramatic texts take place within these geographic and social parameters, although one of his finest plays, *Deporting the Divas* (1996) is set in the southern Arizona desert between Tucson and the Mexican border.[1] Yet, because Reyes has now lived and performed his works for almost fifteen years in the Phoenix area, it is inevitable that a share of them take up the particular circumstances of Latino (which means mostly Chicano) life in the central Arizona metropolis.

It is important to remember that over thirty percent of both the State of Arizona and the Greater Phoenix Area identifies as Hispanic,[2] that Phoenix is the largest state capital, and the sixth most populous urban area, in the country. These are circumstances that contribute synergetically to the growth of the Hispanic population of Phoenix (an important profile of the Phoenix Hispanic population is provided by Luckingham; see also the photographic dossier by Barrios). This despite current economic circumstances and the intense rhetoric of prevailing anti-immigrant ideologies. Anti-immigrant sentiment predominantly translates into an anti–Mexican stance fueled in part because the mostly open border between Arizona and Mexico is at the moment the principal point of uncontrolled crossing of Mexicans (and often others, such as Central Americans) into the United States. There is much cultural work to be done to represent both the stories of longstanding Hispanic families of Phoenix and those of recent immigrants. Reyes, however, has chosen to focus his work — the texts set in Phoenix as well as the majority set in California — in terms of the struggles to compete in Anglo America, which means a significant component of social mobility and the attempts to achieve it. If the self-image of Phoenix (considerably more so than Los Angeles[3]) is that of an all American middle class metropolis, one where it is staggering to grasp the exclusion of Hispanics and other minorities from the halls of power, it is not surprising that a fundamental tension in Reyes's plays involves a lower-class Hispanic interacting with a higher-class Anglo.

Moreover, there is another significant fault line in Reyes's theater, and that is the conflict between heterosexism and gay identity, which plays out along a number of axes that include not only the social disjunction that affects the circumstances of interaction between gay men of differing social classes, but also the differing effects of the closet on Hispanic men as much as on Anglo men (see Fitch; Prieto Stambaugh; Foster, *El ambiente nuestro* for various expansions on this matter). Paradigmatically, this means in the case of the latter, life in the closet as the cost of surviving, and competing successfully, in a homophobic world. By contrast, in the case of Hispanic men, while such a cost may also be present, there is the separate factor of not only the heterosexist presumption of Mexican — and especially Mexican American—society, but also the increased possibility of violence within working-class communities of any ethnic identity. Moreover, the heterosexist presumption of Mexican/Mexican American society may manifest itself in terms of the situation of the individual who has conformed to the imperative to marry and have a family, while at the same time pursuing homoerotic needs, as African American culture would say, "on the down low." Indeed, if the presumption of gay culture is the social and economic freedom to decide against compulsory heterosexism, including the reproductive imperative, members of ethnic working-class communities may not customarily be in a position to exercise such an option, with the inevitable conflict of unsatisfied sexual desire or such desire fulfilled in particularly unsanctioned ways as represented by extramarital affairs: if such affairs are, in terms of "all American norms" scandalous in a heterosexual context, they are even more so in homosexual ones.

In the case of the "all American norms" of a city like Phoenix, characterized by a sense of relative youth (the first settlers date from the 1870s) and intransigently conservative social values, the tensions of the unorthodox are especially enhanced. I use the allusion to orthodoxy advisedly, since, in addition to various other forms of conservative religious beliefs and their effect on sociopolitical and cultural processes, the Phoenix area is characterized by the presence of three conservative mainline faiths: Catholicism (especially in its Mexican dimensions), Southern Baptism, and the Church of Jesus Christ of Latter-day Saints (Mormonism).[4] The moral conservatism of all three, of course, opposes any form of sexual life beyond that prescribed by compulsory heterosexism. Phoenix, to be sure, is not unique in such a conjunction, but it is perhaps the largest American city in which public sociopolitical and cultural debates remain staunchly framed in religious and moralistic terms. Increasingly Hispanics are enrolling in organized religions other than the Catholic Church, but it is notable that their options remain decidedly conservative, as they migrate toward not only varieties of Baptist Protestantism and Mormonism, but also a wide array of Pentecostal sects.

Although Reyes's plays do little more than refer in passing to organized religion (such as the "free-thinking ex–Mormon" in one of the sketches in *Men on the Verge 2: The Self-Esteem Files*; the authoritarian Mormon uncle who threatens to send the main character of *Little Queen* [2009] to a deprogramming camp to rid him of his gayness), conflicts relating to sexual identity resonate precisely to the degree to which the horizons of knowledge of audiences involve an awareness of prevailing levels of homophobia, and this is in particular true of plays performed by Teatro Bravo in Phoenix. Indeed, the very name Bravo, "courageous," refers as much to the daunting task of pursuing bilingual theater in Phoenix, with its majority English Only views, but to promoting forms of sexuality and desire that differ significantly from prevailing social norms. While it is true that theater audiences are mostly self-selecting, both in linguistic and thematic terms, it is significant to note that, as much as there is little Spanish-language theater anywhere else in the Phoenix area, there is also a scant record of queer theater among university, commercial, and amateur groups in the city.[5]

It is within these parameters that I would like to discuss in detail Reyes's play *Places to Touch Him*, first performed in Phoenix in 2002 at Playhouse on the Park in downtown Phoenix, a regular venue for Teatro Bravo productions. Reyes makes a specific reference to the relationship between the play and the place in which its story takes place:

> *Places to Touch Him* became my way of dealing with one man's awakening to sexuality, to obsession, and, yes, to plain carnality all within the milieu of Phoenix where I had come to learn a thing or two about my sexuality — for various reasons I won't go into right now. A lawyer, and aspiring politician, seeks to run for the city council at the same time that he's developed an obsession for a young man who eventually becomes a stripper. This politician is considered safe and asexual, completely non-threatening to mainstream voters. But this relationship will clearly threaten his asexual image. [...] Can the politician maintain his personal private life, and can he afford to fall in love when the issues of the local Latino community have heated up and deserve the attention of serious politicians? [Reyes 178].

The answer the play gives to both these questions is a resounding no. With particular regard to the second of them, it is important to note that, while the Phoenix City Council has and has had very discreet and non-threatening gay members, its record on members drawn from minority communities is decidedly thin. Mary Rose Wilcox (her very name is non-threatening, and one may assume that there are voters who may not know that she is Hispanic) is only one of two Hispanics to serve on the Phoenix City Council; she is currently a member of the Maricopa Board of Supervisors. Michael Nowakowsi — another non-threatening name for those citizens frightened of even Hispanic names — currently serves on the Council.[6]

Places to Touch Him immediately provokes in some the desire to know who the lead, Cesar, the lawyer with political aspirations, might be in "real life" among Phoenix public figures suspected — or known by those who claim to be cognoscenti — to be gay.[7] What is interesting about this response is that one suspects no audience member has ever given any thought as to who the model is for the New York lawyer — the closeted and intensely anguished Joe Pitt — in Tony Kushner's important *Angels in America* (Part One: *Millennium Approaches* [1900]; Part Two: *Perestroika* [1992]), a play in which, incidentally, Mormonism is also a crucial factor, among many others, in sexuality (see Pace on this connection). The fact that Reyes's play, set in Phoenix, where there is limited public discourse with regard to queer issues and where there is even less theater impinging on those issues, provokes such a response is significant to the degree that it is a telling commentary on community values, where being openly gay in a major public service position is still outrageous in a way in which it is not likely to be in the American cities that precede Phoenix on the list of the most populous, with the possible exception of Houston.

The point is that Cesar's personal drama is not really his being gay. If he is identified as an "unsuccessful gay man" in the thumbnails of the characters in the script (179), it is because the circumscriptions on his being able to be a "successful" gay man (whatever that may precisely be) do not derive from internalized psychological or religious constraints. Rather, they are based on the very pragmatic principle that he cannot be unrestrainedly gay and be a successful politician in Phoenix. Being unrestrainedly gay will mean being publicly gay, in a spectrum of demonstrating or performing gayness that runs from the articulation "I am gay" to engaging in public acts of affection with another man. Domingo, the object of Cesar's affection, is a working class man, also Chicano like Cesar, formerly married with children, but like Cesar with aspirations of bettering himself. In Cesar's case, the aspiration means moving from being a lawyer to being elected to public office, while for Domingo it means moving from the working class to whatever the formal education he seeks may provide him.

If Domingo is willing to be openly gay — that is, performing openly his homoerotic desire[8] — Cesar is not, and this disjunction, which provides the major dramatic tension of the play, marks the difference between what to be gay might mean for a working-class Mexican/Mexican American and what it might mean for a professional one. Significantly, Reyes's play does not explore the class differences of being gay and Hispanic (as does Cherríe Moraga's lesbian theater and as she does in important essays such as "Queer Aztlán"; see Foster, "El lesbianismo multidimensional"),[9] but rather the pragmatic ones of Phoenix electoral politics.

Cesar attempts to justify himself to Domingo by appealing to the higher ideal (higher, that is, than the open display of their mutual affection) of getting a Hispanic elected to the Phoenix City Council. This is hard enough given the role that race plays in Phoenix, without confusing matters by being perceived, in addition to being a threatening Hispanic,[10] by being also a threatening gay man: a threatening gay Hispanic male, not exactly a privileged demographic in the context of the high-pitched public discourse over the evils of illegal immigrants and the diseases they bring with them.[11] If such a public discourse is as specious as it is incoherent, it is one factor driving elections, and Cesar is acutely aware of that fact, no matter how much he may agonize over his inability to respond in an uninhibited fashion to Domingo's demanding advances. Matt is Cesar's campaign manager, who frequently expresses exasperation over what he perceives to be Cesar's political ingenuousness:

> CESAR: And if I do [pursue the alleged worst side of Domingo], Matt, that's my business.
> MATT: No, it's our business.
> CESAR: No —
> MATT: And the business of the people of Phoenix, particularly the Latino community, which has not been fairly represented in this town.
> CESAR: The Latino community can survive without me. Maybe I don't need politics any longer —
> MATT: You live for polit —
> CESAR: Maybe it's time for me to live for something else. [...] Why is it too much to ask for after thirty-eight long, long years, that somebody should be there for me? What is it about me that says he's meant to be asexual? Is it written on my forehead? You tell me.
> MATT: Look, personally, I am just used to the idea that you're just a unit, alone, and unencumbered.
> CESAR: A eunuch, you mean?
> MATT: You can keep your balls; nobody has to **touch** them, that's all. [...] I think everyone in this city sees you this way: as the celibate gay politician. And for a campaign manager, that's a big relief [190, my emphasis].

Places to Touch Him—and in the foregoing dialogue part of which I have omitted for reason's of space, is Cesar's heartfelt plea to have someone to touch him; I have included Matt's response — turns on an ironic double meaning of the title. Very transparently, the play is about an "unsuccessful gay man" who needs desperately to be touched by another man, touched as much as he fights being touched for what he perceives to be the political consequences of the sexual narrative that will set in motion; it is a perception emphatically reinforced by his campaign manager. Thus, what is at issue in the first instance is a corporal geography of sexual desire: what it means to be touched sexually, what that touching might be, and what it means for sexual narrative set in motion by touching and being touched. Since one important dimension of the gay movement has meant the insistence on a degree of public visibility, at least some proxemics of sexual interest and commitment between individuals, the denial of touching becomes the denial of desire, the whole basis of how Cesar is such an "unsuccessful gay man."

In the following scene, Cesar does begin to kiss Domingo's neck in the privacy of his office, but the latter brings him brutally up short as to how this is not the touching he has in mind — that is, it is inadequate to what would be for him a satisfactory sexual narrative. All Cesar can do is fabricate a losing narrative of fantasy:

> DOMINGO: See? You're rushing now. There'll be plenty of time for the smoochie stuff later.
> CESAR: You'll be gone soon; I may never see you again.
> DOMINGO: We haven't even dated and you're already feeling abandoned. You've already built an entire life for us together, haven't you? Haven't you fantasized it to death already? You've even imagined the breakup scene.
> CESAR : And my heart's been torn to pieces already, yes.
> DOMINGO: Man, I done nothing. I'm not your lover, so how could your heart possibly be broken, *pinche pendejo*? [195].

Yet, there is another sense to Reyes's title, and that refers to the locales in which touching might take place. If, as the feminist maxim teaches us, the personal is political, corporal geography is also physical geography, in the sense that the life of the body takes place in the context of community, even though much of the life of the body — perhaps the most important life of the body — may not always take place in full communal view. Still, there can never be a full disjunction between, to use a common synecdoche, one's public face and one's private face. Matt may wish to exploit the proposition that Cesar is "just a unit, alone, and unencumbered" (190), but that is precisely Cesar's point about his thirty-eight-year failure as a sexual subject. Any performance as a sexual subject takes place within the confines of a community, and, for this reason, the places where one may be touched must necessarily refer to the sociogeographic places in which such touching may take place.

To be sure, there are domains in Phoenix in which an entire range of touch may take place, such as, clearly, gay bars and other gay hospitality venues. And then there is the public display that is customarily a part of gay pride marches, demonstrations, rallies, and the like. But the sort of relaxed display of same-sex affection that one might find in other metropolitan areas of the country, or the quite unrestricted display now common in most of Western Europe, is simply not to be found in Phoenix. Phoenix area-based Arizona State University may be the largest-enrolling university in the country, but one is pretty hard put to see even timid displays of same-sex affection anywhere on campus, and the student paper, the *State Press*, routinely receives complaints from students and faculty over overt and perceived homophobia in its pages. Now, it must be emphasized that, while random gay bashing takes place in Phoenix as it does throughout the country, there is no organized program of the persecution of gays, and there is a general agreement that law enforcement agencies and other official entities are relatively non-homophobic. Yet Phoenix remains a place in which, generally speaking, one does not engage openly in same-sex touching.

There is much that is metatheatrical about *Places to Touch Him*, particularly in terms of various levels of self-reflexive performativity. There are at least three levels of performativity in the play. There is a common scholarly agreement as to the basic validity of Judith Butler's theories regarding how sexual identity is performative rather than essential—a proposition that she clearly means to pertain to all forms of subjective identity.[12] Concomitantly, if human life is seen as the practice of performance, a theatrical work is necessarily metaperformative to the extent that theater, as a recognized and institutionalized cultural genre, is the studied, formal performance of life as performance. Where these two propositions come together, as in Reyes's play, the audience witnesses the performance of the performance of a performance. This is the case to the extent that the play focuses not just on the question of sexual identity or the performance of sexual subjectivity.[13]

Rather, *Places* makes a specific point about the way in which there is an added level of the performance of sexuality to the extent that Cesar and Domingo are consciously aware of how they are performing sexuality and engage in various degrees of underdetermination and overdetermination of the day-to-day "natural" or "unconscious" performance of sexual identity. Matt wants Cesar to engage consciously in underdetermination, to be a "safe gay man," to which Cesar responds that Matt wants him to be a eunuch. On the other hand, when Cesar comes on too strong to Domingo in the privacy of his office, one could say that he is acting in an overdetermined way, which is why Domingo ridicules him.

The key to the way in which the characters of *Places to Touch Him* perform to a second degree is the metathetrical device by which Matt becomes an internal audience to Cesar's and Domingo's mismatched performance of sexuality for each other. Matt is a voyeur to their performance at several points in the play, as, for example, when the last quote above is prefaced by the stage direction: *"(Cesar begins to kiss [Domingo's] neck. Matt enters on the other side of the stage as if he's been watching all along and watches the last half of this scene.)"* (195). To be sure, it is not uncommon in theatrical works to have a separate party witness/overhear/spy on a character or group of characters in a reduplication of what the audience is seeing and hearing: such a party is the privileged voyeur within the play in the same way in which the audience, on the other side of the proscenium arch, is also, and there are many variants on this moment of privilege. The difference in Matt's case is that he is reduplicating what we really could not see or hear, which is the exchange between Cesar and Domingo in the privacy of the former's office. Of course, the theatrical illusion routinely violates privacy. But what the particular effect of Matt's privileged access here signifies (as it is in the first scene of the play in which Matt witnesses as a flashback the original meeting between Domingo and Cesar [182 ff.]) is the dynamic of the closet that Matt, shrewdly aware of what will work and what will not work for the voters of Phoenix, is complicit in enforcing.[14]

As for Domingo, there is a particularly important moment of overdetermined performativity, which occurs when he performs publicly as a stripper. Not only is he being out about his sexuality in a particularly emphatic way (and assuming for the purposes of discussion here that all male strippers are gay, which is not the case, although it is with Domingo), but his public performance is perceived by Cesar as something like an act of aggression:

> CESAR: And about the stripping.
> DOMINGO: You're asking me to give that up, too?
> CESAR : Well, eventually you're going to have to ... reconsider.
> DOMINGO : I'll eventually get a degree, a better job in an office and a pot belly and nobody will want to see me strip.
> CESAR : Meanwhile, you'll be discreet?
> DOMINGO : How discreet can a stripper be, Cesar?

Production photograph from *Places to Touch Him*; the secret boyfriend performing in a gay strip club (photograph by Sean Kapera, courtesy of Teatro Bravo).

CESAR : I mean don't flaunt it.
DOMINGO : I don't need to go to no boring cocktail parties with stuffy people. My friends accept me as I am. Do you? [205].

Although Cesar protests that he does, it is clear that stripping in public for Cesar is a particularly unsavory performance of sexuality, and there is always Matt to remind him of what the limits are: "Matt: Time for a reality check" (206), as he adds that the saloon where Domingo works may be up for a police raid, because the customers there are "allowed to touch!" (206). Certainly, any indication of Cesar's relationship to a saloon raided in Phoenix for not "following the rules" (206) would be devastating for his political aspirations.

To summarize, then, *Places to Touch Him* involves the performance of sexual identity around various issues related to being gay and being public about it. Since social subjects perform as much for other social subjects as they do for themselves, outed performances are a particularly important dimension of the gay movement, and the outing of the other is ethically complex (see Mohr). For many — and this is reasonably considered a dimension of homophobia — any performance of sexuality is overdetermined, and even more so in the case of queer sexuality. Thus, the rhetorical question "Can't they think about anything else?" and the trope about "The love that won't shut up." In the universe of the play, both overdetermination and underdetermination of queer sexuality are part of the dramatic texture of the play, which is underscored in part by the particular form of Matt's witnessing. Finally, this particular mix of questions of queer sexual identity — its performance and the degree of its performance, its legitimacy in terms of the particular sociogeographic milieu in which that mix is performed — is the performance piece that is the text itself. Finally, all three levels of performativity in the play involve the visibility of sexual or sexualized activity, such that the play itself involves displaying forthrightly much of what Cesar must renounce to fully realize his political ambitions.

In the end, Cesar, coached by Matt, must engage in one other round of overdetermined and underdetermined sexual performativity when Cesar wins his election bid to the Phoenix City Council. At the end of the second act, he and Domingo part definitely, although perhaps it is not the break-up scene Domingo earlier accused Cesar as imagining: "DOMINGO: You will be a great leader for the Phoenix community, and now that you've learned line dancing, you can have a social life" (218). In the Epilogue to the play, what Cesar must perform is the meet-and-greet ritual of his new identity as a Phoenix politician: "*(Cesar speaks to the masses)* CESAR: Tonight, we've made history, and I'm proud that you've elected me to represent you on our city council" (219). As Cesar engages in this overdetermined political theater, Domingo tries to shake his hand; Matt, however, intervenes:

> DOMINGO: Look, bitch, I just want to say hello to him, Okay? As a citizen, as a voter.
> MATT: He doesn't want to see you.
> DOMINGO: Let him tell me that.
> MATT : He doesn't answer your phone calls, does he now? I have built a good network of security around him.
> DOMINGO: So you keep him alone where nobody will **touch** him [220, my emphasis].

In political parlance, to be untouchable means to exercise a high degree of unblemished power and influence. In order to enjoy the fruits of this form of overdetermined political performance, Cesar, acquiescing to Matt's counsel, must return to a definitive underperformance of his sexual desire. Domingo and Matt do get to have one final friendly goodbye, but there is no longer any question of the extent of Cesar's renunciation:

> MATT: Cesar! Cesar!
> CESAR: Coming!
> *(One final look and wave of goodbye and he's out of there as he goes to join the happy supporters)* [221].

And so ends another chapter in Phoenix's political history.

The importance of examining *Places to Touch Him* in terms of its intended sociogeographic setting is the way in which it remains underinterpreted in cultural production to a degree far removed from the number of plays and novels that explore the sense of place with reference to at least the top three metropolitan areas of the country: New York, Los Angeles, and Chicago. This gap is also the case when one examines the record of Hispanic-marked cultural production between, at least, Phoenix and Los Angeles. While it is true that Los Angeles has a Hispanic history dating back to the mid-sixteenth century, the fact that today Phoenix counts over a third of its population as Hispanic means that there is a large ethnic history that remains underrepresented by the cultural production.[15] While Reyes has used a Los Angeles setting extensively for his plays, he has emerged as the strongest theatrical voice in the Phoenix area, and Teatro Bravo, which he leads as Artistic Director, is the most important Spanish-language and bilingual theater project the Greater Phoenix Area has known. It is within this context that the relationship of *Places to Touch Him* to the social and political life of Phoenix assumes its prominence.[16]

Phoenix as Dystopia in Cherríe Moraga's *Hungry Woman*

> The land of the exile. Phoenix, Arizona. What never rose up from the ashes of destruction. (Moraga, *Hungry Woman* 14)
>
> And we made a kind of gypsy ghetto for ourselves in what was once a thriving desert. (Moraga, *Hungry Woman* 24)

Los Angeles has a long if not very enviable history as a space where life can be baleful, noxious, and even lethal: if people leave their heart in San Francisco, many are convinced they'll loose their soul if not their lives in Los Angeles. There are hundreds of Los Angeles-based literary works of fiction and films about Los Angeles as dystopia. The works gathered in Ulin's anthology repeatedly underscore the dystopian aspects of Los Angeles, and I doubt if any audience members of Ridley Scott's *Blade Runner* (1982) thought the City of Angels was being given a bad rap. Mike Davis's *City of Quartz* (1990) is unrelenting in surveying the historical and political reasons as to why such interpretations of Los Angeles are well founded, and there seems to be no escaping the two extremes, one grim and sinister as touted by Davis and a cultural producer like Scott, or one inane and ridiculous as evinced by Woody Allen's dismissal of Los Angeles in *Annie Hall* (1977) as Munchkinland. Indeed, there is a certain measure of sinister Munchkinland exuberance in John Rechy's *Bodies and Souls* (1983), perhaps one of the best Chicano novels on the city and one of the most intransigent in portraying why no one survives with either body or soul intact, and much less the Chicano who is part of the pre–Anglo pollution of land and society (see Valle and Torres for a study of Latinos in Los Angeles; Villa addresses himself to all of California).

With all of this emphasis on Los Angeles as the figure of the tarnished West, few other cities in the West enjoy the opportunity to serve an iconic function, save the Barbary Coast underbelly of the fabled Golden Gate City or the sleaze of Las Vegas, the source of Hunter Thompson "fear and loathing." Not Seattle, not Portland, not San Diego, and much less Phoenix or Tucson. There are signs this is changing: there are something like a dozen crime novels published in the last decade that are set in Phoenix, and Tucson has a wholly negative polarity in Miguel Méndez-M.'s classic and foundational *Peregrinos de Aztlán* (1979). Yet Phoenix by and large continues to thrive on its tourist-brochure capital: the city's only truly famous author, Erma Bombeck, was more zany than trenchant in her depictions of the middle-class crises of North Phoenix/Scottsdale/Paradise Valley denizens (women, mostly, who in the decade after Bombeck's death would come to be called soccer Moms), and the scathing terms of Terry McMillan's nicely feminist *Waiting to Exhale* (1992), in a league of its own for many reasons, did little to undercut Bombeck's essential benevolence and tourist-brochure narratives.

Cherríe Moraga's *Hungry Woman* (first performed in 2000, although five years of staged readings preceded) is unique because of the way in which Moraga chooses to interpret Phoenix, and it is unique in her creative writing, most of which is set in her native California. I do not know why Moraga chose to use Phoenix as one of three spatial anchors of her play and the locus of the totality of its action, although one suspects that it has to do with the city's self-image of having arisen from the ashes to become a symbol of the prosperity of the West, a new Los Angeles where, perhaps, things will not end up falling apart. The whole idea of the Phoenix rebirth is, of course, preposterous hokum: there are no ashes from which to arise again, but rather the sempiternally burning floor of the desert, and except for the remote and mysterious Hohokam Indians who disappeared almost four hundred years before any modern dweller arrived, there was no one before upon the ashes of whose destroyed society for the Anglo city to be built, and if there were no Native Americans, there were also no Hispanics to trod over, as in the case of Los Angeles and Tucson: Phoenix springs full grown from the hostile desert at a great expense in terms of the infrastructure of resources to make it habitable, and the proud sense of the absence of any historical memory is one of its perversely enduring qualities.

For Moraga, who sets her play in the second decade of the present century (on the play as furturistic fiction, see Gant-Britton), Phoenix has lost whatever it had to make it livable, which is indeed a constant fear for the environmentalist and ecologically minded, fearful of what the consequences will be down the line for the staggering growth the city has been experiencing in the past fifty years. In Moraga's vision, by 2020 the worst has indeed come to pass:

> Phoenix is now a city-in-ruin, the dumping site of every kind of poison and person unwanted by its neighbors.... Phoenix is represented by the ceaseless racket of a city out of control (constant traffic, low-flying jet planes, hawkers squawking their wares, muy "Blade-Runner-esque"). The lighting is urban neon. Most people look lousy in it [6–7].

The basic premise of Moraga's play is that America at some point became balkanized as the consequence of an ethnic civil war, which involved the creation of the Mechicano Nation of Aztlán which includes parts of the Southwest and the border states of what was once Northern Mexico. Rebels scorned the ballot box and made alliance with any man or woman of any race or sexuality that would lift arms in their defense. "Several years after the revolution, a counter-revolution followed in most of the newly-independent nations. Hierarchies were established between male and female, and queer folk were unilaterally sent into exile" (6).

The place of exile from Aztlán is Phoenix, and Medea, the main character of the play, is exiled there for being a lesbian with her son, Chac-Mool, and her lover, Luna. The action of the play turns on the estrangement between Luna and Medea, who suffers profoundly from her exile and yearns to be able to return to Aztlán, but she ends up confined to a mental hospital; the play also focuses on her rage because of Jasón's attempt to take back his son as he approaches manhood. The play ends with Chac-Mool resisting his father's demands and his decision to assist his mother in returning to Aztlán, although it seems fairly certain that the herbs he gives her as he puts her to bed in the final scene will provide her with a release from Phoenix and a return to Aztlán that is only hallucinatory, as Jasón has made it clear that she can only return physically to Aztlán by renouncing her lesbianism and agreeing to "take up residence in my second bed" (69), as he has taken a young woman as his new wife. This option is in opposition to remaining to "rot in this wasteland of counter-revolutionary degenerates" (69). But Medea realizes there is no real option for her: she can neither accept Jasón's conditions for her return to Aztlán nor can she, in effect, remain to rot in Phoenix, which would appear to be why she so docilely accepts the herbs her son offers to her.

Phoenix, thus, is a potent anchor for the play, in that it represents not the denial of social justice to the Chicano (a frequent theme, to be sure, of the novels set in Los Angeles, as elsewhere), but to the loss of a measure of social justice — particularly for women and queers — that had been attained with the revolutionary acts of the ethnic war. In a word, Chicano men have reduplicated Anglo patriarchy in the newfoundland of Mechincano Aztlán. When Jasón informs Medea that the courts have made their decision regarding her expulsion, she explodes:

> What courts? Those patriarchs who stole my county? I returned to my motherland in the embrace of a woman and the mother [i.e., her status as a mother] is taken from me [71].

In this sense, Moraga provides a reprise to her brilliant essay "Queer Aztlán," in which she takes to task the sexism and homophobia of the Chicano movement and challenges Chicano macho mentality to engage in the sort of revolutionary structuring that came from the ethnic war, only to be destroyed by the counter-revolution.[1] When Moraga states that her play deals with "a future I imagine based on a history at the turn of the century that never happened" (6), I believe she is not only referring to the fact that the ethnic wars did not take place, but that the creation of the Queer Aztlán envisioned by her 1993 essay did not come about either: it is an often remarked fact that, while Chicana lesbianism has prospered — and Moraga is certainly an icon in this regard — Chicano (i.e., male) writing has remained quite resolutely heterosexist (see, however, Foster, *El ambiente nuestro*). As Marrero remarks with regard to *Hungry Woman*: "[Moraga's play] suggests the problematic juncture of the lesbian motherhood of a male son [*sic*], lesbian desire and cultural exile. It creates an overwhelming sense of the inescapability of the symbolic order of the Father within Chicano culture" (xxvii).

I referred above to how Phoenix is one of three spaces that anchor the universe *Hungry Woman*: in addition to Phoenix and Aztlán, there is a third space, the Motherland. However the Motherland is a eutopia, a realm of felicity for women that was to be part of the establishment of Mechincano Aztlán, but was lost in the counter-revolution. Precisely it is because the Motherland does not exist (MEDEA: I have no *mother*land [15]), that her confrontation with Jasón over the impossibility of her return to his bed is grounded in her realization that there is no place for her: "Aztlán, how you have betrayed me" (15).

Phoenix is called by the outcast women Tamoachán, which means "we seek our home" (24), a fact that underscores both the fact that they are exiled from their home and the possibility that such a home may not (any longer) exist. Thus, Medea, Luna, and the other women with whom they relate are cast out into the Biblical desert, and they inhabit a "gypsy ghetto" (24). Throughout the play, the city is described in terms of urban noise and pollution, a place of pure chaos, where no one "gives a shit about the environment" (35). The noisy chaos of the city is not just the circumstantial nightmare of the space Medea and other women now inhabit, but rather the material conditions that conspire to silence Medea's cry, as a spiritually hungry woman, for social justice. In this sense, the play, as a cultural enunciation, is the opportunity for Medea to speak out and to allow her voice to rise above the volume of the police sirens. Although the stage is not the missing eutopia, despite the fact that the play takes place in the ruined Phoenix provides, no matter how tenuous, the opportunity for Medea to make her case.

The way in which the play as play means that Phoenix is not simply the hellish cemetery of what Aztlán has expelled is clear in the way in which there is a fundamental contradiction in its figuring of loss and the attempt to recover what has been lost, which are the qualities of queer womanhood Medea articulates and, through real life as a culturally productive xicanadyke (Moraga's own self-attribution and spelling, including noncapitalization [ix]). This is the way in which Phoenix is both the place of the outcast's abjection and, yet, a place where some measure of meaningful expression may be engaged in. Medea struggles self-destructively against any attempt to retain a significant relationship with Luna, and certainly Luna's attempt, first, to continue the relationship with Medea and then to forge new relationships with other women is a melancholic reduplication of what life was like for queers in the time before the revolution — which is, of course, the time of the spectators of the play.

Medea's refusal either to return to Jasón, which is an accommodation to the ideology of the counter-revolution, or to acknowledge Luna's love, which is a return to a prerevolutionary form of the closet (the "queer ghetto," as Medea calls it [48]) is what brings her to a dead end, provokes the insanity for which she is institutionalized, and leads her son to provide her with an out through (fatal?) drugs.

After their exile, Medea and Luna end up living in Phoenix in "a cramped government-funded urban apartment" (14), an image that immediately evokes a number of existing slum-like places in the downtown core of the city. Later Medea will be confined to a mental institution, a fact that evokes the Arizona State Hospital on East Van Buren, bordered to the east by North 24th Street. It is important to note that East Van Buren

Street in the area across the street from the State Hospital is dotted by run-down motels from the era when the street was a major part of east-west routes through the city, accessing Los Angeles to the west and El Paso to the east. Although none of these establishments are, to the best of my knowledge, government-funded housing, counted among prostitutes and their pimps, drug dealers, and undocumented aliens are those who are on some sort of government relief. This is an area of considerable blight. For some it might represent the decomposition of the old (i.e., the historical relevance of these establishments as part of the function of Phoenix as a way station in the east-west travel of the region), necessary in order for urban renewal and gentrification to take place, of which there are some notable signs along this corridor that runs from North 7th Street to approximately North 48th Street. For others, Van Buren, while knowing that its current condition of urban blight cannot survive, given the enormous growth of the area and the demand for land in the central corridor, the East Van Buren strip (which is matched by a similarly rundown West Van Buren strip on the other side of the downtown financial area) is a vivid reminder of how explosive urban growth will always necessarily produce an excrescence of blight.[2]

One of the curious features of the street layout of the original urban center of Phoenix is not just the way in which the primary cluster of east-west streets are named after the U.S. presidents, from Washington to Theodore Roosevelt. This would have been too easy. Rather, taking Washington as the east-west ground zero (Central Avenue is the north-south ground zero, with numbered avenues to the west and numbered streets to the east, staggered so that the important streets to the east are even numbers and the important avenues to the west are uneven ones), the chronological inventory of the presidents leapfrogs over Washington. Thus, Jefferson is to the south of Washington, while Adams is to the north; Madison is to the south, while Monroe is to the north, and so on for about a mile-wide block of streets.

One of the most important presidents of the early national period of the United States was Van Buren, and the street that bears his name is one of the most traversed — and one of the most colorful — of contemporary Phoenix. At times a favorite runway of streetwalkers, both women and transgendered men, Van Buren is most prominent for having been a major thoroughfare, before the creation of the I-10, between the United States to the east of Phoenix and California to the west (get on the I-10, which parallels Van Buren about three-quarters of a mile to the north, and you will essentially end up, going west, at the Santa Monica Pier on the Pacific Ocean, as great of a terminus ad quem an internal American migrant could hope for). Long before the cold-war interstate system, when all the country had were the post-depression U.S. highways, there were the original entrepreneurial highways built to stimulate local business. Van Buren was part of US Route 80, which in turn was originally the Dixie Overland Highway, the first complete east-west highway built in the nation (Weingroff). Additionally, Van Buren was something like a parallel spur of the legendary US Route 66, which ran from Chicago to Los Angeles, carrying the migrants who would create modern Southern California and the goods that brought the country out of the Great Depression. Route 66 did not run through Phoenix, but through Flagstaff, several hours today north. US 66 and US 80 were relatively dismantled by the interstate system (there is not a nostalgia-driven project to reconstruct US 66). Yet segments like Van Buren remain, part of the vital interurban transportation network by which metropolises survive: freeways are convenient, but there are times in which an urban thoroughfare is preferable, and Van Buren (along with Washington, Jefferson, McDowell, Thomas, Indian School, and Camelback) fulfills that role.

One might, to use such a metaphor, identify five geological layers with respect to Van Buren.

The original U.S. highway system basically served to link cities with each other across the country. This was in contrast with the three-decades-later interstate highway system, which was designed to connect the country as well, but in doing so it bypasses urban centers or utilizes business loops that connected the cities to them. In contrast, the U.S. highway system typically went through towns of all sizes, linking them together as part of the construction of modern America. When cities could not be connected in as straight a line as the lay of the land allowed, secondary highways were developed, with the goal of providing the maximum degree of urban connectivity. Since Phoenix — which in the 1930s had not yet begun to emerge as a major population center: this would begin after World War II — did not lay on the straight line of Route 66, it was, as a consequence, connected via a secondary route that linked it to the east with Albuquerque, New Mexico, and Amarillo, Texas, and to the west with Los Angeles (the Pacific terminus of route 66) and San Diego. Van Buren Street was the path that that secondary route took through Phoenix, Route 60.[3] Along the several miles that passed through Phoenix there sprung up the typical infrastructure of such routes, which were important, first, as part of the migration of the great depression, the movement of the war period, and, then the postwar prosperity when Americans took to the road in growing numbers. This infrastructure included gas stations and garages: the latter necessary because automobiles were still mechanically unreliable over the long haul, particularly through the unrelenting desert. It included coffee shops and convenience stores, as well as curio shops that sold kitschy mementos of the changes in the geosocial landscape along the trajectory of travel. And, most singular of all, the infrastructure meant the overnight motor lodge, which would develop into the great American institution of the motel, complete with kitchenette, coin-operated radio, and even the coin-operated vibrating bed to ease away the tensions of the road.

With the development of the interstate system, it no longer became necessary to drive through cities, and motel rows like Van Buren Street began to decline. By the 1970s, this strip, bounded on the north by modest residential areas and on the south by industrial parks had begun to see its overnight lodges turn into low-cost housing. Since Phoenix only minimally engaged in urban renewal during this period, much of the downtown began to be abandoned, a phenomenon from which it still has a lot of recovery to experience. Little low-cost housing was specifically built to handle the poor among the population influx of the period, and the motels along Van Buren were — and continue to be — one alternative.

A third stratum, after the first two of a U.S. highway route and low-cost housing, of Van Buren demographics, however, involved prostitution. Although other strips may serve the purposes of prostitution, Van Buren became notoriously associated with street solicitation, although it mostly meant soliciting customers in passing vehicle traffic. Street presence of this prostitution did not survive the late 1990s, and its last hurrah was during the Super Bowl game held in Phoenix in 1996. Van Buren served as an excellent venue for pickups, with its proximity to the Sky Harbor International Airport and downtown Phoenix; the proximity of Van Buren to Arizona State University (it is one major alternative route to the freeway for traffic from downtown Phoenix to Tempe) was an added factor in the last boom of prostitution it hosted in the late 1990s.

Today, a good number of the residents in the motels that have been turned into low-cost housing are so-called illegal immigrants. The ongoing Latin Americanization of Phoenix (it is now 40 percent Hispanic) has involved not only the arrival from across the border of individuals seeking low-cost housing, but also the migration north from so-called South Phoenix, where racial discrimination had confined the (mostly) Mexican population throughout the city's urban history. The South Phoenix border is flexible, but it usually has meant south of the Salt River, which lies approximately two miles south of Van Buren. However, numerous other factors have contributed to the northward migration of Hispanics, as well as the eastward migration necessitated by the destruction, through residential creep, of agricultural communities where Hispanics formerly constituted the majority of the workforce, toward massive sectors of the western Valley of the Sun, where Phoenix is situated.

Today, there is an insistent interest in the revitalization of downtown Phoenix, and this includes major streets around it. Since Van Buren flows into the downtown area form both east and west (and this chapter has given little attention to West Van Buren, although some of the geological layers mentioned are to be found there as well), it is inevitably going to be part of urban redevelopment. In particular, East Van Buren (the focus of this chapter) is privileged because of its proximity to Sky Harbor International Airport, the displacement of the industrial parks around it by gleaming office buildings and their infrastructure, such as new business hotels), and the emerging importance of Arizona State University as the paradigm of the new urban university. Indeed, this segment of Van Buren will play a privileged role in linking the original Tempe-based campus (Van Buren ends at the Mill Avenue Bridge, which takes one into the uni-

Typical mobile home park on Van Buren Street in downtown Phoenix.

versity village across the Salt River from Phoenix) with the downtown campus that will be developed blocks north of it along the Central Avenue Corridor. The gentrification of Van Buren, which has already begun with the aforementioned office buildings and business hotels, in addition to new condominiums catering to young urban professionals and their particular infrastructure, means that the layered historical references of Van Buren will inevitably lost forever: this is the fifth geological layer. Whatever continuity there is, through existing sites and structures, among the first four geological layers I have described, will be permanently displaced. Perhaps a name or two will remain, but that will be all.

Given the rundown and often dangerous nature of Van Buren, there is little reason for nostalgia. But there is every reason for a sensitivity to the historical record. Part of the westward migration that came about as integral to the Great Depression, World War II, and postwar prosperity and its transformations of the demographic landscape of America, as the belief always that such migration would bring with it a better life: movement meant the possibility of acceding to the American dream, the promised land of economic security and the good life. The myth of this American Dream, so inoperant for most Hispanics, is unquestionably referenced by Moraga's play. The Dreamland Mobile Home Park trades on the notion of movement as a way of changing one's life through changing

Typical trailer park on Van Buren Street in downtown Phoenix.

one's residence as a means of attaining the good life. If the invention of the mobile home meant the possibility of taking one's home on the road, the mobile home park afforded an instant installation upon arrival in the place of one's dreams. Phoenix, in its initial growth after the Second World War, certainly marketed itself as a dreamland, for the winter visitor, who could plug in a residence for months at a time in any one of dozens of home parks across the Valley or become even a permanent residence. The mature trees in the second image of this park are an index of how long it has been around. Many parks like Dreamland remain dotted around the Valley, although most have been replaced by urban renewal or the rapidly expanding residential subdivisions on the east and west ends of the metropolitan area.

But, the anchors of Van Buren remain, without a doubt, the motels, which are also referenced by Moraga's play. These include what are now noticeably rundown installations, along with some that have been condemned as structurally unsafe and unsanitary because of deteriorated plumbing and pest infestation. Several demonstrate the theme orientation by which establishments, built often one after the other along a major road, sought to distinguish themselves from one another. This is particularly true in the log-cabin or California cottage motifs, both of which are represented on Van Buren (the former is still maintained in almost mint

Short-stay motel on Van Buren Street in downtown Phoenix.

144

condition). Others are larger installations, and some have been kept up and remodeled (like the one on the cover), which indicates that Van Buren still attracts the traffic of travelers needing a place to spend the night.

Many of the motels cater to more or less permanent residences, often illegal immigrants, drug dealers, and prostitutes (who, however, are now less frequently engaged in public solicitation outside the motels than they were in the 1990s); one motel touts its offer of "quick rent apartments," which one could suspect is a euphemism for rental by the hour. Some motels trumpet the fact that they are "American owned and operated," a claim that indicates rival establishments are in the hands of so-called ethnics, typically Indians or Pakistanis. These circumstances underscore how the historical layers of Van Buren, in addition to being chronologically distributed, also intersect: the low-income resident, the prostitute, the foreign arrival — all of which contribute to a distinctly diverse demographics along this urban site.

One example of something like a gentrification of the motels is the Salvation Army retirement village that makes use of one of the more modern hotels along this strip.

It is not unexpected to encounter along Van Buren Street bars and liquor stores: they are undeniably part of the overall creatural needs of both the transient as well as the fixed population of the street. Sundays, however, bring out the sign board of the Love Tabernacle, whose founder is Jesus Christ. I thought at first this must be a euphemism for prostitution; I now see that it is a minimalist attempt to counter the area's reputation for raw sin. Without a question, there are established-denomination churches located within reasonable distance from this segment of Van Buren; there are, however, none actually along it.

In addition to the Love Tabernacle, a Spanish-language congregation is located a few blocks away in a former strip mall. The arrival of organized religion in the vicinity may not exactly be a manifestation of gentrification, but it is most assuredly a response to the bad reputation of Van Buren that is pointed to with reference to the taverns and prostitution.

The relatively recent "Latino-Americanization" of Van Buren and the area north of the multiple boundaries (Salt River, Washington Street, the Union Pacific railroad tracks) that held the Mexican population, so to speak, in check and out of sight of the white urban core and also referenced in Moraga's play is evident in a network of commercial sites relating to the needs of Hispanics. In the early years of the twentieth century, whites and Hispanics were pretty evenly divided within the city, but beginning with

Strip mall evangelical church on Van Buren Street in downtown Phoenix.

the post–World War I boom and continuing with the World War II boom, the Hispanic presence fell to around ten-percent of the metropolitan population. But the influx of Hispanics in the last decade — casually denoted in a virtually racist manner as "illegal immigration" — has brought the Hispanic population up to around a third of the city and meant that (in addition to a civil rights consciousness) Hispanics could no longer be confined (along with African Americans and Asians) out of sight to the south. Moreover, the southern rim of the Valley, up against the skirt of the southern mountains, is seeing an explosive growth in middle-class and upscale residential areas that may well come to destroy the ethnic neighborhoods of what has always been called South Phoenix.

Because of the use of the Spanish language to one degree or another by most Hispanics, their presence along Van Buren is immediately apparent in the names of business and in the goods and services announced as being offered. Indeed, in some cases these businesses have meant the take over of establishments that were formerly, and long, known as Anglo businesses.

In addition to an open-air flea market, albeit of modest proportions, this segment of Van Buren could boast of one of the first enterprises to provide direct bus service from downtown Phoenix to Mexico. Although the company soon outgrew this space and has moved to a location closer to the Sky Harbor International Airport, its sleek modern busses were, in their arrival and departure, another sign of the intersection of a possible new prosperity for Van Buren Street (precisely because they did so well at this location they had to move into larger quarters) and the sizeable Hispanic presence in the area.

Several *taquerías* along Van Buren mark the Hispanic presence. What is notable about these businesses (which complement traditional Mexican restaurants) is the way in which they include outdoor eating, either in the form of a seating area attached to a permanent building, or in the form of a mobile cart with picnic tables next to it. The nature of these business as specifically Latino, which also include a dance hall now several decades old, the El Capri Dancing, and a bar, El Presidente (which seems now to function more as a special events venue), is marked, of course by the Hispanic flavor of their names. Thus the Capri complements the more Anglo Blue Moon Lounge; Tacos Campos the now disappeared — displaced ethnically? — Carrow's eatery. The Hispanic nature of these establishments, moreover, is often reinforced by the typically Mexican flare of color and exuberant announcement of menu options.

This world of Van Buren Street will soon disappear. I do not know if it will happen within ten years or if it will take longer. Nor do I know if the incursion of Latinos, both new arrivals in the state or those who are being displaced from the old rural areas to the south and west, will slow

Fast food enterprise on Van Buren Street in downtown Phoenix.

the gentrification along Van Buren, since they would have to be displaced to somewhere else in the city. Of course, the regrettably slow but inevitable affirmation of a Latino middle-class in Phoenix has already meant that both old and new residential areas include fully integrated Latino neighbors. Yet it is also true that traditional middle- and upper-class neighborhoods like the downtown Palmcroft-Encanto area remains resolutely Anglo. Nevertheless, this is a consequence of economic rather than the racial/ethnic discrimination of the not-too-distant past.

When Medea is subsequently confined to the state mental institution on East Van Buren Street, this becomes, in its infernal dimensions, a reduplication of the abject life outside its walls, which in turn is the byproduct of abjection generated by the processes of the counter-revolution. In this sense, the mental institution only (re)confirms Medea's radical otherness as, to use Moraga's eloquent term, a xicanadyke. Although Luna attempts to pull Medea back into her emotional orbit, Medea resists:

> It doesn't matter now. I am the last one to make this journey. My tragedy will be an example to all women like me. Vain women who only know how to be beloved. Such an example I shall be that no woman will dare to transgress those boundaries again. You, and your kind, have no choice. You were born to be a lover of women, to grow hands that could transform a woman like those blocks of faceless stone you turn into diosas. I, my kind, am a dying breed of female. I am the last one to make this crossing, the border has closed behind me. There will be no more room for transgressions [46].

Despite the fact that Luna insist to Medea "you won't ever be able to go back to Aztlán or to any man. You've been ruined by me. My hands have ruined you" (48), Medea is impervious to Luna's insistence that they continue as lovers, and she sinks deeper in deeper into her crippling despair, which is permanently sealed when her final encounter with Jasón makes it evident that there is no return possible for her to Aztlán: the material ruin of her present life in Phoenix, reduplicated by her confinement to the mental hospital, figures her *huis clos* damnation, from which only drug-induced hallucinations or death are a remittance.

The spectator may be unwilling to invest much faith in Luna's attempts to make do. Although she acknowledges that "upstairs it's pure chaos" (34), she finds some sort of refuge in the basement laundry room of the apartment building: "I come down here just to get away from Medea sometimes. I sit up on top of the dryer and my thighs stay warm in winter. In the summer its cooler down here in the darkness" (34). Another woman remarks sarcastically, "Yeah, a regular paradise down here" (34), which may well be a figure of how an audience might react to Luna's carrying on despite the miserable conditions exile from Aztlán has brought her and Medea. Nevertheless, this is the world of the play, and as such it is meaningful and productive for the dramatic emotion of this fragment of human — Chicana, feminist, lesbian — it generates: "We were not as we are now. We were not always fallen from the mountain" (60). I am not saying that we would not have the theatrical text if it were not for Medea's and Luna's tragic fall, but only that as much as Phoenix is the dumping ground for the outcasts of Aztlán, it is also the material space of the drama of their fall, and it is within that space that we understand the anemia of Luna's desire to continue as before and the depths of despair of Medea's realization that the course of history has left her nowhere to turn.

The categorical bleakness of Moraga's *Hungry Woman* is certainly at odds with the optimistic boosterism that is an integral part of Phoenix's self-image (as is to be seen in Luckingham's expansive *Discovering Greater Phoenix*), both, as one might expect, on the level of the discourse promoted by the Chamber of Commerce and the Tourist Board and also on the level of men and women at the shopping mall.[4] It is worth speculating as to why Moraga, who has never lived in Phoenix, might have chosen this city as the material space for her play. Phoenix is undoubtedly on the margins of an image of Aztlán. Although Latinos now make up something like 40 percent of the population of the greater metropolitan area, the Chicano community has never had a major presence in Phoenix, such as it has had in Tucson and other clearly major Hispanic cities of the Southwest. The vast majority of the Chicanos who were a part of the historical development of Phoenix through most of the twentieth century inhabited farming communities on the (subsequently greatly expanding) periphery of the city and, as one might expect, they suffered considerable discrimination within its metropolitan boundaries. Today, there are large Latino communities in various parts of the central core of the city, and it is notable that the Van Buren area I have discussed above — not just the blighted area, where what were once Anglo establishments now cater to the Latino community, but nearby residential areas — now hosts a particularly burgeoning presence. Yet perhaps Moraga might see this demographic development as part of the exile from Aztlán for Chicanos in late-capitalist America:

> CHAC-MOOL: I don't want to be here no more.
> BORDER GUARD: Where?
> CHAC-MOOL: Tamoachán.

BORDER GUARD: Phoenix?
CHAC-MOOL: Yes
BORDER GUARD: Where do you want to be?
CHAC-MOOL: Aztlán [77].

The hubris of Phoenix as the quintessence of progressive modernity in the Southwest, as a magnet city for the important demographic changes that have taken place since World War II, and as a rock-bed of neoconservativism leaves it particularly vulnerable to the sort of radical revisionism of the city Moraga's play engages in. There is in general in Phoenix an "I don't ever go downtown" attitude and, despite its crucial location in the central core of the city, there are many residents who have never seen the East Van Buren strip, certainly not even driving through in a car and much less on foot. In choosing to use Phoenix as the geographic locale of her play and what is the real area of the location of the state mental hospital that figures in it, Moraga is playing off of an interpretation of the collapse of the foundational myth of Phoenix, which is also the collapse of the foundational myth of lost Aztlán she postulates in this play.[5]

Cecilia Esquer:
Establishing a Public Voice
for a Chicana Activist

When Cecilia Esquer died unexpectedly in late 2010, she left an extensive legacy of activism as a Hispanic woman that spanned almost fifty years of the history of the Mexican American community in Arizona and, specifically in Phoenix. After some self-doubt as to its viability, Esquer had decided to bring out in the fall of 2010 a book of her memoirs, *The Lie about My Inferiority: Evolution of a Chicana Activist*, published by Latino Book Publisher, an imprint of the HISI, the Hispanic Institute of Social Issues. HISI is a first-rate editorial program located in the Mesa suburb of Phoenix, devoted to the publication of bilingual materials as part of enhancing the visibility of Hispanics in Arizona. Esquer's book is one of the most important projects HISI has undertaken, because not only does it provide historical material relevant to Hispanic life in Arizona, but it highlights the career of one of the state's first and most committed Hispanic feminist activists.

It would be difficult to exaggerate the invisibility of Hispanics in the history of Arizona, and even more so in Phoenix, which did not form part of the original Spanish presence in the state, which was confined to the southernmost region, with Tucson as its administrative center. Although scholars like Daniel Arreola and Eduardo Pagán have worked tirelessly to demonstrate that there was a larger Mexican/Mexican American community in Arizona than originally believed,[1] scholars of race and minority in Arizona (Bradford Luckingham, Matthew C. Whitaker) have shown that the numbers have always been low and that the participation in public, political, and commercial life has historically been low. As Luckingham notes, "By the end of the 1950s, modest progress had been achieved [for

Mexican Americans in Phoenix] in areas ranging from school desegregation to professional attainment, but it was slow and hard" (*Minorities* 4).[2]

And in terms of culture, with the exception of major Spanish-language writers associated with Tucson, like Miguel Méndez-M. and Aristeo Brito, the state has been noticeably impoverished as regards Chicano writers in either Spanish or English, and even more so in the Phoenix area. Arizona State University has brought into the area many important Chicano scholars, such as Arreola and Pagán (a native), along with Manuel de Jesús Hernández Gutiérrez, Margarita Cota-Cárdenas (a major novelist and poet and one of the first Chicana writers), Jesús Rosales, Francisco Arturo Rosales, Cordelia Candelaria (also a writer), Alberto Ríos (from Nogales, on the border with Mexico), Carlos Vélez-Ibáñez, only to name some of the most prominent. But none can really be said to have a consciousness of Phoenix in their work. An author who does have such a consciousness, Justo Alarcón, was originally born in Spain, but has made significant contributions to Chicano culture in Phoenix, both through his teaching, his community activism, and his creative writing.

Esquer entered Arizona State's College of Law in August 1973, the first Chicana woman to study there and very much the beneficiary of the determination of the founding Dean, Willard Pedrick (the college's first class enrolled in 1967), to make the school representative of U.S. population demographics at that time. As a strong champion of affirmative action, Pedrick knew that Phoenix was very much behind the curve of social development in the 1960s, and he knew that even among his handpicked founding faculty there would be enormous resistance to his ideas for student diversity. Yet he knew that the study and the practice of the law would serve as a very effective vehicle for bringing great social progress to Phoenix, and it was only his own prominence in the profession and acceptance in the local legal community that enabled him to prevail against often open hostility from university administrators, themselves frequently too beholden to municipal and legislative fears over the rising voice of minorities in Phoenix.

While certainly Hispanic minorities did not have an easy path anywhere in vying for a public presence and the creation of a social voice,[3] it is important to recall the extent to which, of the four border states, Arizona is the most marginal as regards any historical visibility of the Hispanic population.[4] It often seems like everyone loves Mexican food, but no one respects the Mexican Americans themselves as social subjects.[5] If today approximately one-third of the population of the state is Hispanic, a statistic that is also true of Phoenix, there is a noticeable dearth of Hispanic politicians. Only one has served as governor, Raúl Castro from Tucson, and one has served as mayor of Phoenix, although currently two of the nine City Council members are Hispanic.[6]

Much of this would explain the rhetorical framing of Esquer's book: the underlying proposition that there are two versions of her autobiography, one that she is an inferior Chicana woman, and one that her life as an activist, including important professional initiatives as a lawyer, serves effectively to counter the first version. Ironically, the first version is essentially a non-existent or only a sporadically existent one. The claims of inferiority directed toward a person on the basis of any one of the number of criteria of importance to the dominant imaginary — in this case, race and gender — mean, in practical terms, that the story of that person cannot be written. It cannot be written because there is nothing to write about, except perhaps in terms of the accumulation of evidence of failure. However, for the social discourse regarding the inferiority of others, an intense degree of synecdoche and metonymy apply: one or two examples of failure, ineptitude, inconsequence are more than enough to demonstrate that the individual, or group of individuals, can be safely dismissed as irrelevant to the historical account at issue. Indeed, they may not even be mentioned at all, and the norms of narrative accounts render it useless to attempt to inquire after their existence.

Thus, if one of the functions of autobiographical *apologiae* is to provide a contrary account to the prevailing one, the simple fact being that there may not be a coherent or sustained prevailing one, that the silence of the account is, in fact, its total textual presence. Or the prevailing account may be of the slenderest fragmentary nature, a brief glimpse into what the absent text might look like were it to have been fully developed as evidence in support of the premise it sustains. Yet, this is unlikely to be the case, and, as Esquer demonstrates over an over again, what she, as an examplar of the discrimination against minorities, is up against is only the most passing abstraction, the scantest articulation, of the extensive brief against them. In discussing her experiences at Arizona State's Law School, Esquer demonstrates very effectively this process of the barest presence of the original version of the social imaginary against which she must construct an entire book of refutation:

> [During] Orientation Week, we were divided into small groups of
> fifteen students. Professor Hal Bruff was the discussion leader for our
> group. I was the only minority in the group. The purpose of the group

was to address student fears and concerns and to answer any questions. Toward the end of the discussion, one of the students asked it if was true that if we looked to our left, then to our right, that one of us would not make it to the third year. Professor Bruff quickly discounted that. He said ASU only admitted students they thought would be successful in law school, so they expected all of us to make it, "except for those minority students we admitted." Miraculously, I did not say anything. But, I was very upset.

Having come to law school after having picketed and marched for the UFW [United Farm Workers], I went to Dean Pedrick's office. He told me Professor Bruff had already told him what had happened and that Bruff felt badly about it. Professor Bruff said if I wanted an apology, I could go to his office. I told Dean Pedrick I would do no such thing, and he could tell Professor Bruff to go to hell [81].

As is immediately apparent, Bruff's reported words come to exactly seven words, but it requires no stretch of the imagination to envision the vast social discourse on which they rest, one in which, with no need to provide statistical evidence beyond the anecdotal (which implicitly cannot be questioned, since if I as an authority figure say it is so, it must be so), there is an entire and intricate argument with regard to the inferiority of those to whom the words apply: in this case, the one minority student present in the room. By contrast, Esquer's account of the incident requires almost two hundred words, and one could well wonder if this is an adequate response to the extensive underlying discourse of discrimination. It is important that Esquer includes the account of Bruff's admission of regret for his words, because, while the words can be withdrawn, the effect they have in the highly charged moment of their articulation cannot, and, in this way, they are only one of a number of examples from the historical account of inferiority around which Esquer constructs the counterdiscourse that is the text we read.

It is important to be absolutely clear about the juxtaposition I am framing between a mostly unarticulated system of discrimination and the fully articulate one of contestation to it. Systems of discrimination and oppression are accustomed to project themselves as allegedly natural. In such a paradigm, it is natural that women be inferior to men, that people of color be inferior to those who consider themselves "white," that the poor be lesser than their betters the rich, that Europeans be better than those they have colonized, that heterosexism be righteous but homosexuality a sin. The system that touts itself as natural is rarely called upon to justify in detail how it is natural, to the detriment of the excluded other:

its rhetoric of self-conviction is accepted at face value at it imposes itself as unquestionable on that basis. It may deign to explain the defects, limitations, failings, perversions of the excluded other, but the natural, because it has effectively imposed itself as natural (often through violent means, such as imperial conquest or the intransigent imposition of sanctions), does not allow itself to be questioned and does not yield to the demand to explain itself. The only option is to mount an unrelenting discourse of contestation, toward denaturalization and the exposée of the fiction of the natural. It is on this front that works such as *The Lie about My Inferiority* acquire their importance.

Esquer's account of what we might call the "primes" of the attribution of inferiority to her constitute, necessarily, the organization basis of her memoir: she recalls incidents of marginalization, accusations of inferiority, actions of discrimination, and provides a response to them. It is a response based, essentially, on the logbook of her professional accomplishments as a high-school and university-level teacher, as a practicing lawyer, as a member of a presidential commission (with Hillary Rodham, under President Carter), and a member of state government under Attorney General Bruce Babbitt (who would go on to be one of the state's most successful governors, with a strong commitment to minority representation). This inventory is supplemented by the enormous range of Esquer's participation in local politics (principally in the university suburb of Phoenix, Tempe, which has a long history of Chicano residents[7]), her work with the United Farm Workers and Chicanos por la Causa and her ubiquitous presence in rallies and protests through the city and elsewhere in the state.

The result is that the various chapters and accompanying photographs of *The Lie about my Inferiority* effectively constitute a cartography of Chicano life in Phoenix from the time of the emergence of the Chicano movement in the 1960s, both on her own (particularly at ASU's Law School) and in conjunction with her husband Elías, who actually held elected office as a member of the Tempe School Board. Since this is a personal memoir, Esquer does not attempt to provide a systematic and documented account of the challenges, battles, and accomplishments of the Chicano movement in the Phoenix area, a history that remains to be written. Rather, her text is a response to the particular primes, as I have called them, of discrimination and oppression that it was her lot to encounter. Many of those primes are a reliable index of the experience of Chicanos in Phoenix, throughout the Southwest, and the country from the 1960s on, but the particular emphasis she gives to them, frequently from the added point of view of gendered politics, are, first, part of her personal memoir, and, second, indicative of the specific circumstances of Chicano life in Phoenix.

Public education was a particular nightmare for Hispanics, not only because it was mandatory and schools wanted the head count for state revenue purposes, but also because there were always those families who recognized the need for education as part of the access to American public life. Arizona was ever as retrograde as Mississippi or Alabama in meeting the educational requirements of its minority populations.[8] Moreover, unlike the South, the enormous influx of outsiders who came into Phoenix beginning with World War II diminished or diluted whatever presence and influence Mexican Americans might have once had (Luckingham, *Minorities* 192; see also Oberle, 240–43). Much can be said about where these outsiders came from and what their social imaginaries were. Suffice it to say that few had any interest (beyond liking Mexican food) in the state's Hispanic population. Although the current prevailing political ideology in Arizona may believe that the state in recent decades has been flooded with illegal immigrants from Mexico and Central America, the simple fact is that, through most of the twentieth century, Hispanics were very much a minority in at least the Phoenix area. As a consequence, there was little in the form of any progressive attention to the educational needs of Hispanic students, who were, in effect, warehoused in schools as marginal as the "separate but equal" facilities of the South.

However, the 1960s brought affirmative action, Head Start, special education, bilingual education, and other minority programs. This was the time in which both Esquer and her husband Elías became teachers in the Tempe School District. The administration of schools of the time was dominated by a white male old guard who were very much the repository of the sort of discourse of inferiority that only manifested itself in underarticulated but powerfully effective manifestations of discrimination. In the case of Esquer, her contact with the spokesman for such manifestations was Bill Boyle, her principal at McClintock High School, who had little use for her outspoken activism and may have even gone so far as to search her classroom for subversive material in addition to listening in on her classes on the school intercom. Esquer recounts confronting Boyle (whom Esquer always respectfully refers to as Mr. Boyle) on the latter activity:

> Some of my fellow teachers had told me that Mr. Boyle would listen to my class through the intercom. I went to see Mr. Boyle. "I didn't know you were interested in learning Spanish. You are welcome to sit in on the class anytime." He said some of the parents complained that I was

putting ideas into their children's minds by discussing political issues. I assured him there was no time to do other than to teach Spanish during the class period. Mrs. Chilton and I sponsored the Spanish Club. The members of the club were interested in hearing about César Chávez [an Arizona native who co-founded the National Farm Workers organization] and the farm worker's movement. Apparently some of the parents thought that was too radical [38–39].

There are three features of this passage that bear noting. One is the way in which Esquer meets in a direct and confrontational manner challenges to her integrity, authority, competence. The phrase "I went to see" and its synonyms and associated actions recur through *The Lie about My Inferiority* as a key to the way in which the often indirect, underhand, and often quite devious way in which the dominant discourse of racism proceeds. Esquer's strategy is to meet such manifestations of racism head on, and in her recounting of the numerous, and on occasion distressing repetition of one and the same manifestation over and over again, to frame rhetorically the manner in which she did so. Hence the verbal formula "I went to see." In these confrontations and in her recounting of them, it is not an apology she is seeking, but a clarification and redress of circumstance of racism. The fact that some of these circumstances, fifty years later, seem almost ludicrous, such as that of the principal spying on a class via intercom, does not diminish their significance at the time nor the compelling urgency Esquer feels to immediately counter them with her contestational voice.

Moreover, this quote underscores the way in which Boyle's act of oppression toward Esquer is underhand and unarticulated. It is underhand in the sense that, until someone let her on, Esquer had no idea that Boyle was listening in on her classes. That is, his hand is hidden, as it far too often is in the discourse of oppression: the victim may perceive that oppression is taking place, but she cannot easily identify its source and exactly what its structure may be. And it is underarticulated in the sense that oppression does not speak its name: Boyle listens in on Esquer, but he does not speak to her, does not signal verbally his presence, and does not, therefore, allow for a dialogue of engagement to take place. The latter can only possibly happen if the victim of the act of oppression discovers that it has taken place and "goes to see" the oppressor, forcing an open dialogue to take place.

The third characteristic is that of Esquer's sense of humor. Chicano humor and satire is sly and circuitous. While Chicano activists learned the need to "be in your face," a merciless but understated ironic approach is much more frequent in everyday social intercourse. Although, as Guillermo Hernández points out in his study, Chicano satire may be very broad and very brutal, but, as Esquer's text demonstrates, the individual holds on to her dignity by engaging in more subtle forms of the ridiculing of the expressions of racism. In another of several anecdotes involving the redoubtable Mr. Boyle, Esquer relates:

> The School Board held a yearly dinner in which they included the spouses and school administrators. Mr. Boyle made sure I was seated next to him at these dinners. At one of the yearly dinners in 1973 he said: "I hear you are going to law school."
> "You heard right."
> "Well, too bad you won't get to sue me because I'm going to retire in four years."
> I poked him in the ribs and said: "Law school only takes three years, so you'd better get ready!" [44].

I have emphasized the first segment of Esquer's book, not only because it is prelude to the sophisticated forms of resistance and contestational encounter that she will evolve through her multifaceted career, but because it most vividly represents the circumstances of margination and oppression that characterized life for minorities in the Phoenix area during Esquer's young adulthood and early career. The honing of the survival skills she reports on allows for the accumulation of professional successes in her role as an activist that the bulk of *The Lie about My Inferiority* reports on.

One of the most moving subsequent experiences Esquer reports on, however, is not related to an unqualified professional success, and that is her experience with discrimination in Mexico as a *pocha* (feminine form of *pocho*), a person who represents the corruption of the "real" Mexican by contact with Anglo culture. Specifically, it refers to what racism calls mongrelization, and here it means that Mexicans lose their identity in the U.S. without gaining anything in return, and it characteristically refers to a manner of being in the world, cultural traits along a vast array of axes, and command of the Spanish language. While the emergence of Chicano identity has meant a counter to both Anglo racism and Mexican racism, for a long period of time, at least since the 1848 Treaty of Guadalupe Hidalgo in which northern Mexico became the U.S. Southwest, Mexican Americans were as unwelcomed in Mexico as they were in the U.S. Thus, when in late 1976, Esquer is part of a delegation of the American Council of Young Political Leaders who visit Mexico, she discovers — but this time fully articulated — the ally of the racism in Phoenix:

> In the van the next morning, one of the hosts asked about my nationality and how my parents got to the U.S. When I told him my grandparents were from Mexico, but lived in the Arizona territory from a very young age, he became irritated. He said my ancestors were traitors to Mexico, that they probably fled the country to avoid the Mexican Revolution [of 1910]. This was quite a surprise to me. I felt that, from the day I arrived, they did not see me as an equal to the other delegates. Now I knew why.
>
> He then asked what I called myself. I told him I considered myself a Chicana. He told me I was a Yankee. Shocking! I always thought of Yankees as being Anglo. How could a Chicana be a Yankee? Then he told me I was a gringa; another amazing statement. I always thought gringos were fair skinned Anglos. All of a sudden I felt as if I had no identity. In Arizona, where politics got rough, we would be told to go back to our country (Mexico) [99].

In this passage, Esquer describes her sense of alienation. During the conversation, which is clearly controlled by the agent of racism and not, as elsewhere in her book, by her voice of resistance, she describes experiencing surprise, the shocking, amazement. These are all rhetorical notes in her text used to underscore the sudden descent into the nonsensical that derives from the class between her identity and the identities imposed by a totally previous unknown discourse of racism. This discourse she specifically characterizes by direct reference to the Spanish phrase "Ni fu, ni fa" (not one or the other). Although Esquer's eventual reaction, as she describes it, is to laugh and savor the subsequent recounting of the incident to her husband, this incident underscores how the lies of inferiority are not so easily and conclusively inventoried. As Esquer's book amply demonstrates, with its particular emphasis on her experiences with Phoenix, a city that continues to experience profound tensions over racism and the accommodation of diversity, the work to be done remains extensive. Her life was devoted to that work as an activist. Her personal memoir testifies to the complexity and yet viability of that work by the way in which the text itself is a vigorous response to the discourse of racism, in general and in terms of concrete historical events, in the Phoenix area.

Conclusions

> When I lived in Paris, I wished I were in the 1860s, as the city was undergoing dramatic social and urban transformations that marked its destiny. When I lived in New York, I wished I had been there in the 1910s when massive migration and city building were forming its inimitable character. And when I lived in Los Angeles, I wished I were there in the 1950s, when it gained prominence as a hub for postwar innovation. Living in Phoenix over the last eight years, I have felt that I am finally in the right place at the right time. (Nan Ellen in *PHX*, n.p.)

I undertook this study with a series of premises in mind about Phoenix cultural production, and the likelihood that it would be possible to generate a monograph that would not only provide an account of interesting examples of the production of culture about Phoenix, but also constitute a model for future research on this and other similar urban areas.

My initial point of departure was to take a stand against the often directly uttered proposition, although it is far more often simply passively accepted, that there is not much to say about culture in Phoenix. When I first started teaching a course on the subject, first for an interdisciplinary humanities program, then for the graduate program in the School of Architecture, and most recently as an undergraduate seminar in the Honors College, people would say, "What culture in Phoenix?" I always query students as to why they are taking the course, and invariably there are those who say, "Because I never thought there was any culture in Phoenix, and I want to see what there is."

Of course, Phoenix is proud of the legacy of Frank Lloyd Wright, who did so much of his major work in suburban Phoenix from 1937 to his death in 1959, and everyone felt they knew and loved Erma Bombeck, whose columns and appearances were followed by legions of fans in Phoenix, where she moved to from Dayton, Ohio, in the 1970s and from where she wrote virtually all of her engaging chronicles.[1] Phoenicians are perhaps less enthusiastic about Alice Cooper's local roots, and few seem to remember that Steven Spielberg was already making amateur films when he was a high-school student in Phoenix. The building that housed the temple where he was bar mitzvahed stills stands, abandoned, in downtown Phoenix, although feeble efforts to have it renovated and preserved because of the famous member of the Beth Hebrew Orthodox community have not been successful. But there is no denying that a quick survey of Phoenicians at the mall is unlikely to reveal much in the way of any familiarity with culture in Phoenix. And while it is true that there is a vast production of the plastic arts in Phoenix, with an appropriately extensive infrastructure of galleries and museums that feature this production, it is difficult to refer to any one artist whose work is truly memorable or influential.

Thus, this study began with the simple challenge to discover what there might be. By contrast, as one would expect, with cities like New York, Chicago, San Francisco or Los Angeles, which are cultural centers for the nation with important names that have local recognition, or even by contrast with a similar historical trajectory like Seattle or Portland, the lack is notable of any perceived artistic or intellectual record for a city like Phoenix, which seems to have gone, almost overnight, from being a drowsy backwater to constituting a major population hub. To be sure, one can always find bits and pieces of cultural production that could justifiably merit a degree of passing commentary. I think, for example, of Reg Manning's editorial cartoons from the days in which the *Arizona Republic* (the morning newspaper) and the *Phoenix Gazzette* were locally owned by Eugene Pulliam (as is customary, I make note of the fact that Pulliam was Vice President Dan Quayle's maternal grandfather). Pulliam's politics were very much on the hard-rock conservative end of the spectrum, and Manning loyally represented, with a certain amount of creative flair, Pulliam's position on the local and national affairs of the day. Manning draw editorial cartoons for Pulliam between 1926 and the 1970s, and won a Pulitzer Prize for Editorial Cartooning in 1951 for the cartoon "Hats," which dealt with the Korean War. It is, quite simply, a brilliant cartoon, juxtaposing the silk top hats hung on a rack of world leaders who met at Lake Success to attempt, futilely, to resolve the Korean conflict and the bullet-pierced helmet of a U.S. soldier hung on a battlefield cross. But much of Manning's work today, while sometimes very creative, is almost unintentionally comical in its right-wing naïveté (by which I mean the failure to engage with the profound complicity of political issues and the appeal to alleged simple

American pieties). Manning also published several books of cartoons dealing with topics of interest on Arizona, typically oriented toward newcomers and tourists, which increased steadily in number after World War II.

But Manning's work, which I have chosen not to examine in this study, would constitute, to adopt a term from linguistics, a cultural isolate. Like a language occurring in isolation from other languages (e.g., Basque, with no scientifically demonstrable relationship to any other known language), a cultural isolate stands out for its uniqueness against a backdrop of otherwise rather dull and uninteresting efforts.

I suppose in a certain sense much of the cultural production examined in this study exhibits features of the cultural isolate. Take, for example, the case of Jon Talton's outstanding crime fiction. There is a lot of dreadful crime fiction set in Phoenix. Much of it is painful to read, and much of it, for all too apparent reasons, is published with vanity presses. One can access an inventory of such writing by searching a universal database like the Library of Congress or the OCLC WorldCat under the subject heading "Phoenix (Ariz.)—Fiction." I don't know if the fact that virtually none of what I have found listed in the universal databases is to be found in the library collection of Arizona State University, based in the Phoenix suburb of Tempe, but with two branch campuses in Phoenix proper, is due to the fact that so many of the works are so bad or if the university is a co-conspirator in the effort to underacknowledge writing about the city!

But Talton's writing, which is now published by the Scottsdale-based Poison Pen Bookstore, is truly exceptional. Scottsdale is another of Phoenix suburbs, a major tourist center and, therefore, a major arts center and entertainment venue. Poison Pen specializes, quite successfully, in publishing crime fiction and in selling the works of authors from all over the English-speaking world. One cannot accurately speak to the motives for the many works of crime fiction set in Phoenix, but, with the exception of Talton's writing (and very few other authors—Marc Savage's excellent novels come to mind), there is scant evidence that these writers have any identification with Phoenix, any real interest in Phoenix, and any tangible knowledge about the city historically or socially. Insouciantly inventing details about the city that make little sense in terms of the actual lived experience of Phoenix, it is as though these authors hit on the idea of setting their works in the Arizona capital because there is something exotic about the desert, as though it offered new terrain, so apparently unexplored that one really need not know anything about the city to write about it. In order to write about New York or Los Angeles, cities that have such a specific density in the national imaginary that one could hardly dare to get the details of the locale wrong, such as making Broadway an east-west street north of Central Park or putting the famous Hollywood sign on the side of a cliff facing the sea in Santa Monica.[2] Prues and Heffron's *Writers Guide to Places* is meant to assist writers aspiring to portray cities and states with some measure of accuracy as locales for their fiction, down to listing "Facts and Peculiarities Your Characters Might Know" (Phoenix is covered on pages 21–24, and the information provided is impeccable). But most writers who opt for the novelty of Phoenix (or Tucson) give the impression of never having visited the city or, if in fact they live there, of never having explored the city beyond the nearest shopping mall: like most of my students, they also appear never to have gone anywhere near downtown Phoenix or, if they have, to have conducted their business there (downtown Phoenix, in addition to municipal agencies, houses the county seat, the state capital, and myriad federal installations) and gotten quickly out, as though it were a barren no-mans-land.[3]

Talton, on the other hand, really knows Phoenix, having grown up in the central corridor, about two miles north of the downtown area. His narrative device is an exceptionally clever one of a has-been history professor who is employed as a cold-case expert by an old friend, a Chicano who is sheriff of Phoenix-based Maricopa County (in itself a hilarious boutard, given the current Sheriff of the County and his bullying stance toward the Chicano community). In having his detective, David Mapstone (who, like Talton, has deep family roots in the Phoenix area), revisit cold cases, Talton hits upon a very effective way of bringing the history of Phoenix into the attempt to bring major unsolved crimes to resolution. For those who may believe that Phoenix, whose first settlers came in the late 1870s as part of the project to provide supplies to the U.S. Army in its final subjection of Native Americans, has no real historical depth, Mapstone's cold cases reach way back, to use Jana Bommersbach's metaphor in her investigation of the Winnie Ruth Judd murder case, into the dirty linen closet of Phoenix's past. Phoenix was always pretty much of an open wild west town, with enough police corruption to satisfy any novelist or filmmaker. Examples of illicit narcotics and recreational drugs, alcohol, prostitution, money laundering are rife, as in the case of the Las Vegas-based Jewish mafia's involvement with Durant's, a venerable downtown steakhouse, now one of the best in the state, but in its day, mid-century, a meeting place for assorted questionable business transactions with Mob connections.[4]

Conclusions

Some (perhaps all) of Mapstone's cold cases appear to be based on real crime stories in Phoenix history, although, necessarily, considerable fictionalization is involved. Talton could have opted to pursue Bommersbach's interest in the Winnie Ruth Judd case as a real crime story that requires (re)investigation, with a scrupulous adherence to the historical record, but Talton's fictionalization allows greater latitude, as is customary with fiction, in interpreting matters such as human relations and personal motivations that may not, routinely, be supported by the documentary evidence available. Thus, where Bommersbach can do no more than lament the fact the Judd went to her grave never, not even sixty years after the events, speaking even in private to Bommserbach, who had done much to befriend her, Mapstone is able conclusively to close the case in Talton's 2003 novel, *Camelback Falls*, which has some significant parallels to the Judd case. As Aristotle says in the *Poetics*, poetry tells us not how things were, but how they might have been, and Talton's fictional riffs on Phoenix history, with all their meaty elaborations of the worse and the worst of the protagonists of the city, including allusions to alluringly unsavory power brokers that many readers will enjoy attempting to identify with historical persons, go well beyond the record historians customarily adhere to. Barry Goldwater may have tried to get away with sending the message to Bommersbach to lay off the digging deep into the evidence of the Judd case, but no such injunction can be made to a novelist. After all, it's only fiction isn't it?

What happens, then, in Talton's novels is that, unlike the bulk of the dreary bibliography of crime novels set in Phoenix, Phoenix is not such a novelty, not just a far-fetched outpost of what passes for known civilization in the United States.[5] Rather Talton uses the conceit of the crime novel as a means to engage seriously the authentic social and political history of Phoenix. His novels project an accurate sense of the city, and his characters move across the vast territory that is now the Greater Phoenix Area. In Mapstone's specific case, he fans out from the old historical center of the Phoenix downtown and, a few miles to the north, the stately Willow historic bungalow district where he lives and where Talton grew up and then later lived. In so doing, the novels chart the significant differences between one area and another, the distinctive demographic compositions, and the ways in which different sectors of the city interact with the meaningful space of the city. I am not saying that Talton's novels only make sense if you know Phoenix. But if you know Phoenix, you know that Talton is talking as much about the specific place that is Phoenix as Raymond Chandler is about the specific place that is Los Angeles or Dashiell Hammett about the specific place that is San Francisco. The result is an immensely satisfying reading experience in terms of the meaningful space of lived human experience, and not the nonhistorical convience setting of the majority of the works found in the library database under Phoenix (Ariz.) — Fiction.[6]

Equally, Stella Pope Duartes fiction projects a profound sense of Chicano life in Phoenix. In her case, however, there is virtually no competing writing, as so few Chicanos have written about life in the city (Phoenix appears in some texts by Alberto Ríos and Justo Alarcón, for example). The presence of La Sonorita is unmistakable in the novel analyzed in this study, *Let Their Spirits Dance*, although the novel moves out of the Valley as the family undertakes its journey to the Vietnam memorial. Duarte's most recent book, a collection of marvelously wicked short stories, *Women Who Live in Coffee Shops* (2010), are all set in firmly achonored locals in downtown central Phoenix.

Another premise that I began with is that there are, in fact, interesting things to say about Phoenix, that there is historical depth to the city, despite the abiding belief that everything relating to Phoenix happened yesterday, except maybe for Barry Goldwater, who was there at the birthing: born in 1909 and deceased in 1998, Goldwater was essentially the major face of twentieth-century Phoenix, which pretty much covers the entire historical trajectory of a city that, while first settled in the 1870s, was never really a city until the next century. There are now several excellent museum and archive collections and published photographic dossiers of Phoenix history (especially useful are published volumes like (Melikian; Barrios; Luckingham and Luckingham; VanderMeer and VanderMeer; Pagán; Dutton; Scharbach and Akers; Spears and Wildfang), some of them of the "then and now" genre, which juxtapose a photograph (taken, say, 100 years ago) with a recently taken photograph of the same spot (Brian Dutton's work is perhaps the best known in the state). However, there is little in the way of an interest in systematically photographing contemporary Phoenix, although my own work is an attempt to make a beginning in that regard (Foster, "Here Today"; Foster, "Historic Catholic Churches"; Foster, "La Sonorita"; Foster, "Can You Get There"). Material from "Can You Get There" is included in the chapter on Cherríe Moraga; while material from "La Sonorita" is incorporated into the chapter on Stella Pope Duarte.

One can take a certain delight in these photographic dossiers, par-

Conclusions

ticularly Melikian's. His organizing principle of "Vanishing Phoenix" (a trope on Martha Summerhayes's classic memoir *Vanishing Arizona: Recollections of My Army Life* [1908]), necessarily implies historical depth because of the multiple processes that lie behind the circumstances by which buildings, homes, institutions, and landmarks may disappear. This is a much more complex process than the simple justaposition of then and now photographs, as useful as that may be in providing a sense of the enormous growth of the city over a period of 100 years. There are the dossiers prepared by Luckingham and Luckingham and by VanderMeer and VanderMeer, which do deal with contemporary Phoenix (the Luckingham's include more of a historical trajectory), but these are coffee table books meant for the tourist and, especially in the case of the VanderMeers' book, the business community, evident in the way in which the focus is explicitly on the growth narrative of Phoenix and the opportunity for investment and future development. As a consequence, little in the way of cultural development in Phoenix, beyond reference to high profile museums, is included. This is not meant as a criticism of these volumes: indeed, they are enormously important as indexes of a specific imaginary for Phoenix that someone like Jon Talton has thematized in his novels. But it does mean that there is still the gap of interpretive photography of the contemporary city to be filled as part of the cultural record. Such photography will allude, if only implicitly, to the narratives that can be told about Phoenix, in the way in which my own essay on the vanishing Cuatro Barrios area of Phoenix references the way in which essentially Anglo development has impacted on the Mexican American community, in this case the creation and successive expansions of the downtown Sky Harbor International Airport ("Here Today"). By contrast, my essay on La Sonorita, which complements Stella Pope Duarte's novel examined in this book, underscores the survival of one of the most important remaining Mexican American neighborhoods in the area south of downtown Phoenix (the other is the Garfield historic district that borders the downtown to the east). In sum, photography has an important, but unexplored, role to play in the stories to be told about Phoenix.

There are stories that have been told about Phoenix that are not covered by the book, although I will stand by the significance of the work that is studied here. My critical decision to examine a few key works with some extended analytical detail, rather than to provide an author and title inventory, followed by brief descriptive notes, has meant that the range of works included here is necessarily limited. But as I have insisted, this is an essential bibliography. I hope that, precisely, the probability that readers will say, "But why didn't you include so and so?" will serve to prompt adequate critical study on that production that is absent from these pages. For example, I hope those who have the training I do not will wish to concern themselves with the cultural record of art and music in Phoenix, and architecture certainly deserves more attention than it has received, by which I mean not just the listing of important names and important buildings, but the critical and interpretive analyses of them as Phoenix cultural artifacts.[7] As one of the largest cities now in the nation, there is surely serious scholarship remaining to be done on the lived human experiences of the city.

Appendix I:
Glendon Swarthout and
The Cadillac Cowboys

> Phoenix is the only city in America building new slums; the others are content with their old. (Swarthout, *The Cadillac Cowboys* 18)

> "We're goin' t' have us a cor-ral full. Mebbe ah'm a might old t' daddy, but Chris, she's in the prime t' calve." He sobered. "Carleton, we're going t' have us ev'rythin' ev'rybody roun' heah's got. An' then some." (Swarthout, *The Cadillac Cowboys* 55)

About a decade before Erma Bombeck and family moved to Phoenix, Glendon Swarthout wrote about the construction of the Phoenix suburbs where the Bombecks ended up living and which Erma Bombeck used as one of her points of reference.

Swarthout's novel, *The Cadillac Cowboys* has a considerable acheological flavor to it. Published in 1964, it captured the sociocultural conflicts in Phoenix at the time of the enormous growth inspired by the prosperity of the 1960s. Although Phoenix's population had grown appreciably as part of the war effort and during the postwar boom, the development of the 1960s, propelled by the definitive installation of domestic air conditioning and the mobility of the country in general, was especially notable. By the time of *The Cadillac Cowboys* there was a well established Phoenix lifestyle — at least one that could be a major selling point of the Chamber of Commerce and its allies, particularly the land developers — some of whose principal facets included the anchor of the venerable Biltmore Hotel, a gentrified Scottsdale and a very upscale Paradise Valley. One way of reading a novel like *Cadillac*, and, indeed, one of the ways in which it is "archeological," is in terms of an inventory of these facets.

Appendix I

Swarthout aims essentially at producing a parody of life in the northeast suburbs in the early 1960s, and in order to make this goal explicit, he engages in an archness of tone that works essentially on two levels. One is the broadly drawn silliness of life in the Valley, especially for newcomers. Although some locales are identified by their verifiable names, such as the Biltmore Hotel and Scottsdale, other receive soubriquets that are even more absurd than the often delirious naming of the land developers: Temptation Valley (presumable Paradise Valley), Sarcophagus Mountain (Mummy Mountain), Dromedary Mountain (Camelback Mountain), Social Security City (Sun City), the Tuwee Indian Reservation (Pima Reservation), the Casa del Alma (the Franciscan Renewal Center, known as the Casa de Paz y Bien), among others. Since many places are identified by their own names, droll renaming, rather than out of any concern for libel, represents the parodist's underscoring of metonymic and synecdochic meanings through exaggeration. On the other hand, Swarthout's narrator has read his Frederick Jackson Turner, Joseph Wood Krutch, Erna Fergusson, and John C. Van Dyke, whose writings about the development of the West and the allure of the Southwestern deserts. In quoting them and in demonstrating that what they have to say, in some cases almost a century before, has direct application to developments in Phoenix and the Valley of the Sun in the mid–1960s.

The central core of *Cadillac*, indeed, is a consideration of the fate of the cattle commissioner turned Paradise Valley homeowner, Eddie Bud Boyd. In Eddie Bud the narrator has a synthesis of the Arizona native who is being displaced by the transplanted Easterners: the narrator is one H. Carleton Cadell, failed college history teacher who married a wealthy widow and convinced her to resolve the boredom in their lives by moving to Phoenix. Because he is a well read professional historian, with a bona fide liberal point of view,[1] Cadell understands, in a way his neighbors do not, the plight of the old hands who are only remembered as tourist attractions, but who are no longer welcome in the flesh in the land they originally settled. Another dimension of the novel is also the running reference to the Native American, although Swarthout's narrator here is mockingly racist, and it is the late nineteenth-century cattleman (and, one assumes, by extension, the farmer) whose displacement deserves sympathetic treatment. Eddie Bud's plight is handled in a comic mode, with one disaster after another, as he attempts to have everything the newcomers have and then some. While the principal axis of Eddie Bud's disasters is the swimming pool he attempts to have built but which becomes a bottomless pit for his construction outlays, the Cadillac he purchases and uses instead of the modern-day cowboy's legendary pickup truck becomes a symbol of his social and, ultimately, financial overreach. However, Swarthout's tale is a comedy of Eddie Bud's plight within the parody of the Phoenix lifestyle, and Boyd reverses Cadell's trajectory and finds new fortune in the East as a Malboro Man–type icon. Meanwhile, the recounting of Eddie Bud's misadventures in his failures to adjust to the ethos of the New West is interspersed by a half-dozen obituaries of stalwart pioneers whose harsh frontier lives have little to do with those of the denizens of Paradise Valley pool parties.

Swarthout's novel is passingly funny on the level of Eddie Bud's social failures and his descent into bankruptcy, and it is appropriately scathing on the level of the parody of the Phoenix lifestyle. Joining a large bibliography of fiction on the growth of suburban America after the war,[2] *Cadillac* is moderately interesting as fictionalized social commentary, although one will find a more sustained and consistent version a decade later in Erma Bombeck's often hilarious and black-humor tinged Paradise Valley chronicles.

One distinctive note about *Cadillac* is the language used. While Eddie Bud is represented as speaking in a folksy, often crude English that the reader is to understand as the plain speech of the pioneer Arizonan, Cadell, as both an Easterner and a university man, speaks with a presumed professional class register that Eddie Bud often cannot quite directly understand. Moreover, although Cadell seems never to patronize Eddie Bud when speaking to him (indeed, the narrative only functions on a bound of manly trust between them, such that the former enjoys a privileged, if not always credible, access to the cattle commissioner's universe), he engages in a pseudo–Shakespearean English qua narrative voice, replete with words that might send readers to the dictionary and with flourishes of inverted syntax. One assumes that this linguistic disjunction serves to mark the cultural chasm between himself and his woefully out of place neighbor, while at the same time it constitutes a self-mockery of aspirations of the Eastern transplant to bring civilization to the nation's last frontier.

Swarthout is implacable in his characterization of the thin veneer of culture available in Phoenix in the 1960s, the knee-jerk conservatism of a society in which any independent opinion is "communistic" and true patriotism is embodied in the John Birch Society, and, above all else, the naked opportunism of the land developers and their allies,[3] including the tourist industry. The narrative stance, however, throughout is more ridicule than nuanced analysis. Calling himself a "dilettante Quixote gone daft from reading" (5; even if his reading has been some of the most distinguished opinion on the West), Cadell the narrator, in what he characterizes as his "journal" (8) rarely rises above the witticism of comments such as "Should Heaven ever apply for admission as the fifty-first of these United States, we [in Arizona] would be opposed" (56).

What I have called the archeological flavor of Swarthout's novel is, therefore, its own thinness as a narrative text. Mildly entertaining but ultimately too self-consciously cute, its main valor today is as a still accurate account of life in Phoenix for the comfortable, professional-class Eastern transplants in the early and mid–1960s.

Appendix II:
The Matter of Jack Swilling

When the rowdy and often dissolute trajectory of Jack Swilling (1830–78) finally lead him to Arizona in 1867, like many of the other recent arrivals the major allure was for the potential the state offered to find gold. While old-timers and mountain men lamented what they saw as the threat to the last remaining frontier within the contiguous states and territories of the continental United States, Arizona, which had been established by Abraham Lincoln in 1863 as a separate territory through its separation from New Mexico, was hardly being overrun by individuals seeking the opportunity to homestead there. Yet they had begun to come, and the U.S. Army established a post in 1865 at the site of what was subsequently to become Fort McDowell, in large part to ensure the safety of arriving settlers, who would in the next decade establish the city of Phoenix: if the Fort provided safety to the settlers, the settlers serviced needs of the Fort, and this symbiosis began the development of Phoenix, which less than a hundred and fifty years later would become the largest of the fifty state capitals and the sixth largest demographic concentration in the country. But by then Jack Swilling was long dead.

Yet Swilling had a premonition that something would come of the new territory, especially in the area in which he finally settled (although he was to die in the Yuma Territorial Prison, ironically, given the many notches on his gun, for a murder he did not commit). In *I, Jack Swilling, Founder of Phoenix, Arizona* (1961) by Tempe-based writer John Myers Myers (1906–88), Swilling, who narrates his own story from the cell in Yuma where he lies dying, recalls the words of his associates in the heady adventures of the West:

> "[...] Arizona is going to be one of the nation's garden spots."
> "Perhaps you mean rock-garden spots." The author [John Ross

Browne] glanced at the bleak, hot mountains piling up to the north of us. "But assuming your words are to be taken at face value, how is this to be accomplished?"

"I haven't worked out that detail yet," Posten admitted, "but even the Sahara blooms lushly when water is present, and I don't see why an oasis couldn't be created artificially."

"We could run an aqueduct down from the Great Salt Lake," Brown suggested [238].

Of course, Brown's proposal is facetious, as the waters of the Great Salt Lake, as its name suggests, would hardly have been effective for agriculture. Rather the detail that Posten has not yet worked out, but which Swilling and his associates will with the organization in late 1867 of the Swilling Irrigation Canal Company and the initiation of the digging of Swilling's Ditch. This was to become the basis of the still extant canal system in Phoenix by which run-off swollen rivers with headwaters in the north of the state are diverted in order to make the Arizona Sahara lush, first with cash crops and, much later, with tourist attracting greenery. A hundred years later, in 1968, President Lyndon Johnson signed into law the authorization for the construction of the Central Arizona Project, but by then few people in Phoenix, the overwhelming majority of them newcomers who had little interest in the history of the area beyond scattered folkloristic images of primeval indigenous peoples, even remembered who Jack Swilling was. (The recent renovation of North Second Avenue north of West Van Buren Street has involved the creation of a historical marker in memory of Jack Swilling, but one doubts few have yet to read it beyond the homeless, who make up the majority of the foot traffic in the area.)

Myers's novel is heavy on Swilling's swashbuckling past, enhanced by the seductiveness of a first-person narrator who is intelligent, wittily articulate, and urbane. Although much of what Swilling relates can be viewed with the grain of salt due a self-serving first-person narrator (self-serving in the sense that his story is motivated by the injustice of having been incarcerated for one of the few crimes attributed to him that he actually did not author), it serves the dramatic irony of the novel for Swilling to contrast his prescience regarding the future of Arizona with either those who do not see how anything civilized will ever come of the new territory or those who agree with the latter is hoping it will not because of the threat to their frontier life. The overarching dramatic irony of Myers's novel is that readers in 1961 and thereafter, know very well the consequences that will flow (punning metaphor advisedly used here) from Swilling's ditch. And there is a parallel irony in that even in 1961 it was difficult to grasp what Phoenix would become as of this writing in 2007, when some are predicting that the abuse of water resources may well lead Phoenix to the same sort of crisis faced in the fifteenth century by the Hohokam Indians whose long abandoned canals were the basis of Swilling's ditches.

It is appropriate that Myers has Swilling speculate only minimally about the future of the desert he sees given (by Darrell Duppa in 1868) the pretentious name of Phoenix, a name that reflects the shared classical education of men of the privileged upbringing of their long-lost origins (Swilling in Georgia, Duppa in Europe). Yet, while he is still alive he is very much involved with the tugs of war that characterize the competing interest that may go with the founding of any new site:

> To begin with, Phoenix had not stood for a town but the entire area we were trying to bring to life again [after the previous life it had with the Hohokam]. I had taken it for granted that there would be a town so called, though, and that it would develop where I had established irrigation service and a postal station. I still don't see that it wasn't as good a site as that a half-a-dozen miles away where Darrell Duppa and a group of others chose to settle. Before I knew it, however, that spot was coming to be known as Phoenix, while the settlement where I lived [to the west] had the drab name of Mill City, applied because a couple of brothers named Heller had established a flour mill.
> That was the status quo as of 1870. The following year, Mill City and Phoenix clashed because a by-product of my canal digging was the creation of a new county to go with the three Arizona already had. Reading from north to south, as Pah-Ute had been lost to Nevada, these were Mohave, Yavapai, and Pima. From the last two Maricopa was carved in 1871, and the tug of war was to see which would get to be the county seat.
> Mill city lost [...] (279).

Swilling's narrative is matter-of-fact here and neatly serves whatever bare-bones interest Myers's readers may have had for the basics of Phoenix's founding. From the point of view of plot, Swilling suspects that these controversies played a role in his being railroaded to the Yuma prison; from the implied historian's point of view, Swilling's brief, albeit significant, intervention in the founding of Phoenix might well explain why he effectively disappears from any historical collective consciousness regarding the city: Duppa's name is at least recorded in a housing development (the 1940s Duppa Villa project at North 20th Street and East Van Buren, to house workers and their families at the defense contractor, AirResearch); there appears to be no such recorded evocation of Swilling's name.

Thus, despite its subtitle, the overall plot of Myers's novel is an effective, although perhaps unplanned, objective correlative of Jack Swilling's place in the founding of Phoenix. Less than one-fourth of a novel of 308 pages is devoted to Swilling's activities in what will eventually be called the Valley of the Sun. His brief intervention in the area's history (and it is appropriate that he sees Phoenix not just as the designation of a city but of an area), while it has the advantage of the emphasis accorded the close chapters of a story, chapters that are something like the cumulative consequence of what has gone before, is ultimately not firmly inscribed in that history. The relative brevity of that story, in the context of all the stories Myers has Swilling tell about himself, signals the superficial nature the people of Phoenix still seem to see as regards Swilling's role as the "founder" of Phoenix (which is shared by the historians of Phoenix: Luckingham accords Swilling only three brief references in the 316 pages of his history of the city).

Myers, who attracted some critical attention with the fantasy novel *Silverlock* (1949), approaches Swilling basically in the fashion of the history buff, and he seems to see little of interest in Swilling as a human being beyond his alleged role as the "founder of Phoenix." The result is a novel of only passing interest in the archeology of Phoenix cultural production, and its one note of eloquence remains Swilling's contemporary invisibility. Part of this invisibility is that the child he bore with his Mexican wife, Esperanza, must, by all accounts, be the first native Phoenician and Phoenix's first, founding Mexican American. And, too, the degree to which Swilling was pretty much of a rake and a rogue is also part of the unsavory Arizona past rendered invisible.

Chapter Notes

Introduction

1. None of the standard works on the film, such as Rebello, even mentions Hitchcock's decision to film in Phoenix. The Bates Motel locale was in Indio, California.

2. http://www.ermamuseum.org/life/default.asp.

3. I will throughout use the terms "Phoenix," "Phoenix area," and Phoenix metropolitan area interchangeably, although mostly the texts refer exclusively to the city of Phoenix proper.

Erma Bombeck

1. Actually, Bombeck had been doing freelance and bit writing since 1952, but she always considered that her career as a writer really began with this job and the column "At Wit's End."

2. In a gathered anthology, several books are reprinted with one binding and an overarching title, such as *Four of Kind* (1985); a sampler anthology collects pieces taken from several previously published titles, such as *Best of Bombeck* (1987) or *Forever, Erma: Best Loved Writing from America's Favorite Humorist* (1997).

3. The state of Arizona, at the beginning of the twenty-first century is approximately one-third Hispanic, and Phoenix now counts over 40 percent of its citizens as Hispanic. Of course, not all are Catholic, as protestant groups and the Church of Latter-day Saints count many faithful in Latin America and among Hispanics in the United States.

4. One would have liked to see Bombeck discussed in the section of "Housewife Discourses" of Wheeler's *Uncontained: Urban Fiction in Postwar America.*

5. To be completely accurate, Bombeck lived in Paradise Valley, a northeastern suburb of Phoenix; Barry Goldwater was her immediate neighbor. However, the name Phoenix is customarily used to refer to the Greater Phoenix Metropolitan Area, and not just to refer to the municipality of Phoenix proper.

6. One supposes that the innocence of the moment caused Bombeck to overlook the implied permission for individuals of the same sex to sleep together.

7. More recently, Marcia Fine has established a body of chronicles about upper middle-class life in Scottsdale. See, for example, *Stressed in Scottsdale* (2010).

Wallace and Ladmo

1. *Arizona Memories from the '70s.*

2. Another major artist of Phoenix origin, Steven Spielberg, claims to have idolized the show as a teenager. He went on to produce his own brand of subversive children's shows: *Tiny Toon Adventures* (1990), *Animaniacs* (1993), *Freakazoid* (1995), *Pinky and the Brain* (1995).

3. Ruelas, *Thanks* is a biography of Bill Thompson; it also contains much descriptive material about the show.

4. Steve Hoza runs a website, "Wallace Watchers," devoted to memorabilia about the show, including some recordings of segments. My Works Cited indexes some of the recordings of the show that are available. See also comments on the show at KPHO's website, "Brief History of 'Wallace and Ladmo.'"

5. There has been a tradition of virtual mythification as regards the show, but relations between Thompson and Kwiatowksi eventually went sour over franchising aspects of the show. Phoenix playwright Ben Tyler wrote *The Last Wallace and Ladmo Show* to detail this pathetic, human side of their long relationship; see the commentary on the play by Robrt [*sic*] Pela, "The Last Days."

6. Along with Frank Snell, Sr., founding partner of Snell and Wilmer, one of the first major law firms in Phoenix, and Walter Bimson, president of the Valley National Bank.

7. This is the sense of her first chapter, "Children's Desires/Mother's Dilemma."

8. See the special KPHO-TV5 show on LADMO, March 4, 1994.

9. Occasionally the name is found spelled as Maude.

10. As opposed to cross-dressing, in which the male body intends to mask itself completely under/behind/within feminine clothing, or the female body the same in male clothing, drag undermines the male-female binary that heterosexuality overdetermines in large measure through gender-distinctive clothing. In drag, the gender "abandoned" or "suppressed" by the ostentatious nature of the clothing of the so-called opposite gender "shows through," such that there is a tension between the two. That tension may range over various modalities, although in the case of Aunt Maud it is primarily ludicrous. In drag, the spectator always knows what the "real" gender is supposed to lie beneath appearances, and no one involved with the *Wallace and Ladmo Show* ever forgot for a second that it was Pat McMahon performing Aunt Maud, beginning with the fact that his voice and gestures were the same that characterized all the characters he played. At the same time, other McMahon characters also toyed with gender issues: Captain Super was not always as thoroughly virile as the models he is based on, and, again referencing Valley of the Sun's legally enforced homophobia, Captain Super is on one occasion supposedly arrested in the satellite city of Scottsdale for wearing pantyhose. Marshall Good is prone to display an effeminate cowboy posture.

11. See my analysis of Steven Benson's editorial cartoons on snow birds elsewhere in this volume.

12. There is a scattering of other characters, such as The Wizard, Boffo the Clown, and Bobby Jo Trouble, a biker who may have been meant to reference James Dean or any of the mythic figures underlying the biking culture prominent in Phoenix. McMahon was also the lead guitarist of Hubb Kapp and the Wheels, a parody of Beatle-type rock bands. Other musical groups that we part of the show include Commodore Condollo's Salt River Navy Band and The Ladmo Trio, with the LaChords. See the CD *Mike Condello Presents.*

13. McMahon came from a vaudeville background. His parents were a duo, McMahon and Adelaide.

14. The Florian/Maud interaction became a running gag on the show, and the cover of Aunt Maud's Storybook features an image of Maud in her rocking chair with a portrait of "Harry" on the wall behind her.

15. VanderMeer (106–11) places the Arizona State Fair in the context of other similar Western-themed phenomena in Phoenix. VanderMeer also discusses *Wallace and Ladmo* (116).

16. In the sense that a city that has little value for its real, material history clings to phantasmal images of an imagined and impossible past. Phoenix was never a cowboy city and, although it does have an important agricultural history, with its dependence on Mexican labor and accompanying culture bears little resemblance to the Mid-Western county or state fair the Arizona version seems to have at its core.

17. Luckingham and Luckingham include a reference to the Rodeo and provide an illustrative image (93).

18. I would like to acknowledge the contributions of Paul Bergelin to this essay, in the form of notes on the episodes and conversations about the dynamics of the show.

Truthful Misrepresentations

1. Stephen Reed Benson was born in Sacramento in 1954. Although the grandson of Mormon Church president, Ezra Taft Benson, Benson has been very public in his renunciation of the church ("Editorial Cartoonist's Journey"). He left the church in 1993 and is a proclaimed atheist, although in his youth he served a mission in Japan. After receiving his BA in political science from Brigham Young University, he graduated in 1973 from the Art Instruction Schools in Minneapolis. Benson has been a cartoonist for the *Arizona Republic* for over twenty-five years. Benson professes no partisan political identity.

2. Lamb includes numerous references to Benson's work: "He is one of he most provocative cartoonists working in the United States" (182).

3. An overview on Benson, including a listing of additional awards is to be found at the online site "Steve Benson."

4. *Editorial Cartoon Awards 1922–1997* includes a selection of Benson's work (277–80).

5. Letters to the editor from readers and subjects often achieve a level of vitriol correlative to Benson's hyperbole, and his published volumes repeat the best of them with notable glee, as though red badges of courage. One of the comments on the back cover of *Fencin' with Benson* (1984) says succinctly: "one of the finest collections of garbage I have seen."

6. It was reissued with the title *Back at the Barb-B-Que* (1991). The cover of this edition shows Benson wielding a paintbrush dipped in Sacred Cow Sauce and slathering an enormous animal lashed to his barbecue.

7. Kush never did lead ASU to the Rose Bowl; ASU would not go to Pasadena until 1987; ASU also played the Bowl in 1997.

8. Webb's projects landed him on the cover of *Time* on August 3, 1962; see VanderMeer and VanderMeer 66–67. For an official history of Sun City, see *Silver Anniversary Jubilee*.

9. The use of "geezer" here is inspired by one of the names Benson gives to the many snowbird vehicles that are featured in his cartoons. One is called "Geezer Pleaser."

10. It is difficult not to perceive a degree of racial problematic in such a resistance, although Benson does not take this question up. This is because the residents of Sun City and similar communities (called by many "geriatric ghettos") are, in their vast majority, Anglos, while their taxes would go — clearly not for schools in their residential enclaves — to fund education in surrounding communities, which are the vestiges of the farming society that those enclaves have displaced. Because of the demographics of farming in Arizona, the vast majority of the children involved are Hispanic. (Although when the issue of school taxes was a burning matter in the early 1980s, the question of educating so-called illegal children was not a foregounded component, as it is — and to a very alarming degree — at the time of this writing in mid-2009). The Anglo nature of Sun City is amply abundant in the photographs included in *Silver Anniversary Jubilee*. Distribution of people of color in Phoenix and discriminatory housing covenants in Phoenix are discussed by Whitaker (esp. 104–12), although there is no specific reference to Sun City.

11. In fact, September 11, 2001, had a severe impact on the Arizona economy. Coming on the cups of the tourist season, this attack and the threat of other terrorist attacks kept winter visitors to the Valley and the state away in droves. The severe 2008–2009 economic downturn has had a similar deleterious impact on tourism.

12. Another cartoon (*Evanly Days!* p. 133) also involves troping of cultural referents, this time two: (1) the text is to be sung to the tune of "Frosty the Snowman," and is appropriately titled "Frosty the Snowbird," while (2) the title of the strip is "Invasion of the Valley Snatchers," a reference to Philip Kaufman's 1978 film *Invasion of the Body Snatchers*. Another cartoon from *Where Do You Draw the Line?* (p. 3) speaks of the "Legend of the Abominable Snowbird," whose tell-tale droppings are coins and bills.

13. Again, there is a racial dimension here, since the mostly Anglo sun-birds would not feel kinship with the many people of color that make up the ranks of the transient and the homeless.

14. There are two other Valley cartoonists whose work should be noted here. Bil Keane (1922), whose *Family Circus* (1960-date) has long been carried in the *Arizona Republic*; and Benson's predecessor as *Republic* editorial cartoonist Reg Manning (1905–86). Manning had a well defined political agenda, conservative and often reactionary (reflecting the editorial opinion of the paper's founder and editor, Eugene Pulliam, Vice President Dan Quayle's grandfather), but he is now more known for his cartoon books on Arizona than for his editorial work. Of particular interest are *Cartoon Guide of Arizona* (1938 and many subsequent editions) and *What Is Arizona Really Like; A Guide to Arizona's Marvels* (1968 and numerous subsequent editions).

Phoenix, Say What?

1. Harr and Fessler review this trope in the American imaginary as it relates to social justice.

2. The fact that Notaro's misfortunes now continue in the totally different environment of the Pacific Northwest, in Eugene, Oregon, as evinced in her only novel and in her last collection of chronicles (*The Idiot Girl and the Flaming Tantrum of Death; Reflections on Revenge, Germophobia and Laser Hair Removal* [2008]) does detract from the specificity of place in her Phoenix writing, although it does signal that her persona has taken on an added identity. The fact that the town in which *There's a (Slight) Chance I May Be Going to Hell* (2007) takes place is neither Eugene nor any

known Pacific Northwest city, but rather only a generic tree-hugging milieu attests to the way in which Phoenix is where, so far, Notaro possesses geographic specificity. If, in her subsequent writing, Notaro eschews specific locale in favor of a narrator whose misadventures are not as specifically anchored geographically, this in no way diminishes the concreteness of Phoenix in her first five collections of chronicles.

3. It should be evident that Notaro is working of what is by now a well established feminist trope: the nonconformist woman as "mad" (a key adjective for a considerable semantic chain of metaphoric and metonymic equivalents). This is a trope famously identified with Gilbert and Gubar; see also Quay on "insanity."

4. A recently observed bumper sticker: "Yes. I'm a bitch — I'm just not your bitch."

5. Hence, the existence of a website, www.idiotgirls.com.

6. The precise location of the house is a consequence of personal communication with Notaro, who does not provide as clear a designation in her book.

7. So-called illegal immigrants may not be always destitute, but they congregate in, among other areas, the old inner core for mutual support, access to social services, and the jobs available to them.

8. I remember visiting a mansion in the 1960s in the Phoenix Country Club enclave. The house lacked central air-conditioning, except in the English bulldog kennels out back. The lawyer who owned the house was from an old pioneer family that had learned to survive without it. Such hardy types are long gone in Phoenix, and one civic goal, despite energy concerns, is universal air-conditioning.

Desert Noir

1. Basing himself on Bommersbach and others, Scott Coblio has produced a DVD, *Murderess: The Winnie Ruth Judd Story*, in which puppets enact the story.

2. See the fine collection of Phoenix noir short stories, *Phoenix Noir*. Talton's story, "Bull" (17–36) is not only the lead story, also one of the best.

3. Fine's chapter, in which Chandler is only one of several detective writers of Los Angeles discussed, nevertheless specifically honors him by titling the chapter "Down These Mean Streets: The Tough-Guy Detective Story."

4. Marc Savage's *Flamingos* is an excellent contender for a bibliography of desert noir novels. Del Rebus is driven by the obsessive need to avenge his father's personal and commercial failures at the hands of the cruel and indifferent desert city. Aided by Elvis Mahoney, a would-be restaurateur whom Rebus protected from an Aryan brotherhood during a shared stay in prison for capital crimes, Rebus sets out to mastermind the con of the Scorcese family's Phoenix operations. No match for the family's superior organization, he is killed in the attempt. Mahoney, however, survives, and moves to New Jersey to cook for the aging Don. Savage constructs a fairly complex story with excellent ironic nuances regarding motivation and behavior. What is noirish about the novel is the exploration of the seedy dimensions of Phoenix beyond the façade of desert tranquility and tourist gloss. The desert receives the sawed up bits of the enemies of the mob, while a Paradise Valley mansion is the control center of the con operation. Savage knows Phoenix well (the novel's jacket flap has him living there) and he deftly moves his characters among various locales that are important signs for what the reader suspects from the start will be an operation ending in bloodshed. These icons include the Phoenix Greyhound Race Track (underscoring the contest between Rebus and the Scorcese family) and Phoenix Sky Harbor International Airport, which is an integral

part of the glossy tourist industry, but here hosts the bloody denouement of the story. The fictional Sport Time Lounge, located near the racetrack and the airport in the area directly south and east of the city's historical core, is the only specifically seedy locale in the novel, but it is the base of the Scorcese family's Phoenix operations. If the Paradise Valley mansion is the pole of the con operation and the lounge that of the resistance to it, this axis of Phoenix's seediness prevails. Mediating between the two of them is the Phoenix Zoo, the home of the eponymous flamingos. Zoo exhibits like flamingos, so out of place in the desert setting, point to the way in which most of the life displayed in the desert is an exercise in incongruity. Everyone is out of place in the dreadfulness that is Phoenix, which everyone in the novel clearly sees as being the where in which there is no there there. There is an interesting queer dimension in the novel which, although it is not handled in an exactly homophobic fashion, seems to be meant to serve as an index of nonbenevolent nature of the city: queerness is as infelicitous as every other sincerely humane endeavor in the novel.

5. Mexican American Peralta is a nice conceit of these novels. The "real" Sheriff of Maricopa County is the Italian American Joe Arapaio, who touts himself as "the toughest sheriff in America." It is debatable whether Arapaio is particularly unsympathetic to Mexican Americans, in the aggressively so-called anti-illegal immigrant climate of Arizona. But there is no doubt that Talton in his editorial columns suffers lightly the frequently disingenuously buffoonish publicity grabbing antics of the Sheriff.

6. Talton begin writing the novel in the context of the emerging political football of so-called illegal immigration in Arizona. One of the major players in the intense campaign against Mexican Americans perceived as immigrants was Sheriff Joseph Arpaio (re-elected in November 2012), who is of Italian American origins. Talton, however, makes his fictional counterpart a Mexican American, a member, precisely, of the minority group most harassed (according to a Justice Department suit against Arpaio that is still pending as of late 2012) by Arpaio and his political allies.

7. It is, therefore, a significant coincidence that Talton is both a journalist and narrative voice behind the notably autobiographical detective Mapstone.

8. This is the recurring motif of photo-essay books like those of Luckingham (*Discovering Greater Phoenix*) and VanderMeer, as well as photographic "then and now" projects such as the one by Allen A. Dutton. Significantly, the photo-essay books in question are principally exercises in the selling of Phoenix to the business and commercial community, both investors and specialist newcomers, on the beneficent qualities of Phoenix's meteoric growth.

9. Maryvale was developed by the Valley's mega-developer, John F. Long. According to Philip VanderMeer, it was named after his wife Mary: "The models opened in 1955 to huge crowds; at $7,950 for a three-bedroom house, Long was selling 125 houses a week" (39; there is an accompanying photo that records the circus-like opening of the development).

10. The east-west railroad tracks in Phoenix serve as part of the imaginary north/south divide in the city which has, historically, been also an Anglo/Chicano divide.

11. Pointedly, while both Willo and Maryvale are "historical" districts in the academic sense of the word (as I have said, Maryvale was an important development for middle-class housing in Phoenix after World War II), only Willo is one of the thirty-some officially designated historical districts in Phoenix.

12. There is a moment during the difficult trial featured in Gordon Campbell's *Missing Witness*, in which Douglas MacKenzie is defending as second to the legendary

Daniel Morgan when he wishes he had not returned to Phoenix. Raised in a semi-Mormon family in Mesa, the so-called second capital of the Church of Latter-day Saints, McKenzie, who went briefly to Arizona State and then to Brigham Young, only to return to ASU for Law School, had been offered a position with a prestigious law firm in San Francisco. But he chose to return to Phoenix, in great part to work with Morgan, whose fame in defending the downtrodden and in opposing the death sentence (definitely a minority stance in law-and-order Arizona), was as much a part of his fame as his cross-examination talents.

In this passage, McKenzie has gone to San Francisco to track down a witness. Beginning to sense despair at winning the murder case he and Morgan are trying, he muses "[W]ith an ache somewhere deep in my should I asked myself why I hadn't stayed in the city where I stood and taken up my proper position among decent people who lived their lives in gracious ways" (231). It is immaterial what would, indeed, by McKenzie's "proper position" and whether law in San Francisco is practiced by people who are more decent and who live more graciously than in Phoenix. What is material is that this is the sense of the profession as McKenzie has been experiencing it up to that point in Phoenix. As a senior partner in the law firm which he has joined observes, after one messy trial had led to another, "You don't have to be an asshole to be a trial lawyer. That having been said, you never want to lose sight of the fact that you are part of the social milieu" (362).

The plot of *Missing Witness* is a complex one and turns on whether a mother or her daughter shot the former's husband to death, a man who, turns out, is both the nominal father and, biologically, the half-brother of the child. Because the daughter develops catatonia, after the shooting, she is the missing witness that allows Morgan to have the mother declared innocent, as the child is allegedly, in fact, to have killed her father/brother and gone into catatonia as the result of it; the mother also claims that the victim had sexually abused the child. After the mother's having been found innocent, the prosecuting attorney thereupon charges the daughter, who has come out of her Catania, although the daughter tells a very different story, part of which is that her husband had accused his wife of being lesbian, whereupon she shot him in the girl's presence. The mother is now the missing witness in her daughter's trial, and when she is found she refuses to testify and then runs out of court never to be seen again. The daughter is finally acquitted, in part because of the mother's refusal to face what she knows will be the revelation of her lesbianism, dashing any hope of inheriting from her husband's father, to whom she has been a lover in order to gain access to his estate through her daughter, one presumes.

In the process of working through the details of these two trials, the novel has much to say about the seedy side of power politics in Arizona and the implications of the law-and-order mentality, such that a judge has no problem in sending a child to the gas chamber and then boasting about it at church and the persistent denial of the rights of suspects. It is also a social milieu in which judges are wont to play fast and lose with criminal trial procedures and incompetent lawyering is as much a way of life as a frontier mindset of taking no hostages and winning at all costs. As the narrator recounts in his memoir written twenty-five years after the events, the man he works with has no qualms about treating his closest associates like shit in order to prevail. Set against what had become by that time a certain measure of gentility in Phoenix — fancy clubs, expensive clothing stores (Goldwater's, of course), shaded neighborhoods, and upscale suburbs (both the new wealth in Mesa and Paradise Valley), Campbell has both a good sense of what Phoenix looked like in 1972–73, while at the same time capturing what could still be a very raw professional legal world.

Campbell is near pitch-perfect in his details of Phoenix and environs, and there are only a few bloopers: insects do now swarm around porch lights in mid–January; the famed Arizona Club was at the top of the First National Bank Building (it was popularly called the "lawyers club") and not the Valley National Bank Building, although it did move to the latter (now called the Chase Building) in the late 1970s (Campbell gets it right once and wrong once); and there is no residential Encanto Circle in central Phoenix, although there is an Encanto Boulevard and an Encanto Drive, both adorned by the sort of mansions/luxury homes attributed to one of the founding partners of the firm McKenzie works for. Many of the characters in the novel could be taken as à clef for prominent historical figures, including supposed prominent Phoenix lesbians. Although I did not have sufficient contact with the Phoenix legal scene in the early 1970s to be able to make any knowing connections, there is one prominent law professor mentioned by name, Edward H. Cleary, who was one of the founding faculty of ASU's Law School and an expert on legal procured and who helped draft the uniform rules of evidence used in federal courts.

It is possible to see the reference to lesbianism in the novel as homophobic, since two of the three are presented as "greedy bitches": one is the mother who, despite her guilt, is exonerated, and the other is a lover who lies for her; the legal team finds this out too late to correct their error in calling her. Yet, the novel also refers to the references to lesbianism as nasty charges, but only an appeal to an actual historical record will save this detail from seeming disingenuously exploitative, especially since the world McKenzie portrays in 1972–73 in Phoenix is still overwhelmingly one of sexist male dominance, down to having the one female lawyer in the firm model sexy clothes in the choice of a seductive wardrobe for the accused mother and having secretaries make and fetch coffee. Indeed much is made of the hypersexuality of Morgan, who "seduces" men and women alike as his awed allies and, as one of the other founding partners of the firm says, he "had so much musk on him that when he walked into a courtroom, he made the rest of us feel like fairies" (427).

One interesting dimension of the novel is its Mormon inflection. Mormon-referenced fiction is gaining some public currency, especially with Phoenix-based Stephenie Meyer, whose novel is a successful Hollywood film, *Twilight* (2008). One of the recurring issues in Mormon-referenced literature is a strong moral base, whether or not it is translated into specific religious commitments and behavior. McKenzie comes out of a Mormon background and is quite close to his Grandmother, who is disturbed that any lawyer can defend a client sensed or known to be guilty. McKenzie does have moral reservations throughout the novel as to Morgan's morality, if not his legal ethics, but in the end he throws his lot in with him: he has become assimilated to the social milieu.

Arizona State University's Law School website has an article about Cambell's relationship to the School: http://www.law.asu.edu/?id=1110 (accessed January 4, 2009).

Jana Bommersbach

1. An anonymous donation of unattributed crime scene photographs, "Winnie Ruth Judd Photograph Collection," may be consulted at the Arizona State Archives.
2. The only other book on the Judd case is by J. Dwight Dobkins and Robert J. Hendricks (1973), who because of when the book was written change some names to protect individuals who are still alive ("Authors' Note" vi). Thus, the crucial figure of Jack J. Halloran (see below) becomes Carl Harris.

3. See essays in the volume *Women, Violence, and the Media* to understand the way in which reporting on both women criminals and women victims of criminals is heavily influenced by prevailing gender politics and ideology.

4. The house where the murder took place still stands on North 2nd St., although the numbering has changed from 2929 to 2947. It is part of a small residential pocket surrounded by high-rises, which means it will probably disappear as part of continued commercial development in the central Phoenix corridor.

5. Luckingham, *Phoenix*, discusses briefly the Judd case in the context of how by the early 1930s "Phoenicians enjoyed a variety of social activities, not all of them constructive" (114), which included, in addition to the partying activities in which Judd and her female friends were involved, narcotics trafficking.

6. Crime was rampant in Phoenix throughout the period, as was political corruption. In one sense, Judd's railroading was of a whole with this panorama. Prostitution was particularly an issue, especially in the context of the influx of the military and war-related industries as part of World War II (see both Luckingham, *Phoenix*, and VanderMeer, *Desert Visions*).

7. Such as Meagan Abbott's novel *Bury Me Deep* (2009) and Scott Coblio's performance video, *Murderess: The Winnie Ruth Judd Story* (2007), in which puppets are used to enact the story. Yet a recent collection of crime texts about Phoenix, Patrick Millikin's *Phoenix Noir*, contains no fictional account of the Judd case.

8. It does seem that, in subsequent years, Halloran was known to get drunk and babble about how "'if you knew the right people, you could fix anything in this town. He laughed and said Winnie Ruth was out in the state hospital paying for what he'd done'" (296). But this could hardly ever rise to the level of counternarrative able to undo the original, successful conspiracy against Judd.

9. I have in mind writing by Mary Daly, Andrea Dworkin, Catherine MacKinnon.

10. Bommersbach has also authored another account of murder in Phoenix, written from an equally strident posture of feminist rage. *Bones in the Desert: The True Story of a Mother's Murder and a Daughter's Search* (2008) deals with domestic abuse and the financial exploitation of women by predatory men.

Out of the Barrio

1. Approximately five years ago, Phoenix ranked fifth in the nation in size, ahead of Philadelphia, which now ranks fifth. Phoenix's loss in ranking likely reflects in part the departure of Hispanics, scared away by recent anti-immigrant hysteria in the state, fanned opportunistically by sectors of the state government, the state legislature, and some law enforcement agencies.

2. South Phoenix is given little more than passing reference in Luckingham's *Phoenix* (94, 98) and, as one might expect, none in his coffee table book, *Discovering Greater Phoenix*.

3. Much research has been conducted in recent years by Daniel D. Arreola of Arizona State University and his associates in reexamining the history of Hispanic barrios in Phoenix. See papers by Lukinbeal and Oberle, both of whom Arreola has worked with. *Recuerdos* is a more informal account of barrio life.

4. Mexicans with the name of Jesús, which was offensive to Anglo sensibilities when pronounced in English, often say their name changed to Jesse, and many Chicanos ended up, officially or otherwise, with Jesse as their name rather than the more

Hispanic Jesús (María, by contrast, never provided a problem when pronounced in English).

5. I have been unable to identify any study dealing with the representation of the Vietnam conflict in Chicano literature, although numerous Chicano texts refer to the conflict. Another important novel by a woman is Gina Valdés's *There Are No Madmen Here* (1981; rev. 1996).

6. Except, of course, those who go through the prison system.

7. Or, to use a useful neologism, Hurban (Hispanic + urban).

Phoenix in Guillermo Reyes

1. For an analysis of the queer dimensions of this play, where the othered divas to be deported are as much "illegal" Mexicans as they are "illegal" gays, see Foster, "Queer as Border"; and Fitch Lockhart, "Gender Bending" and "Queer Representations."

2. I will from this point use the term "Hispanic," since that is the one preferred by Reyes in the bulk of his works.

3. As in plays like *The Seductions of Johnny Diego* (1990), *Farewell to Hollywood* (1993), and *The West Hollywood Affair* (1993).

4. The 2000 Association of Religious Data Archives for Maricopa County, of which Phoenix is the county seat, report 38 percent churchgoing Catholics; 11 percent churchgoing Mormons, and 5.5 percent of church going Southern Baptists, for a total of over 50 percent of the survey base. The Center for Arizona Policy is an ultraconservative action group that, during the past decade, has been very successful in driving the agenda of the Republican-controlled state legislature.

5. The one exception would be the productions, since 1999, of the Nearly Naked Theatre, which is based out of the Phoenix Little Theater in a space that is part of the campus of the Phoenix Art Museum.

6. As of this writing, December, 2012.

7. I regularly use *Places to Touch Him* in my seminar on Phoenix and Urban Cultural Production, and there are inevitably students who want to know what politician Cesar is based on. Reyes, in a personal communication and in class visits, insists that he had no interest in basing Cesar on any known public figure.

8. The audience is thus asked to suspend any reservations regarding what this may mean for Cesar's ex-wife and children.

9. Moraga, who lives and works in the Bay area, set one of her plays in Phoenix, *Hungry Woman* (see analysis elsewhere in this book).

10. Note that it is Cesar G. Gutierrez, not César G. Gutiérrez: written accents are the damning trace of threatening Hispanics; even better than getting rid of the accents is to Anglicize names and drop those that cannot be Anglicized. The writer Richard Rodriguez may be Richard Rodriguez because of his commitment to assimilation, but Mary Rose Wilcox, who was born in Superior, Arizona, to a fourth-generation Mexican American pioneering family, does not use her maiden name Garrido; it is not clear if her birth name is Rose Mary or Rosa María or some variant of the latter. One of the monologues of Reyes's *Men on the Verge of a His-panic Breakdown*, "The Marriage of Figaro," is built around Federico, who is definitely the prototype of the threatening Hispanic:

> Knock, knock, knock... Hello, it's me... I'm back... Remember me?... I'm Federico.

Last year you refused to open the door for me. Well, I'm still around —
and I haven't forgotten you, pendejo! [Reyes, *Men* 47].

11. Rossini, in his brief comments on identity negotiations in *Deporting the Divas*,
speaks of how the internal voice in the play of anti-immigration sentiments, Marge
McCarthy: "Marge's 'horrible fantasy' of having an illegal alien is expressed in the
same language of coming out as the supposed lesser of two evils, gay identity" (133).

12. It is important to consult the preface to the second edition to understand
Butler's clarification of ways in which she feels her formulations have been misunder-
stood, especially to the extent that if gender is performed, it is not "real," not socially
relevant.

13. Although he is not specifically interested in performance theory, John M.
Clum cleverly titles his anthology of gay plays *Still Acting Gay*, fusing the concept of
theatrical acting with the display of sexuality.

14. There are a few instances in the play in which Matt's watching is not metatheatrical in the sense I am insisting on here, as he watches Domingo attempting to teach
Cesar to line dance at the beginning of Act II (201).

15. For that matter, Phoenix remains underrepresented in studies of Hispanic
society in the U.S. Phoenix is not mentioned in collections like *Latinos in a Changing
Society*, *Latinos: Remaking America*, or *Orbis/urbis latino: los hispanos en las ciudades de
los Estados Unidos*. However, see Oberle, "Se venden aquí," which appears in a collection
edited by Daniel D. Arreola.

16. In addition to the already mentioned Phoenix reference in *Men on the Verge
2: The Self-Esteem Files*, the original *Men on the Verge of a His-panic Breakdown* contains
a monologue, "Castro's Queen," involving Paco, who is president of the Arizona Gay
Republicans and runs a Cuban restaurant in Phoenix.

Phoenix as Dystopia in Cherríe Moraga

1. "El Movimiento did not die oue in the seventies, as most of its critics claim;
it was only deformed by the machismo and homophobia of that era and coopted by
'hispanicization' of the eighties. In reaction against Anglo America's emasculation of
Chicano men, the male-dominated Chicano movement embraced the most patriarchal
aspects of its Mexican heritage. For a generation, nationalist leaders used a kind of
'selective memory,' drawing exclusively from those aspects of Mexican and Native cultures that served the interests of male heterosexuals" (156).

2. I am fully aware that the notion of "blight" requires some theorization, especially as it tends to be a classist term and, from there, a racist and anti-ethnic one as
well. If I am leaving it undertheorized here and limit myself to echoing Moraga's mag-
nification of existing sectors of Phoenix, I do so by meaning not that which has been
recycled for uses that go against the grain of middle-class order, but rather to refer to
what has become and remains so rundown, if not abandoned, that the property risks
legal condemnation for building rot and accompanying hazards. Clearly, "rundown"
is a subjective and relative word, but I am not using it here in any sense of bourgeois
aesthetics: one citizen's blight may be another citizen's welcome refuge.

For an excellent example of Chicano cultural production dealing with the injustices
of the definitions of blight, see Culture Clash's play *Chavez Ravine*. On the history of
Chavez Ravine, a Mexican/Mexican American neighborhood destroyed in order to
construct the Los Angeles Dodger Stadium, see Pitt. Ethington's brilliant essay on the
"ghost neighborhoods" of Los Angeles (i.e., those destroyed in the name of blight-

erradicating progress) contains the following observation: "Specific agents made the future of this area [Bunker Hill, in what is now north downtown Los Angeles] highly questionable by creating a damagin' representation of it in explicitly racial terms" (42). This is a strategy not unknown to the discussions of blight in Phoenix today, where Chicano barrios have been destroyed both for the construction of the international airport (and others are already threatened by plans for expansion) and downtown sport arenas (see Foster, "Here Today").

3. The principal segments of Route 60 today are Interstate Highways 10 and 17 as the run through central Phoenix and the Superstition Highway that separates from the I-10 and bisects the East Valley communities of the Greater Phoenix area.

4. Certainly, in the case of a city like Phoenix, the phrase "man in the street" requires a fundamental reconfiguration, as Phoenix is not a place where one is likely to be found in the street.

5. Although Phoenix is not mentioned, nor is Moraga's *Hungry Woman*, I want to call attention to Brady's superb study on space in Chicana literature, the whole first chapter of which is devoted to the dual imaginary of Anglo Arizona and Nuevomexicano New Mexico.

Cecilia Esquer

1. For example, the WPA guide to Arizona, *Arizona: The Grand Canyon State*, states: "Mexican residents comprised about half the population prior to 1900 despite the fact that Phoenix always prided itself as being a "purely American town." In 1938, however, they numbered less than 10 per cent (218).

2. Quino E. Martínez, the first Chicano to teach at Arizona State, joined the Spanish faculty in 1957.

3. And this was even more the case for minorities within the minority, such as women and queers: the dynamic of social margination would seem to increase to a higher power within the minority group the processes of discrimination within the overall society, such that sexism, for example, might be greater among a minority than even in the general population. As Sonia Saldívar-Hull writes:

> The New Mestiza refuses to wait patiently for the men to liberate her. Given her history as a woman of a culture that insists that its women be submissive, [Gloria] Anzaldúa "refuses to glorify those aspects of [her] culture which have injured [her] in the name of protecting [her]" [...] "[...] I abhor how my culture makes *macho* caricatures of its men" [...] [73].

Cherríe Moraga has written about this particularly with reference to women and queers.

4. Mary Pat Brady examines the "production of Arizona as the Anglo complement to the Nuevomexican other" (46) when the two states were created out of the New Mexico Territory.

5. Thomas Macías speaks of "'Real' Mexican Food and 'Bad' Mexican Ethnics" (27–29). The cover of his book is the image of a mock Chicano barbecue at the tomb of Arizona's first governor, George W. P. Hunt, in Papago Park in downtown Phoenix. The image is Robert C. Buitron's staged photo, "The Legend Continues."

6. As Matthew C. Whitaker, director of Arizona State's Center for the Study of Race and Democracy, states, statistics are even more depressed to Afro Americans in Arizona and Phoenix.

7. The university exists (since 1889) thanks to the destruction of the San Carlos

barrio; one of the first Catholic Churches in the Phoenix area, Mount Carmel, was built in 1903 basically as a barrio church, but also as a bridge between the Anglo and Hispanic communities. See Foster "Historic Catholic Churches of Phoenix," posted at http://www.public.asu.edu/~atdwf.

8. See Whitaker (113–19) on school segregation; on school segregation for Mexican Americans, see Luckingham (*Minorities* 49–51), who speaks of alleged "language deficiencies" [49] as one major justification for segregation.

Conclusions

1. Phoenix is very much a city of new beginnings, whether it is the opportunity for Bombeck to develop as an urban chronicler or for a mob man like Jack Durant to go legit. Jon Talton's David Mapstone has a new beginning in Phoenix as a cold case investigator. I owe the insight about the importance of new beginnings in Phoenix, whether for authors, real-life individuals, or literary characters to Marshall Shore, a fellow devote of Phoenix stories.

2. Even when Raymond Chandler renames Santa Monica Bay City in his crime fiction, the city is so accurately present in its material details that any reader familiar with Southern California feels right at home.

3. Much has changed in the past decade, with the construction of sports facilities, the creation of attractive cultural venues (e.g., the Herberger Theater, the Arizona Science Museum, the Convention Center), and an admirable flourishing of entertainment venues, along with bars and restaurants, many in recycled commercial and residential buildings. The Arizona Center shopping and business complex, which opened in 1990, has not, at least as a commercial operation, really paid off, or has paid off only minimally, does manage to stay open (the 24-screen AMC theaters are usually a ghost pavilion). But it has been the installation of the vibrant Arizona State University Downtown Campus that has done much to recreate a livable or functional Phoenix downtown that was lost with the flight to suburbs beginning in the 1950s, enabled, among other things, by the availability of effective domestic air conditioning.

4. Mabel Leo has written a self-published investigative document on Jack Durant, *The Saga of Jack Durant* (1996), specifically linking Durant to Jewish mob boss Bugsy Siegel; see also the sequel, *Jack's World.* (2005). Terry Earp's unpublished play, *In My Humble Opinion,* based on Leo's book, had considerable success in the mid–2000s; it was restaged as recently as spring 2012 by the Carefree (Ariz.) Theatre Company. There is a filming in DVD of one of the performances; I have not been able to determine the date of this filming. See Pela's excellent review of Earp's play, "You Don't Know Jack," which is basically an opportunity to supplement Leo's biography with additional historical information.

5. For example, Darian Land, plugs his 2003 satire *The Teasdale Primer (for MBAs)* in the following fashion: "Dr. Jacques LePere accepts a tenure track teaching position at the Teasdale Intensive Business School located in posh Scottsdale, Arizona that acts like a land-locked island state with no accountability to person or high governing authority" (back cover). Although the syntax is ambiguous here, such fiction might easily be referring to Scottsdale as the land-locked island state or to the Teasdale School. Scottsdale is only partially posh, there being many middle-class neighborhoods and pockets of poverty in Scottsdale, and internal evidence suggests the novel is really referring to the Thunderbird School of Global Management (aka the American Graduate School of International Management and originally just the Thunderbird School),

located across town in the old agricultural suburb of Glendale, now predominantly a solidly middle-class enclave; the conjunction of posh and Glendale would be an oxymoron. But, then, Scottsdale is, at least superficially, a far more interesting and sin-inspiring setting. Scottsdale also serves as a setting for Marcia Fine's 2010 slapstick *Stressed in Scottsdale*: "With the absurdity of desert living set in her literary crosshairs, Fine [...] skewers some of Scottsdale's finest while her protagonist [...] has to find sanity in a world where it rains dirt and blind sheep fall off mountains" (back cover). Now, neither of these works are crime novels, but both exemplify the use of the Phoenix area as exotic or perversely different. Both are published by marginal (vanity?) presses. Marc Savage's aforementioned very good 1992 crime novel (published by Doubleday), *Flamingos*, a title that seems more to evoke Miami than to allude to Phoenix, contains as a plug a quote from the novel: "Do I have to go down to south Phoenix to find someone big enough to beat some sense into you?" (back cover). The reader is left to surmise what the particular resources of south Phoenix are (the area south of the dry Salt River bed immediately south of downtown), and knowing that it is historically the area of people of color (Afro Americans, Mexican Americans, Asians) unwelcome in the predominantly Anglo neighborhoods north of the river (although long since no longer so) only adds precise information. The quote is cast effectively to suggest the marginal and sinister.

6. One other highly successful novel about Phoenix is Donald Rawley's 1998 *The Nightbird Cantata* (the nightbird is an authentic Phoenix ornithological detail). Rawley died at the age of 40 right after the publication of *Cantata*, his only novel, whose richly layered narrative includes one of the few powerful representations of south Phoenix Afro American life, which is woefully underrepresented in the cultural production of the city. Rawley was not Afro American. Alas, Phoenix has no Afro American writer of the stature of Tucson's Terry McMillan, whose 1993 novel *Waiting to Exhale* is one of the best novels ever written in Arizona. Set in Phoenix, it was made into an excellent film in 1995 by Forest Whitaker, who actually filmed in Phoenix proper and the upscale suburb of Paradise Valley, the Beverly Hills-Belair of Phoenix. The only Afro American novel I have discovered for Phoenix is Murad Kalam's 2003 *Night Journey*, about boxing clubs and abandoned Afro American teenage boys. While the novel is interesting enough, the representation of Phoenix is so superficial that it might as well be Phoenix, North Dakota. The novel speaks of the south Phoenix Third Ward, but Phoenix, unlike, say, Chicago, never followed the ward system. Also of Afro American interest is Mark Crockett's 2002 *Turkeystuffer* about a serial killer who stalks the homeless in Phoenix (one of the city's notable demographic details), but has little insightful Afro American content.

7. One isolated example of such an analysis is *Historic Homes of Phoenix*.

Appendix I

1. During the period from the mid–1950s and the beginning of the 1960s, there is a considerable influx of Eastern liberals into Phoenix, an influx that changes notably the Democratic Party, originally heavily influenced by Southern Democrats. The lawyer John P. Frank and his wife Lorraine are among the most outstanding representatives of this influx; they settled in Phoenix in 1954. The so-called outside liberals come into conflict with the growing strength of the Republican Party, which embraces many Arizonans with a commercial, financial, and professional background but also contains its own contingent of Eastern "conservative liberals." The most famous Republican of

the day is Senator Barry Goldwater (former mayor of Phoenix), whose presidential bid occurs at the time of the novel. Characteristic of the many silences in Swarthout's novel, this is perhaps the most significant one, since Goldwater, an old Arizonan, exemplifies those who are not displaced by the Easterners, like Edie Bud is, but in fact become part of their power base — indeed, Goldwater is their icon. Goldwater's famous *The Conscience of a Conservative* (1960) may have served many political uses — the 1990 edition contains a forward by Pat Buchanan — but many Arizonans at the time considered it the virtual founding document of their state's social ideology.

2. See the studies Beuka; Lukin; Jackson; Jurca on the growth of suburbia and its fictional interpretation.

3. The only development promoter mentioned by name actually predated the great mogols of the 1950s and 1960s: Darrell Duppa, although he is identified in the novel as Walt Duppa. Given the cutesy nature of some of Swarthout's naming, it is easy to speculate that this developer was chosen because of his suggestive surname (=dupe), while the change to Walt might perhaps suggest the Disneyland nature of the promotion of land developments and residential "communities" (now "new urban villages") in Phoenix (see Luckingham, *Phoenix* [15, 16] on Duppa); the Duppa Villa residential area, originally built as part of wartime housing, is named after him (Luckingham 141).

References

Abbott, Megan. *Bury Me Deep*. New York: Simon and Schuster, 2009.

Abril, Joe. *Echoes of Life in Phoenix: Living, Loving and Growing in the Barrio*. Apache Junction, AZ: Hispanic Institute of Social Issues, 2007.

Arizona: The Grand Canyon State: A State Guide. Comp. by Workers of the Writers' Program of the Works Project Administration in the State of Arizona. Complete rev. by Joseph Miller. Ed. Henry G. Alsberg. New York: Hastings House, 1956.

Arizona Memories from the '70s. Videorecording. Producer, writer, director, John Booth. Tempe: KAET Eight, 2008.

Association of Religious Data Archives. "County Membership Report. Maricopa County, Arizona. Denomination Groups 2000." Internet, accessed August 26, 2008.

Barrios, Frank M. *Mexicans in Phoenix*. Charleston, SC: Arcadia, 2008.

Benson, Steve. "Editorial Cartoonist's Journey from Jesus to Journalism — and Beyond." http://www.lds-mormon.com/benson2.shtml Accessed, August 28, 2009.

_____. *Evanly Days! A Cartoon Journey into the Wacky World of Arizona Politics — and Beyond*. Phoenix: Phoenix Newspapers; Many Feathers Books and Maps, 1988. Reissued as *Back at the Barb-B-Cue: An Expanded Cartoon Collection*. Phoenix: Phoenix Newspapers; Wide World of Maps, 1991.

_____. *Fencin' with Benson: A Cartoon Collection*. Phoenix: Phoenix Newspapers, 1984.

_____. *Where Do You Draw the Line? Cartoons*. Phoenix: Wide World of Maps, 1992.

Bergelin, Paul. "'Thirty-Five Years of Corrupting Minds': Pat McMahon and *The Wallace and Ladmo Show*." *Studies in American Humor* 3.23 (2011): 66–76.

Beuka, Robert. *Suburbian Nation: Reading Suburban Landscape in Twentieth-Century American Fiction and Film*. New York: Palgrave Macmillan, 2004.

Bishop, Bill, and Robert G. Kushing. *The Big Sort: Why the Clustering of Like-Minded America is Tearing Us Apart*. Boston: Houghton Mifflin, 2008.

Bombeck, Erma. *Family — The Ties that Bind ... and Gag!* New York: Fawcett Crest, 1987. Originally New York: McGraw Hill, 1987.

_____. *Four of a Kind: A Suburban Field Guide. A Treasury of Works by America's Best-Loved Humorist: The Grass Is Always Greener of the Septic Tank; If Life is a Bowl of Cherries — What Am I Doing in the Pits?; Aunt Erma's Cope Book; Motherhood: The Second Oldest Profession*. New York: Galahad, 1985.

_____. *A Marriage Made in Heaven ... or Too Tired for an Affair*. New York: Harper-Paperbacks, 1994.

Bommersbach, Jana. *Bones in the Desert: The True Story of a Mother's Murder and a Daughter's Search*. New York: St. Martin's, 2008.

_____. *The Trunk Murderess, Winnie Ruth Judd*. Scottsdale, AZ: Poisoned Pen, 2003.

References

Orig., with the subtitle *The Truth about an American Crime Legend Revealed at Last*. New York: Simon and Schuster, 1992.

Brady, Mary Pat. *Extinct Lands, Temporal Geographics: Chicana Literature and the Urgency of Space*. Durham, NC: Duke University Press, 2002.

"Brief History of 'Wallace and Ladmo.'" http://www.kpho.com/station/11552995/detail.html/.

Butler, Judith. *Gender Trouble: Feminism and the Subversion of Gender*. 2d ed. New York: Routledge, 1999.

Campbell, Gordon. *Missing Witness*. New York: William Morrow, 2008.

Chandler, Raymond. "The Simple Art of Murder." *Later Novels and Other Writings*. New York: Library of America, 1995.

Clum, John M., ed. *Still Acting Gay: Male Homosexuality in Modern Drama*. New York: St. Martin's Griffin, 2000.

Colwell, Lynn Hunter. *Erma Bombeck: Writer and Humorist*. Hillsdale, NJ: Enslow, 1992.

Culture Clash. "Chavez Ravine." *American Theatre* 20.9 (2003): 40–61.

Daly, Mary. *Gyn/ecology: The Metaethics of Radical Feminism*. Boston: Beacon, 1978.

Davis, Mike. *City of Quartz: Excavating the Future in Los Angeles*. London: Verso, 1990.

Dobkins, J. Dwight, and Robert J. Hendricks, *Winnie Ruth Judd: The Trunk Murders*. New York: Grosset and Dunlap, 1973.

Duarte, Stella Pope. *Let Their Spirits Dance*. New York: Rayo, 2002.

_____. *Women Who Live in Coffee Shops*. Houston: Arte Público Press, 2010.

Dunn, Betty. "The Socrates of the Ironing Board." *Life* 71 (October 1971): 66+.

Dutton, Allen A. *Arizona Then and Now: Text and Contemporary Photography*. Rev. ed. Englewood, CO: Westcliffe, 2002. Orig. 1981.

Editorial Cartoon Awards 1922–1997. Ed. with general and special introductions by Heinz-Dietrich Fischer in cooperation with Erika J. Fischer. München: K. G. Saur, 1999. Added title: *The Pulitzer Prize Archive: A History and Anthology of Award-Winning Materials in Journalism, Letters, and Arts*.

Edwards, Susan. *Erma Bombeck: A Life in Humor*. Carmel, NY: Guideposts, 1997.

"Erma (Louise) Bombeck." *Contemporary Authors Online* (Gale, 2003). Accessed through the online index Literature Resource Center, 4 October 2007.

"Erma Museum." Online: 6 October 2007. http://www.ermamuseum.org.

Esquer, Cecilia D. *The Lie about My Inferiority: Evolution of a Chicana Activist*. Introd. by Christina Marin. Mesa, AZ: Latino, 2010.

Ethington, Philip J. "Ghost Neighborhoods: Space, Time, and Aleination in Los Angeles." *Looking for Los Angeles: Architecture, Film, Photography, and the Urban Landscape*. Ed. Charles G. Salas and Michael S. Roth. Los Angeles: Getty Research Institute, 2001.

Fine, David. *Imagining Los Angeles: A City in Fiction*. Albuquerque: University of New Mexico Press, 2000.

Fine, Marcia. *Stressed in Scottsdale*. Scottsdale: L'Image, 2010.

Fitch, Melissa A. "Gender Bending in Latino Theater: *Johnny Diego, The His-Panic Zone*, and *Deporting the Divas* by Guillermo Reyes." *Latina/o Popular Culture*. Ed. Michelle Habell-Pallán and Mary Romero. New York: New York University Press, 2002. 162–73.

Fitch Lockhart, Melissa. "Living Between Worlds: An Interview with Guillermo Reyes." *Latin American Theatre Review* 31.1 (1997): 117–21.

_____. "Queer Representations in Latino Theatre." *Latin American Theatre Review* 31.2 (1998): 67–78.

References

Foster, David William. *El ambiente nuestro: Chicano/Latino Homoerotic Writing.* Tempe, AZ: Bilingual, 2006.

_____. "Can You Get There on Van Buren? Urban Flashes: Phoenix, Arizona." *Border-lines* 2 (2008): 4–22.

_____. "Here Today, Gone Tomorrow: A Vanishing Phoenix Chicano Barrio." *El culturadoor.* http://www.culturadoor.com/Foster.htm. Accessed 29 January 2010.

_____. "Historic Catholic Churches of Phoenix." http://www.public.asu.edu/~atdwf.

_____. "El lesbianismo multidimensional: conflicto lingüístico, conflicto cultural y conflicto sexual en *Giving up the Ghost: Teatro in Two Acts* de Cherríe Moraga." *XVIII Simposio de Historia y Antropología de Sonora.* Hermosillo, Son.: Instituto de Investigaciones Históricas de la Universidad de Sonora, 1994. 2.331–40.

_____. "Queer as Border Culture/Border Culture as Queer." *El ambiente nuestro; Chicano/Latino Homoerotic Writing.* Tempe, AZ: Bilingual/Editorial Bilingüe, 2006. 139–50. Orig. published as two separate but connected articles: "Queer Theater." *Gestos* 27 (1999): 17–24; "Guillermo Reyes's *Deporting the Divas.*" *Gestos* 27 (1999): 103–08.

_____. "La Sonorita: Survival of a Chicano Barrio." *Confluencia* 27.1 (2011): 212–18.

"Gammage Controversy — African Dance Haltered." *State Press* [Arizona State University], 29 October 1968: 9.

Gant-Britton, Lisbeth. "Mexican Women and Chicanas Enter Futuristic Fiction." *Future Females: The Next Generation: New Voices and Velocities in Feminist Science Fiction Criticism.* Lanham, MD: Rowman and Littlefield, 2000. 261–76.

Gilbert, Sandra M., and Susan Gubar. *The Madwoman in the Attic: The Woman Writer and the Nineteenth-Century Literary Imagination.* New Haven: Yale University Press, 1979.

Goldwater, *The Conscience of a Conservative.* With a new introd. by Patrick J. Buchanan. Washington, D.C.: Regnery Gateway, 1990. Orig. New York: Hillman , 1960.

Greater Phoenix Regional Atlas: A Preview of the Region's 50-Year Future. Tempe, AZ: Greater Phoenix 2100, Arizona State University, 2003.

Gubar, Susan. "The Graying of Professor Erma Bombeck." *College English* 61.4 (March 1999): 431–47.

Harr, Charles Monroe, and David William Fessler. *The Wrong Side of the Tracks: A Revolutionary Rediscovery of the Common Law Tradition of Fairness in the Struggle Against Inequality.* New York: Simon and Schuster, 1986.

Hernández, Guillermo E. *Chicano Satire: A Study in Literary Culture.* Austin: University of Texas Press, 1991.

Historic Home of Phoenix: An Architectural Preservation Guide. Phoenix: City of Phoenix, 1992.

Huerta, Jorge. *Chicano Drama: Performance, Society and Myth.* Cambridge: Cambridge University Press, 2000.

Jackson, Kenneth T. *Westchester: The American Suburb.* New York: Fordham University Press; Yonkers: Hudson River Museum, 2006.

Jurca, Catherine. *White Diaspora: The Suburb and the Twentieth-Century American Novel.* Princeton: Princeton University Press, 2001.

King, Norman. *Here's Erma!: The Bombecking of America.* Aurora, IL: Caroline House, 1982.

Kunstler, James Howard. *The Geography of Nowhere: The Rise and Decline of America's Man-Made Landscape.* New York: Simon and Schuster, 1993.

Kushner, Tony. *Angels in America 1992.* New York: Theatre Communications Group, 1995.

References

Ladmo Remembered: A Wallace and Ladmo Special. Videorecording. Phoenix: Meredith, 1994.

Lamb, Chris. *Drawn to Extreme: The Use and Abuse of Editorial Cartoons.* New York: Columbia University Press, 2004.

Latinos: Remaking America. Ed. Marcelo M. Suárez-Orozco and Mariela M. Páez. Berkeley: University of California Press, 2002.

Latinos in a Changing Society. Ed. Martha Montero-Siebuth and Edwin Meléndez. Westport, Conn.: Praeger, 2007.

Levin, Ira. *The Stepford Wives: A Novel.* New York: Random House, 1972.

Luckingham, Bradford. *Minorities in Phoenix: A Profile of Mexican American, Chinese American, and African American Communities, 1860–1992.* Tucson: University of Arizona Press, 1994.

_____. *Phoenix: The History of a Southwestern Metropolis.* Tucson: University of Arizona Press, 1989.

_____, and Barbara Luckingham. *Discovering Greater Phoenix: An Illustrated History.* Carlsbad, NM: Heritage Media, 1998.

Lukin, Josh, ed. *Invisible Suburbs: Recovering Protest Fiction in the 1950s United States.* Jackson: University Press of Mississippi, 2008.

Lukinbeal, Chris, Daniel D. Arreola, and D. Drew Lucio. "Mexican Urban *Colonias* in the Salt River Valley of Arizona." *The Geographical Review* 100.1 (2010): 12–34.

Macías, Thomas. *Mestizo in America: Generations of Mexican Ethnicity in the Suburban Southwest.* Tucson: University of Arizona Press, 2006.

Manning, Reg. *Reg Manning's Cartoon Guide of Arizona.* New York: J. J. Augustin, 1938.

_____. *What is Arizona Really Like?* Phoenix: Reganson Cartoon , 1968.

Marrero, María Teresa. "Manifestations of Desires: A Critical Introduction." *Out of the Fringe: Contemporary Latina/Latino Theatre and Performance.* Ed. Caridad Svich and María Teresa Marrero. New York: Theatre Communications Group, 1999. xvii–xxx.

McMillan, Terry. *Waiting to Exhale.* New York: Viking, 1992.

Melikian, Robert A. *Vanishing Phoenix.* Charleston, SC: Arcadia, 2010.

Méndez-M., Miguel. *Peregrinos de Aztlán.* Berkeley: Editorial Justa, 1979.

_____. *Pilgrims in Aztlán.* Trans. from the Spanish by David William Foster. Tempe: Bilingual/Editorial Bilingüe, 1992. Trans. of *Peregrinos de Aztlán.*

Mike Condello Presents Wallace and Ladmo's Greatest Hits. Sound recording. Np: Epiphany, 2004. CD, 28 tracks.

Miller, Arthur. *Death of a Salesman.* Ed. and with an introd. by Harold Bloom. New York: Chelsea House, 2007.

Miller, Joseph. *Arizona: The Last Frontier.* New York: Hastings House, 1956.

Mohr, Richard D. *Gay Ideas: Outing and Other Controversies.* Boston: Beacon, 1992.

Moraga, Cherríe. *The Hungry Woman: The Hungry Woman, a Mexican Medea. Heart of the Earth, a Popol Vuh Story.* Albuquerque: West End Press, 2001. Also in *Out of the Fringe: Contemporary Latina/Latino Theatre and Performance.* Ed. Caridad Svich and María Teresa Marrero. New York: Theatre Communications Group, 1999. 289–363.

_____. "Queer Aztlán: The Re-Formation of Chicano Tribe." *The Last Generation: Prose and Poetry.* Boston: South End Press, 1993. 145–74.

Murderess: The Winnie Ruth Judd Story. Written and directed by Scott Coblio. West Hollywood: Scott Coblio Good Enuf Productions, 2007. 83 min.

References

Myers, John Myers. *I, Jack Swilling, Founder of Arizona*. New York: Hastings House, 1961.

Not Aiming to Please, Just Aiming. Columbus, Ohio: Mills/James Productions, 1998. 45 min.

Notaro, Laurie. *Autobiography of a Fat Bride: True Tales of a Pretend Adulthood*. New York: Villard, 2003.

_____. *I Love Everybody (and Other Atrocious Lies): True Tales of a Loudmouth Girl*. New York: Villard, 2004.

_____. *The Idiot Girl and the Flaming Tantrum of Death: Reflections on Revenge, Germophobia, and Laser Hair Removal*. New York: Villard, 2008.

_____. *The Idiot Girls' Action-Adventure Club*. New York: Villard, 2002.

_____. *An Idiot Girl's Christmas: True Tales from the Top of the Naughty List*. New York: Villard, 2005.

_____. *There's a (Slight) Chance I Might Be Going to Hell: A Novel of Sewer Pipes, Pageant Queens, and Big Trouble*. New York: Villard, 2007.

_____. *We Thought You Would be Prettier: Tall Tales of the Dorkiest Girl Alive*. New York: Willard, 2005.

Oberle, Alex P. "Se Venden Aquí: Latino Commercial Landscapes in Phoenix, Arizona." *Hispanic Spaces, Latino Places: Community and Cultural Diversity in Contemporary America*. Ed. Daniel D. Arreola. Austin: University of Texas Press, 2004. 239–54.

_____, and Daniel D. Arreola. "Resurgent Mexican Phoenix." *The Geographical Review* 98.2 (2008): 171–96.

Orbis/urbis latino: los "hispanos" en las ciudades de los Estados Unidos. Ed. Cardenio Bedoya, Flavia Belpoliti and Marc Zimmerman. Houston: Global Casa, 2008.

Pace, David. "'Angels' in Utah." *American Theatre* 13.3 (1996): 49–50.

Pagán, Eduardo Obregón. *Historic Photos of Phoenix*. Nashville: Turner, 2007.

Pancrazio, Angela Cara. "Voice of the Barrio: Latino Spirit Drives Phoenix Author." *The Arizona Republic* (May 27, 2002): E1, E5.

Pela, Robrt L. "The Last Days of Ladmo." *Phoenix New Times* #85 (15–21 August 2002): 17–32.

_____. "You Don't Know Jack." *Phoenix New Times* #158 (6 January 2005): 42+.

Pérez, Daniel Enrique. "Dramatizing the Borderlands: Staging Chicana/o and Latina/o Lives and Deaths." *Borders on Stage: Plays Produced by Teatro Bravo*. Ed. Trino Sandoval. Phoenix: Lion and the Seagoat, 2008. xiii–xxiii.

_____. "Reyes, Guillermo." *Encyclopedia of Latino Popular Culture*. Ed. Cordelia Candelaria et al. Westport, CT: Greenwood, 2004. 2.677–78.

Phoenix Noir. Ed. Patrick Millikin. New York: Akashic, 2009.

"Phoenix's Mexican Heritage." http://www.azpbs.org/arizonastories/ppedetail.php?id=93. Accessed 29 January 2010.

PHX: Phoenix 21st City. Ed. Edward Booth-Clibborn. London: Booth-Clibborn, 2006.

Pitt, Leonard, and Dale Pitt. "Chavez Ravine." *Los Angeles A to Z: An Encyclopedia of the City and County*. Berkelely: University of California Press, 1997. 87

Prieto Stambaugh, Antonio. "La actuación de la identidad a través del performance chicano gay." *Debate feminista* 7.13 (1996): 253–315.

Prues, Don, and Jack Heffron. *Writer's Guide to Places*. Cincinnati: Writer's Digest, 2002.

Quay, Sara E. "Insanity." *Encyclopedia of Feminist Literary Theory*. Ed. Elizabeth Kowaleski-Wallace. New York: Garland, 1997. 212–13.

Rebello, Stephen. *Alfred Hitchcock and the Making of Psycho*. New York: Dembner, 1990.

References

Rechy, John. *Bodies and Souls*. New York: Carroll and Graf, 1983.

Reck, Tom S. "Raymond Chandler's Los Angeles." *The Critical Responses to Raymond Chandler*. Ed. J. Kenneth Van Dover. Westport, CT: Greenwood, 1995 109–15.

Recuerdos: Memories of Life in the Barrios Unidos, Phoenix, Arizona. Phoenix: [Braun Sacred Heart Center], 200?.

Reyes, Guillermo A. *Bush Is a Lesbian*. Dallas: Dialogus Play Service, 1993.

_____. *"Deporting the Divas."* *Gestos* 27 (1999): 101–58.

_____. *Farewell to Hollywood*. Dallas: Dialogus Play Service, 1993.

_____. *Men on the Verge of a His-Panic Breakdown: A Play in Monologues*. Woodstock, IL: Dramatic, 1999. Also *Staging Gay Lives: An Anthology of Contemporary Gay Theater*. Ed. John M. Clum. Boulder: Westview, 1996. 401–24.

_____. *Places to Touch Him*. In *Borders on Stage: Plays Produced by Teatro Bravo*. Ed. Trino Sandoval. Phoenix: Lion and the Seagoat, 2008. 177–221.

_____. *The Seductions of Johnny Diego*. Thesis, MFA, University of California, San Diego, Department of Theatre, 1990.

_____. *Silence of a Kiss*. Dallas: Dialogus Play Service, 1994.

_____. *The West Hollywood Affair*. Dallas: Dialogus Play Service, 1993.

Reynolds, Jean. *The History of Grant Park Neighborhood, 1880–1950*. Phoenix: Phoenix Revitalization, 2000.

_____. "'We Knew Our Neighbors, and It was Like One Family': The History of the Grant Park Neighborhood, 1880–1950." October 1, 1999, for the City of Phoenix, Historic Preservation Office. See summary in *The Arizona Republic* (July 9, 1999): A1, A16.

Ross, Andrew. *Bird on Fire: Lessons from the World's Least Sustainable City*. New York: Oxford University Press, 2011.

Rossini, Jon D. *Contemporary Latina/o Theater: Writing Ethnicity*. Carbondale: Southern Illinois University Press, 2008.

Ruelas, Richard. *Thanks for Tuning In*. Winfield, KS: Central Plains, 2004.

_____, and Michael K. Sweeney. *HoHo!HaHa!Hee!Hee!Haha!Hoho!Haha!HeeHee! HaHa!: The Wallace and Ladmo Show: 35 Years of Laughter*. Phoenix: View Designs, 1994.

Saldívar-Hull, Sonia. *Feminism on the Border: Chicana Gender Politics and Literature*. Berkeley: University of California Press, 2000.

Savage, Marc. *Flamingos*. New York: Doubleday, 1992.

Scharbach, Paul, and John H. Akers. *Phoenix: Then and Now*. San Diego: Thunder Bay, 2005.

Seiter, Ellen. *Sold Separately: Children and Parents in Consumer Culture*. New Brunswick, NJ: Rutgers University Press, 1993.

Shields, Rob. "Fancy Footwork: Walter Benjamin's Notes on *Flânerie*." *The Flâneur*. Ed. Keith Tester. London: Routledge, 1994. 61–79.

Silver Anniversary Jubilee, 1960–1985: A History of Sun City, Arizona. Phoenix: COL, 1984.

Spears, Linda, and Frederic B. Wildfang. *Tempe*. Charleston, SC: Arcadia; Tempe: Tempe History Museum, 2010.

"Steve Benson." http://www.creators.com/editorial cartoons/steve-benson-about.html. Accessed June 7, 2009.

Summerhayes, Martha. *Vanished Arizona: Recollections of My Army Life*. Philadelphia: Lippincott, 1908.

Swarthout, Glendon. *The Cadillac Cowboys*. New York: Random House, 1964.

Talton, Jon. *Arizona Dreams: A David Mapstone Mystery*. Phoenix: Poisoned Pen, 2006.

References

_____. *Cactus Heart: A David Mapstone Mystery*. Phoenix: Poisoned Pen, 2007.

_____. *Camelback Falls: A David Mapstone Mystery*. New York: Thomas Dunne, 2003.

_____. *Concrete Desert: A David Mapstone Mystery*. New York: Thomas Dunne, 2001.

_____. *Dry Heat: A David Mapstone Mystery*. Thomas Dunne Books, an imprint of St. Martin's, 2004.

_____. *South Phoenix Rules: A David Mapstone Mystery*. Scottsdale: Poisoned Pen, 2010.

Thompson, Bill, and Pat McMahon, *The Wallace 'n Ladmo Show Presents Aunt Maud's Storybook*. Phoenix: View Designs, 2000.

Thompson, Clay. *Valley 101: A Slightly Skewed Guide to Living in Arizona*. Phoenix: Primer, 2004.

_____. *The Valley 101 Great Big Book of Life*. Phoenix: Primer, 2005.

Trujillo, Charley. *Soldados: Chicanos in Viet Nam*. San José: Chusma House, 1990.

Trujillo, Richard. "A Class Act: Teatro Bravo Fights to Keep an Edgy Niche in Arizona Theater Community." *Latino Perspectives* (March 2005): 42–44.

Valle, Víctor M., and Rodolfo D. Torres. *Latino Metropolis*. Minneapolis: University of Minnesota Press, 2002.

VanderMeer, Philip. *Desert Visions and the Making of Phoenix, 1860–2009*. Albuquerque: University of New Mexico Press, 2010.

_____, and Mary VanderMeer. *Phoenix Rising: The Meaning of a Desert Metropolis: A Modern History*. Carlsbad, CA: Heritage, 2002.

Villa, Raúl Homero. *Barrio-Logos: Space and Place in Urban Chicano Literature and Culture*. Austin: University of Texas Press, 2000.

Walker, Nancy A. *A Very Serious Thing: Women's Humor and American Culture*. Minneapolis: University of Minnesota Press, 1988.

Wallace and Ladmo: A Whole Bunch of Shows. Tempe, AZ: WallaceWatchers, 2008. 240 min.

The Wallace and Ladmo Show. Park Central Mall's 30th Anniversary Special, September, 1987. Tempe, AZ: Arizona Historical Society, n.d. 60 min.

The Wallace and Ladmo Show. 35th Anniversary Special. Tempe, AZ: Arizona Historical Society, n.d. 60 min.

The Wallace and Ladmo Tribute. Phoenix: Super Boffo, KPHO 5-TV, 1999. 49 min.

"Wallace Watchers: Wallace and Ladmo Official Site." http://wallacewatchers.com.

Weingroff, Richard F. "U.S. Route 80 The Dixie Overland Highway." http:www//fhwa.dot.gov/infrastructure/us80.cfm.

Wheeler, Elizabeth A. *Uncontained: Urban Fiction in Postwar America*. New Brunswick, NJ: Rutgers University Press, 2001.

Whitaker, Matthew C. *Race Work: The Rise of Civil Rights in the Urban West*. Lincoln: University of Nebraska Press, 2005.

Wilson, Sloan. *Man in the Gray Flannel Suit*. New York: Simon and Schuster, 1955.

"Winnie Ruth Judd Photograph Collection." Arizona Historical Society-Papago Park. Call Number: FP FPC #4.

Women, Violence, and the Media: Readings in Feminist Criminology. Ed. Drew Humphries. Boston: Northwestern University Press; Hanover, NH: University Press of New England, 2009.

Index

Index